THE GREEN CHILDREN
OF WOOLPIT

Exeter New Approaches to Legend, Folklore and Popular Belief

Series Editors:
Simon Young, University of Virginia (CET, Siena) and
Davide Ermacora, University of Turin

Exeter New Approaches to Legend, Folklore and Popular Belief provides a venue for growing scholarly interest in folklore narratives, supernatural belief systems and the communities that sustain them. Global in scope, the series encompasses milieus ranging from ancient to contemporary times and encourages empirically grounded, source-rich studies. The editors favour the broad multidisciplinary approach that has characterized the study of folklore and the supernatural, and which brings together insights from historians, folklorists, anthropologists and many other branches of the humanities and social sciences.

THE GREEN CHILDREN OF WOOLPIT

CHRONICLES, FAIRIES AND FACTS IN MEDIEVAL ENGLAND

JOHN CLARK

UNIVERSITY
of
EXETER
PRESS

First published in 2024 by
University of Exeter Press
Reed Hall, Streatham Drive
Exeter EX4 4QR
UK

www.exeterpress.co.uk

Exeter New Approaches to Legend, Folklore and Popular Belief

ISSN 3049-7329 Print
ISSN 3049-7337 Digital

British Library Cataloguing in Publication Data
A catalogue record for this book is available from the British Library

ISBN 978-1-80413-136-7 Hardback
ISBN 978-1-80413-239-5 Paperback
ISBN 978-1-80413-137-4 ePub
ISBN 978-1-80413-138-1 PDF

https://doi.org/10.47788/UVYO7590

EU Authorised Representative: Easy Access System Europe –
Mustamäe tee 50, 10621 Tallinn, Estonia, gpsr.requests@easproject.com

Typeset in the UK by BBR Design, Sheffield

Cover image: Woolpit village sign (photograph by the author)

'I am not ashamed to have related this
wonderful and marvellous happening'

Woolpit village. Photo: David Pike/Alamy Stock Photo.

Contents

Illustrations

Acknowledgements

Any historical researcher should first acknowledge the work of the, usually anonymous, librarians and archivists who have preserved and organized and made available for us the documents and published works on which we depend—and recently those who have digitized and put online so many essential resources. My own special thanks must go to University College London's library and its links to a treasury of online sources, which collegiately facilitated this work for some ten years between 2012 and 2022. I have also had the enviable benefit of living within thirty minutes' reach of the British Library.

I am grateful to all the authors and researchers who have devoted so much time to investigating Woolpit's Green Children or reinterpreting them for new audiences—they are acknowledged in the references, notes and extensive bibliography. My work depends on all that has gone before, and even if I may disagree with some of their conclusions it would have been impossible (or at least much less interesting) without them. A special credit goes to Kevin Crossley-Holland, whose lifelong fascination with the Green Children and contribution to their story I recognize.

Much of my research into the subject was a fairly solitary pursuit—only later, particularly after folklorist Simon Young had publicized my work on his blog, did I realize others might be interested. Some contacted me with suggestions; I approached others with queries. Simon himself was my first port of call, and has been my support throughout, encouraged me to submit this book to the University of Exeter Press and helped me see the project through to completion. Other helpful people include Debbie Bamford and John Stoker of the Mulberry Dyer; Jelena Bekvalac; Keith Briggs; Elizabeth Cockayne of Woolpit Museum; Art Evans; the Rev. Ruth Farrell, Rector of Woolpit and Drinkstone; Samuel Giddes Hogan; Jon Howe; Duncan Lunan; Alan Marks; Caroline Oates; Sonia Overall; James Plumtree; Frances Pritchard; Julia Round; Roy Vickers; and Francis Young. To these I must add members of the audiences at talks I have given on the subject, and the anonymous peer reviewer who advised the University of Exeter Press on the quality of my work and made extensive recommendations for improvements (not all of which I have adopted!). These are duly acknowledged for their specific contributions in my footnotes.

I am also grateful to Jeremy Complin for his work in the index, to BBR Design for the typesetting, and to Anna Henderson, Nigel Massen, David Hawkins and other staff of the University of Exeter Press who have made this all possible.

Finally I acknowledge the unfailing support and enthusiasm I received from my sister Joanna until her sudden death, just two weeks after I had submitted the draft book text to the University of Exeter Press for their consideration. I miss her greatly, her companionship and our adventures together, and I dedicate this book to her.

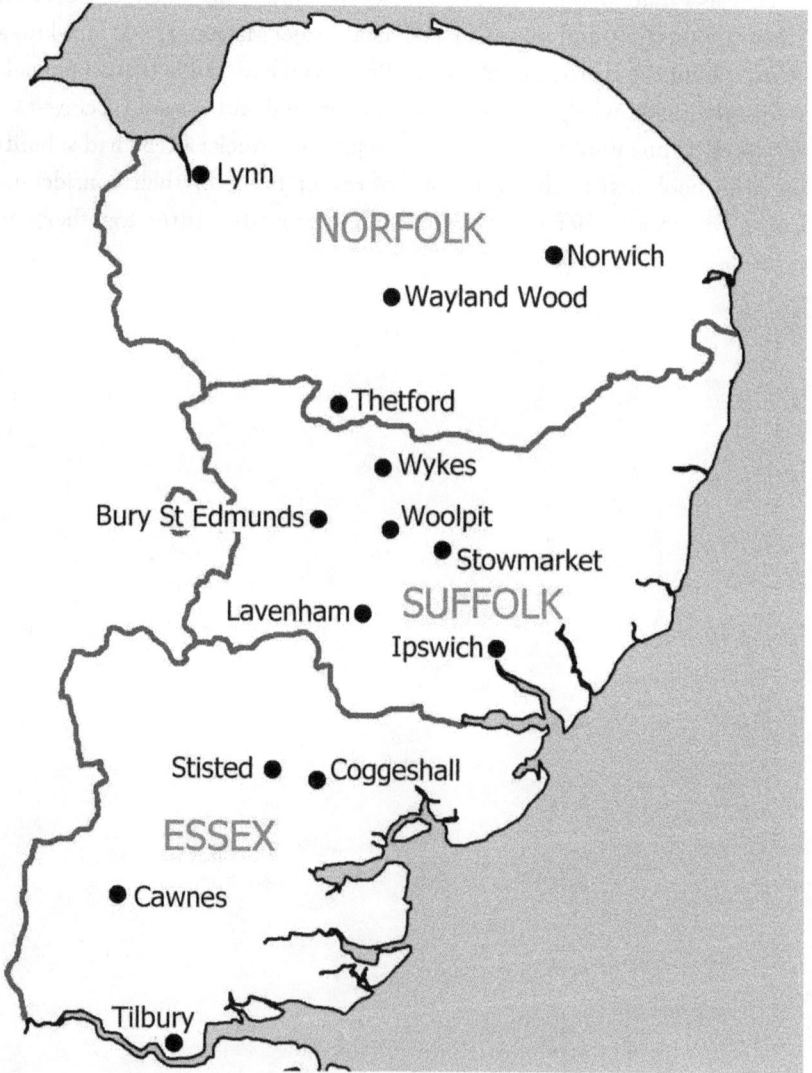

Map 1.   East Anglia, showing places mentioned in the text. Map: John Clark.

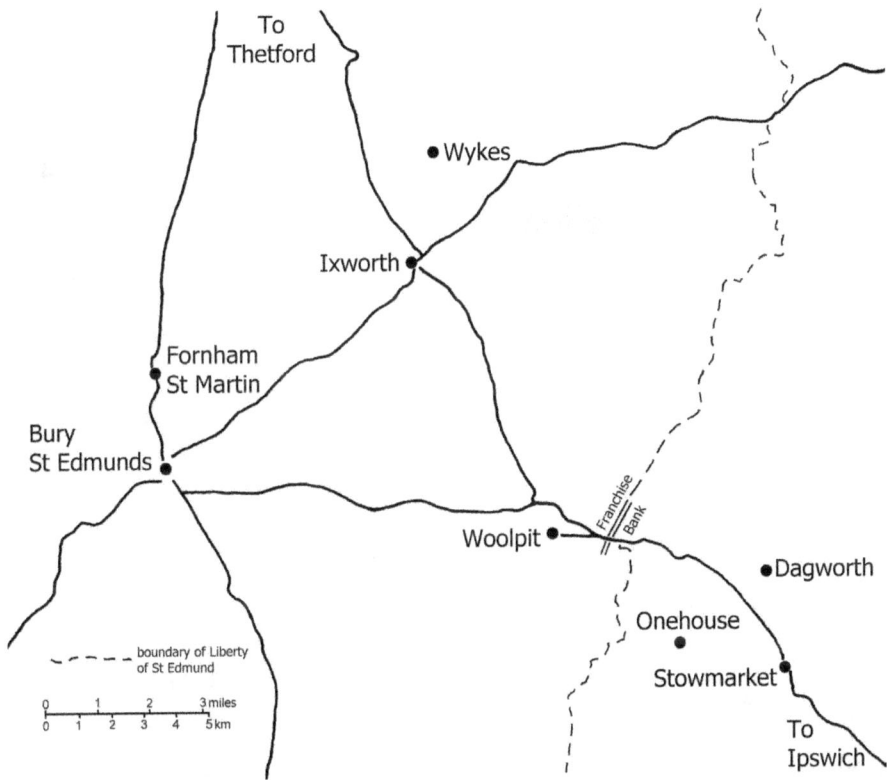

To
Thetford

• Wykes

Ixworth •

Fornham
St Martin •

Bury
St Edmunds •

Woolpit •

Franchise Bank

• Dagworth

Onehouse
•

Stowmarket •

To
Ipswich

boundary of Liberty
of St Edmund

0   1   2   3 miles
0 1 2 3 4 5 km

Map 2.   Sketch-map of the Woolpit area in the Middle Ages. Roads based upon the
First Edition Ordnance Survey map; the eastern boundary of the Liberty of St Edmund
based on the pre-1972 boundary of West and East Suffolk. Map: John Clark.

CHAPTER ONE

An Introduction

In the beginning

In 1966 Anglo-Saxonist, poet and translator Kevin Crossley-Holland (b. 1941) published the first of three short books for children with illustrations by Margaret Gordon, each a version of a traditional tale from East Anglia. In the first of these he retold the story of the 'Green Children of Woolpit', the two strange green-skinned children, a boy and a girl, who reportedly appeared as if out of the ground to harvesters in the fields of the village of Woolpit, Suffolk (Crossley-Holland 1966). Speaking a strange language, they would at first eat nothing but raw beans. Becoming used to more normal food, they lost their green colour. The boy died, but the girl learnt English and explained that they had come from a twilight land called St Martin's Land. The story was reported, apparently independently, by two medieval chroniclers at the end of the twelfth century.

Crossley-Holland was to return to the story several times. In an interview in 2012 he spoke of his long fascination:

> Imagine an eager, anxious boy lying on the top half of a bunk bed. His sister, three years younger than he is, lies on the bottom. Their father sits beside the bunk, eyes closed, and sings-and-says folk tales, accompanying himself on his Welsh harp. That's when I first heard the story … (Crossley-Holland 2012)

My own introduction to the story was probably through Katharine Briggs's compendium of *Folk Legends*, two volumes of her four-volume *Dictionary of British Folk-Tales* (Briggs 1971: 1:262–63). I did not, at first, take notice of the Woolpit story—there were so many other intriguing historical tales in Briggs's compilation. And so it was not as folklore that I was eventually drawn into its study but as 'a classic example of "forteana"' (Minyak 2000: 56).

Many who have come across the writings of the American Charles Fort (1874–1932) or more often references to 'forteana' probably associate them

with sightings of UFOs, with falls of fish, with crystal skulls and lost civilizations established by the intervention of alien astronauts. And, indeed, Charles
Fort devoted much of the latter half of his life to collecting records of anomalous
events, usually from nineteenth- and twentieth-century newspapers, from
unexplained lights in the sky and falls of frogs or fish to strange disappearances,
and between 1919 and 1932 published four extraordinary books, *The Book of the
Damned, New Lands, Lo!* and *Wild Talents* (Fort 1974).

Fort accepted even the most unlikely account of an extraordinary event or
phenomenon, and rarely made any attempt to provide 'scientific' explanations—
and where there are they seem deliberately elusive. Indeed, he used them to
pour scorn on the pretensions of scientists, instead presenting 'A procession of
the damned. By the damned, I mean the excluded. We shall have a procession of
data that Science has excluded' (Fort 1974: 3). For these excluded phenomena
he presents sometimes at first sight tongue-in-cheek explanations.

Since the appearance of Damon Knight's biography of Fort as the 'Prophet
of the Unexplained' some fifty years ago (Knight 1971), the British Library
catalogue has listed over fifty new books with the words *The Unexplained*
forming the whole or part of the title—including three encyclopedias, a
dictionary and a magazine, *The Unexplained: Mysteries of Mind Space & Time*, which
ran to 156 issues and an index volume between 1980 and 1983. Titles such as
Unsolved Mysteries and *Ancient Mysteries* reflect the same late twentieth-century/
early twenty-first-century obsession with the mysterious and the possibly
supernatural or paranormal. To these we may now add many websites and
YouTube channels devoted to similar topics—and most of them at some time
have referred to the Green Children.

In general, writers on 'The Unexplained' have treated the Green Children
as another such mystery—usually identified as 'unsolved', but subject to speculation. However, there is also a strong human desire to present a 'logical'
explanation—to solve the 'unsolved'—and sometimes researchers go to
extraordinary lengths to do so. Thus Harold Wilkins (1959: 187–91) and
astronomer Duncan Lunan (1996; 2012) explained the Green Children in
terms of extraterrestrial interventions in human affairs and 'teleportation',
perhaps through vortices in space, from a human colony on a distant planet.

The term 'Fortean' (now often spelt with a lower-case initial 'f') has come
to be used both to describe such phenomena and to identify those who investigate them (Gardner 1957, 43; Simpson and Roud 2000: 134). And whereas
Charles Fort's own approach entailed a deliberate acceptance of even the most
unlikely accounts, there are now many fortean researchers who treat 'witness
reports' with caution, and readily accept that accounts of anomalous entities and

events are shaped and sometimes inspired by contemporary culture—by folklore and tradition, by literary or fictional models, by media expectation and by the pressure of current opinion. This is the approach adopted by many contributors to the British popular magazine *Fortean Times* and its short-lived offspring, a series of *Fortean Studies* (1994–2001) edited by Steve Moore, which allowed for longer, more academic research papers than were possible in the magazine itself.

Paul Harris's article 'The Green Children of Woolpit: a 12th century mystery and its possible solution' appeared in the fourth issue of *Fortean Studies* (Harris 1998). Harris attempted a 'down-to-earth' (but admittedly rather convoluted) explanation in the context of national events in the 1170s, dismissing the more 'Otherworldly' or 'folkloric' elements as conscious or unconscious elabora-tions by the two medieval chroniclers, William of Newburgh and Ralph of Coggeshall, who first recorded the story—or by their informants. He also printed both Latin and translated texts from William's and Ralph's accounts as a basis for his discussion. I noted some errors in the Latin transcripts and the English translations, and had problems with his interpretations of medieval history—I was no expert on Suffolk history in the twelfth century, but some of his conclusions seemed unlikely.

At that time Curator of the Medieval Collections of the Museum of London, I had a grounding in archaeology and medieval history. I had already become interested in the relationship between London's own history and the legends of its origin inspired by medieval historian and arch-confabulator Geoffrey of Monmouth, and thus in the ongoing interplay between conventional history and archaeology on the one hand and traditional 'legendary' narratives on the other (see, for example, Clark 1981). Though not a fluent reader of medieval Latin, I could make shift with interpreting the original texts. And the subject clearly related to my personal interests in folklore and 'forteana'. I offered the editor a follow-up paper to Harris's, subtitled 'a cautionary tale', setting out my reservations, and it duly appeared in *Fortean Studies* volume 6 (Clark 1999).

So my first venture into the subject was a critique of another author's work. Was it possible to take the subject forward independently, without being simply critical? A review of the literature (and indeed of what was then available on the internet) revealed that not only were a variety of 'explanations' offered by those who thought the story had some foundation in historical 'fact'—explanations ranging from the mundane to the extraterrestrial—but also that folklorists and academic historians had made much use of it.

The early appearance of a translation of Ralph of Coggeshall's Latin original, together with a summary of some points from William of Newburgh's version, in the 1850 edition of Thomas Keightley's *Fairy Mythology* (Keightley 1850:

281–83), set the tone for most 'folklore' interpretations—it was a traditional tale, fairylore. It inspired a unique 'motif' in Stith Thompson's authoritative *Motif-Index of Folk-Literature* (1955–1958).

Academic historians have taken a different approach. They do not investigate the intriguing historical conundra of the original texts—for example, did it actually happen, and if so when, who was our chief witness Sir Richard de Calne, how did the chronicler Ralph de Coggeshall meet him, where was his manor of Wykes, and why did the villagers of Woolpit take the Green Children there? Instead they have debated why and for what purpose(s) twelfth-century historians incorporated stories of 'wonders'—of which the Green Children were just one example—into their texts. Thus Nancy Partner concluded:

> I consider the process of worrying over the suggestive details of these wonderfully pointless miracles in an effort to find natural or psychological explanations of what 'really', if anything, happened, to be useless to the study of William of Newburgh or, for that matter, of the Middle Ages. (Partner 1977: 122)

But even more striking was the extent to which the story has inspired modern writers and creators to retell, rework or reimagine it. Kevin Crossley-Holland's retellings were just some of many, from stories for children to modernist poetry, from village pantomime to opera to psychedelic rock. Thus Olivero rescues the Green Child from her brutal husband and returns with her to the cold perfection of her subterranean homeland (Read 1935); Henry Cope, Regency Brighton's eccentric 'Green Man', reminisces about his ancestress the green girl of Woolpit (Dane 1938); in Suffolk, author Crispin Clare, brought near to death by illness and stress, is renewed by writing fresh versions of Ralph of Coggeshall's tales of wonders (Stow 1980); in Arizona Emily hopes that 'Maybe somebody in that green country will hear me. Maybe somebody will let me in' (Windling 1995); during the American Civil War, Robin, a young Confederate soldier, dying in a brutal prisoner of war camp, muses on the fate of the two strange children (Youmans 2001); in Ukraine in 1656, Scotsman Dr William Davisson jokes that 'It could be we have captured some Polish elves' (Tokarczuk 2018); and the unfortunate narrator of 'A Retelling' is buried alive in Woolpit (Johnson 2020). That two of Britain's most well-known composers of the twentieth century (Peter Maxwell Davies and Benjamin Britten) both planned operas on the subject of the Green Children is significant. That neither project came to fruition may be equally significant in reflecting the story's 'inherent inexplicability and unclassifiability'![1]

The present book began as the draft of an 'essay' that would attempt to unravel the strands of the original story and to put it into its historical context; in doing so, I hoped it might also suggest why and how the story of the Green Children has become perpetually fascinating, and utilized in such disparate ways. The study expanded, and it quickly became clear that it would, if completed, exceed the length of any article that would be accepted by an academic journal.

Perhaps to subdivide it? My 1999 paper had appeared in a 'fortean' context—what of folklorists, what of historians? In about 2004 I offered a 10,000 word 'research paper' on the many possible interpretations of 'St Martin's Land', the Green Children's homeland, to *Folklore*, the internationally respected journal of the Folklore Society. It was rejected, on the basis of well-founded reviews by two anonymous referees—I had, among other things, been tempted into speculation in an area where I had no expertise. So I reduced it to half, made it clearer that I was responding to an article (speculative itself, I thought!) that had already appeared in the same journal, and it was accepted (Clark 2006b).

The other area that seemed ripe for attention was the story's later legacy—the rewritings and reworkings of it as admitted fiction—why was it so fascinating? Among the earliest of references to the Green Children in early modern literature were the allusions in Bishop Francis Godwin's *The Man in the Moone*, published posthumously and anonymously in 1638. This was widely acknowledged to be the first genuine 'science fiction' story in the English language. Later writers who had reused the Green Children story included John Crowley (1981) and Terri Windling (1995), undoubted members of the science fiction/fantasy community. I offered a paper, admittedly borrowing Diane Purkiss's characterization of the children as 'small, vulnerable ETs' (Purkiss 2000: 63) as a title to bolster the claim, to DePauw University's *Science Fiction Studies*. The road to publication was again a rocky one, and I am grateful to editor Art Evans for seeing it through (Clark 2006a). The same theme is dealt with in Chapter 2 here, much expanded, as works I'd missed came to my attention (there had not been *one* opera but at least *four* actual or projected!), and with the apparently impossible task of keeping up with new versions of the story as they appeared.

In 2009 I retired from the Museum of London—what had been an occasional 'Saturday afternoon at the British Library, Sunday on the computer' part-time research project could now take up more of my attention. I opened an academia.edu account and posted a 'Green Children' essay there, continuing to add to it and amend it for the next few years, as well as supplementing it with a few short 'research notes' alongside copies of my published papers.[2]

Apologia

My drafts were of course 'self-published' on academia.edu; they had not undergone any form of peer review, and no academic (or Wikipedia contributor) could cite them. They did, however, attract some academic attention, and I was pleased to receive the plaudits of folklorist Simon Young.[3] It was Simon who suggested my work was worth publishing in full, and he has been supportive throughout its long gestation, and the intensive reworking and expansion of the version that was previously available online.

Unravelling the strands took me into many unfamiliar areas of research, from the horticulture of broad beans to medieval dyeing techniques, from green sickness to little red men, from *The Hierarchie of the Blessed Angells* to Satanic ritual abuse, from the cult of St Martin to St James's fair, from the trapping of wolves to the capture of fairies, and geographically from Carmarthen in Wales to Lutsk in Ukraine, from Utqiagvik in Alaska to the non-existent 'Banjos' in Spain, and even to the Land of the Antipodes. I visited Woolpit several times, and found a village that was clearly proud of its Green Children. On one occasion I walked there from Stowmarket, passing the isolated church of Onehouse, notorious for sightings of sandy-coloured fairies, and strayed into a beanfield.

The results of all those endeavours are presented here.

Our starting point, the Latin texts and modern translations of the accounts by William of Newburgh and Ralph of Coggeshall, is reserved for the Appendix, but we begin in Chapter 2 with a summary of what they tell us, and then look at the legacy—how the story has been interpreted, told and reworked over several hundred years. Chapter 3 considers this in more detail. In Chapter 4 we look at interpretations offered by modern folklorists, by academic historians and by those who seek a down-to-earth or alternatively extraterrestrial explanation for the events.

Having seen how in general others have interpreted it, we can turn to the detail and our own analysis. In Chapter 5 we introduce our two medieval historians, William and Ralph, and their works, before analysing the texts. We suggest that each of the texts comprises two elements: a 'framing narrative'—what, if we believe our authors, actually happened, the children's arrival, how they were treated and their eventual fate (Chapter 6); and 'the children's story'—what the children are reported to have said about their homeland and their arrival in 'our world' (Chapter 7). Under each heading we compare the two accounts and assess their differences. We then study each element of the narrative and try to decide what, if anything, 'actually happened'. This is the opportunity to assess the validity of all the many 'explanations' that have been offered over the years—and offer our own. In Chapter 8 we investigate a potential 'Welsh connection'—speculative, but perhaps no more unlikely than many explanations that have been offered!—and some concepts essential to the study of traditional behaviour and folklore that seem not to have been considered before. We then try to draw together the hopefully unravelled strands to estimate the 'truth' of the Green Children. And finally Chapter 9 provides the nearest thing to an overall conclusion I can offer, and the identification of the Green Children as 'strangers in a strange land'.

CHAPTER TWO

The Story and its Legacy

The story

> [T]hey differed in the colour of their skin from all the mortal inhabitants of our world; for the whole surface of their skin was dyed with a green colour. (Ralph of Coggeshall)

The children were green. There were other strange things about the boy and the girl, but the first thing everybody noticed was that they were green-skinned—dark green like the leaves of leeks, some said. And they appeared suddenly to the villagers in the harvest fields, as if they had come out of a hole in the ground. There was much more to the story, but that's how it began.

Two (nearly) contemporary writers report the strange event that took place at the Suffolk village of Woolpit, in eastern England, one summer in the twelfth century: William of Newburgh, an Augustinian canon at Newburgh Priory in Yorkshire, and Ralph of Coggeshall, abbot of a small Cistercian house in north Essex.[1] William included his chapter 'Concerning green children' in his *Historia Rerum Anglicarum* (*The History of English Affairs*) in about 1198, and based it, he tells us, on reports from a number of trustworthy sources. Ralph of Coggeshall's chapter 'Concerning a boy and a girl who emerged from the ground' appeared in his *Chronicon Anglicanum* (*English Chronicle*). Although the *Chronicon Anglicanum* was not, it seems, completed until the 1220s, it incorporated text written much earlier, and, in the case of the Green Children, information from Richard de Calne of Wykes, who gave the children a home and (as we shall see) died before 1188.

The story is well known, but in relating it many commentators have combined inconsistent features from the two accounts. The following summary draws on both authors, but indicates some of the differences; the similarities and the inconsistencies will be analysed in detail below.

One day (in the time of King Stephen, according to William), the villagers of Woolpit in East Anglia (harvesters in the fields, adds William) saw two bewildered children, a boy and a girl (brother and sister, says Ralph), apparently emerging from a pit—from the 'wolf-pits' that gave the village its name, says William. Their skin was green; they spoke an unknown language and (says William) they were dressed in strangely coloured clothing of strange material. Ralph says that they were taken to the house of Sir Richard de Calne, at nearby Wykes. Both authors agree that they refused all food for several days (according to Ralph, the girl later said that they thought that the food they were offered was inedible). Then by chance they saw some freshly cut bean plants; at first they tried to find the beans within the stalks, but once a bystander had taken the beans out of the pods for them they eagerly ate the beans. For some time they ate only raw beans, but gradually they became used to normal food and (perhaps as a result) lost their green colouring. It was decided to baptize the children. The boy was sickly and died, either before or soon after baptism. The girl flourished.

Once they had learnt our language the children (or the surviving girl, according to Ralph) explained that they had come from a land where the sun never shone, but where the light was like that of twilight here—Ralph adds that everybody and everything in the land was green. William reports that the children said it was a Christian land with churches; they called it St Martin's Land and said St Martin was venerated there. From it another brighter land could be seen across a broad river. According to William the children could not explain how they came to our land; while herding their father's cattle they had heard a loud noise, and suddenly found themselves in the field among the harvesters. Ralph, on the other hand, says that they had followed the cattle into a cavern and had become lost; following the sound of bells, they had eventually come out into our land where the villagers had found them.

Ralph says that for many years the girl was a servant in the household of Sir Richard de Calne, from whom he had heard the story, but that she was said to have been badly behaved; William says that she married a man in Lynn, and he had heard that she was still alive shortly before he wrote. In a postscript, William adds that many illusions are the work of 'evil angels' but that he is unable to explain the Green Children.

This summary does scant justice to a story that, as folklorist Katharine Briggs commented, 'has a curiously convincing and detailed air' (Briggs 1967: 7–8). It certainly convinced a reluctant William of Newburgh, who heard the story from many sources and was 'overcome by the evidence of so many witnesses of such weight'.

However, it is unlikely that the story had continued to circulate widely after its original currency in the twelfth and thirteenth centuries. There are no references to it in literature between the original chroniclers' accounts and the sixteenth century, when it was first noticed by antiquary John Leland from a manuscript copy of William of Newburgh's chronicle (Leland 1715: 2:312) and then by commentators drawing on the first printed editions of the texts. Though it was then taken up by intellectuals speculating about the plurality of inhabited worlds, or of worlds within our own, there is no evidence of any popular survival or local circulation. It probably remained unknown locally until Thomas Keightley included a translation of Ralph of Coggeshall's Latin original, together with a summary of some points from William of Newburgh's version, in the 1850 edition of his *Fairy Mythology* (Keightley 1850, 281–83). It thus became known to the new breed of 'folklorists' interested in local traditional tales and beliefs.[2] And it seems typical that Lady Eveline Camilla Gurdon's version, in an 1893 compendium of Suffolk folklore taken from printed sources (Gurdon 1893: 33–34), printed for the Folk-lore Society, was derived from an earlier guidebook to East Anglia ([King] 1875: 175–76). It seems likely that it was from such guidebooks that it has re-entered local tradition, where it is current today.

The legacy

The Green Children have warranted entries in a dictionary of folklore (Simpson and Roud 2000: 153–54), in three dictionaries of fairies (Briggs 1976: 200–01; Rose 1996: 130–31; Bane 2013: 166), in dictionaries of fantasy literature (Clute and Grant 1997: 437), of 'The Unexplained' (Clark 1993: 133–4) and of 'alien encounters' (Baker 2000: 123–24). They have inspired a long, detailed and much-debated Wikipedia article.[3] To folklorists the story is the primary exemplar of a standard folktale motif (Motif F103.1 in Baughman's classification (1966: 203))—although perhaps it is also unique. And it has been described as 'a classic of forteana' in the magazine *Fortean Times* (Minyak 2000).

The children's story has been cited in academic discussions of medieval cosmology (Bartlett 2000: 688; Bruce 2019: 110–11), of medieval childhood (Orme 1995: 74–75; 2001: 92), of the relations between the races of Norman

Britain (Cohen 2008), of the possibility of medieval 'science fiction' (Campbell 2016) and of, most often, the purposes and methods of twelfth-century historical writers (Partner 1977: 115–28; Otter 1996: 103–04; Freeman 2000: 129; 2002: 194; Watkins 2007: 63–64; Clarke 2009; and Staunton 2017: 120–27). Thus Clarke interprets William of Newburgh's version of the story as an example of the 'literature of trauma' inspired by the Anarchy of King Stephen's reign; to Cohen 'the Green Children resurface another story that William had been unable to tell, one in which English paninsular dominion becomes a troubled assumption rather than a foregone conclusion'; and Freeman concludes that Ralph of Coggeshall's version reflects 'the threat posed by outsiders to the unity of the Christian community'.

Two recent historical papers (Madej 2020 and Plumtree 2022), instead of employing selected aspects of the story in an argument in favour of one or other historical theory or methodology, have gone back to a detailed study of the events as they were recorded by the two chroniclers.[4] Madej, however, concludes by apparently accepting Cohen's interpretation of William of Newburgh's motive in telling the story ('the anxiety experienced [by] a chronicler who considered himself to be English, but lived in an Anglo-Norman society'), and Freeman's interpretation of Ralph of Coggeshall's purpose ('threats stemming from what is different and unknown') (Madej 2020: 130).

Unfortunately, Paul Edward Dutton's brief but important study of the episode of the Green Children, a chapter in his book *Micro Middle Ages* (Dutton 2023: 11–53), appeared too late for me to take it into consideration in what follows.

The tale of the Green Children has been retold many times, usually for young readers or as a 'Suffolk folk tale' (for example, Crossley-Holland 1966; Colwell 1972: 70–73; Mitchell 1996; Hartsiotis 2013: 14–17; Coats 2019). Of these authors we have already mentioned Kevin Crossley-Holland, and shall return to his work again. Kirsty Hartsiotis is a professional storyteller. Her version of 'perhaps Suffolk's most famous folktale' was later reprinted to represent that county in an anthology of English folktales (Gay 2016). In 1980 the story of the Green Children appeared as a picture story in a British comic aimed at teenage girls and specializing in horror and the supernatural (*Misty* 1980) (Fig. 1).[5] It has inspired novels (Dane 1938; Read 1935; Stow 1980), poetry (Robertson 1977; Prynne 1982; Yolen 1993; Burton 2013; Newell 2015), plays (Maxwell 1996; Bignell 2000; Nigro 2021) and a children's opera (LeFanu and Crossley-Holland 1990). Two of Britain's most distinguished twentieth-century composers (Peter Maxwell Davies and Benjamin Britten) independently considered it as the subject of an opera (Falkiner 2016: 465–66,

Fig. 1.   First page of 'The Green Children:
A Misty Special Story' from *Misty Holiday Special* (Summer 1980).
Misty © Copyright Rebellion Publishing IP Ltd. All Rights Reserved.

502). It became the focus for a teaching resource in drama on the theme of 'Community cohesion and the prevention of violent extremism' (Council for Subject Associations [2009?]; Baldwin 2009: 155–63). In the 1960s it even spawned a modern 'unexplained mysteries' doublet of itself, said to have occurred in Spain in the nineteenth century (Macklin 1965: 23–26). And the name was adopted by an Anglo-Norwegian musical duo, The Green Children (TGC 2022).[6]

Diane Purkiss compared the story to the 'magical realism' of the work of Jorge Luis Borges: 'The best thing to do with this beautiful oddity is to leave it alone in its Borgesian glory'—but she then willingly succumbed, as so many have, to the temptation to interpret it as a story of fairy-folk (Purkiss 2000: 62–63).

James Plumtree (2022: 224) recently described the Green Children as 'perpetually figures of lurid interest'. Faced with such a range of historical interpretations and fictional uses and abuses, we can only echo Plumtree's conclusion:

> The green children are an exemplum of the inherent problems of the historical method. Scholars and speculators, like the two medieval chroniclers, show a desire to place, comprehend, categorize and understand, an urge often at the expense of the sources and—if it existed—the original tale, and—if they existed—the original children. The probable story of displacement and the kindness of strangers becomes a fearful parable that can be manipulated to suit a variety of intentions. (Ibid.: 223)

My own research into this 'fearful parable' did eventually lead to some conclusions, but no all-embracing 'explanation' is offered here.

CHAPTER THREE

Transmission

Transmission and early reactions

> Nor does it seem right to omit a wonder, unheard of by the ages,
> that is known to have happened in England in the time of King
> Stephen. (William of Newburgh)

There is evidence, to which we shall return, that the story of the Green
Children was circulating orally, at least locally, in the twelfth century. It was
preserved in written accounts by two authors, William of Newburgh and Ralph
of Coggeshall, which survive in several manuscript versions. Their Latin texts
are reproduced with fresh translations in the Appendix.

Richard Howlett, who edited William of Newburgh's *Historia Rerum
Anglicarum* for the nineteenth-century 'Rolls Series', lists nine manuscripts
of the work dating from the twelfth century to the fifteenth (Howlett 1884:
xxxix).[1] The first printed edition appeared in Antwerp in 1567 (with a reprint
in Heidelberg in 1587) and a new edition by Jean Picard (or Picart) of Paris
in 1610 (ibid.: lv; William of Newburgh 1988: 19), making the text widely
available to the international intellectual community.

In the case of Ralph of Coggeshall's *Chronicon Anglicanum*, Joseph Stevenson
employed only three early manuscripts for his Rolls Series edition (Ralph of
Coggeshall 1875: xvi–xvii). One of these, now in the British Library (MS
Cotton Vespasian D X), seems to be the author's original draft.[2] There was
no printed edition of Ralph's work until parts of it were included in a nine-
volume collection of historical texts published by Edmond Martène and Ursin
Durand in Paris in 1724–1733 (5: columns 801–82; see Stevenson 1875: xvii–
xviii). However, their edition *omits* Ralph's digressions on the Green Children
of Woolpit and other wonders, which the editors perhaps felt unworthy of
inclusion.[3] However, Ralph's account of the Green Children *was* printed in
full in the editor's notes in the 1610 Paris edition of William of Newburgh's
Historia (above), alongside William's own account (William of Newburgh 1610:

704–06). This early association of the two texts was to be very important for the transmission of the story, as we shall see.

In the early sixteenth century, before the appearance of the first printed texts, the antiquary John Leland (c.1506–1552) abstracted some information from a manuscript of William of Newburgh's *Historia* in his four volumes of notes, or *Collectanea* (now in the Bodleian Library, Oxford).[4] He included a short summary of the story of the Green Children: '*de masculo & femina viridibus pueris, è terra subito exilientibus*' ('concerning the male and female green children, suddenly springing out of the ground') (Leland 1715: 2:312). He notes the children's appearance in the wolf-pits, the early death of the boy, their claim to have come from St Martin's Land, the fact that their green colour faded with time and the girl's marriage to a man in Lynn. He quotes in full William's account of the location of Woolpit and the derivation of its name from the adjacent wolf-pits (paragraph 2 in the Appendix below) and goes on to mention three more of William's 'wonder' stories. He makes no comment on the significance of the story of the Green Children and no attempt to judge its veracity.

John Leland's *Collectanea* did not appear in printed form until 1715, more than 160 years after his death (Leland 1906–1910: 1:xix–xx), and although scholars might have had access to the manuscript, Leland's work seems to have played no part in the transmission of the story.

At the end of the sixteenth century, William Camden (1551–1623) mentions the story of the Green Children in the description of Suffolk in his celebrated work *Britannia*. To quote the whole passage from Philemon Holland's 1610 translation of Camden's original Latin:

> *Wulpet* is a Mercat towne, and soundeth asmuch as, The Woolues pit, if we may beleeue *Nubrigensis* who hath told as pretty and formall a tale of the place, as is that fable called the TRVE NARRATION of *Lucian*: namely, how two little boies (forsooth) of a greene colour, and of Satyrs kinde, after they had made along journey by passages under the ground, from out of another world from the *Antipodes* and Saint *Martins* land, came upheere: of whom if you would know more, repaire to the authour himselfe, where you shall finde such matter as will make you laugh your fill, if you have a laughing spleene. (Camden 1610: 463–64; for the original Latin text, see Camden 1586: 257)

So Camden dismisses the story as a laughable fiction to be compared with Lucian of Samosata's *Vera Historia* (a tall story of a voyage to the moon, written in Greek in the second century CE), while identifying the children as putative 'satyrs'—presumably wild men.[5] Although he attributes the story to William of Newburgh (*Nubrigensis*), he seems to have begun the long tradition of conflating (and confusing) William's account with that of Ralph of Coggeshall. Although the reference to 'St Martin's Land' is found only in William of Newburgh's text, the 'long journey by passages under the ground' comes from Ralph of Coggeshall. He could have found William's story in print, in the Antwerp edition of 1567, while his friend John Stow, the London historian, possessed a manuscript of Ralph of Coggeshall's *Chronicon*.[6]

Ralph of Coggeshall and William of Newburgh agree that the children were a boy and a girl—'*duo pueri, masculus et femina*' as William puts it. In Latin *puer* is ambiguous. Although it usually means 'boy' it can also mean 'child (of either sex)'—hence William's need (followed by John Leland) to elaborate 'male and female'. Thus Camden's reference—in Holland's translation—to the children as 'two little boies' is startling. Camden's original Latin '*duos pusiones*' (Camden 1586: 257) indeed means 'two little boys', for *pusio* is unambiguously a 'little male child' (Souter et al. 1968–1982: 1525). Perhaps Camden misremembered William of Newburgh's original. His translators Philemon Holland (Camden 1610: 463) and Edmund Gibson (Camden 1722: 443) followed him unquestioningly. They presumably thought it inappropriate to correct their author, did not refer back to the original Newburgh account or may have been unaware of any other source that indicated that the children were a boy and a girl.

The suggestion that the children's world was the land of the Antipodes seems to be Camden's own addition to the twelfth-century historians—although, as we shall see, their contemporary Gervase of Tilbury identified the Otherworld reached through Peak Cavern in Derbyshire as 'the land of the Antipodes' (Gervase of Tilbury 2002: 642–45; Westwood 1985: 204–06; Westwood and Simpson 2005: 172), and William Camden was aware of Gervase's narrative, referring to it himself in his account of the Peak (Camden 1586: 314).

Camden's account of the Green Children was summarized by John Speed (1552?–1629) in his atlas of maps of the counties of Britain *The Theatre of the Empire of Great Britaine* ... (1611), in a page of notes on the county of Suffolk printed on the reverse of the county map:

> the like fable is formally told by *Nubrigensis*, that at *Wulpet* in the
> Heart of this Shire, two greene boies of Satyres kind arose out of the
> ground, from the *Antipodes*; believe it if you will. (Speed 1611: 33)

Although Camden is not credited, the source is evident in the vocabulary and the tone. The story's presence on a map that would have been the pride of any Suffolk gentleman's library may have drawn it to wider attention locally, but Speed's repetition of Camden's sneering recommendation to 'believe it if you will' would have discouraged anyone from paying much attention to it.

In stark contrast to Camden's light-hearted approach is that of (or attributed to) Spanish Dominican Thomas Malvenda (1566–1628), who in an influential book on the Antichrist, first published in Rome in 1604, apparently attributes the Green Children to a *miracle* performed by the Antichrist: '*Antichristum ea potissimum effecturum miracula, quae magis mirentur homines*'—as noted by James Plumtree (2022: 216 note 50). In the chapter under this heading the author quotes in full both William of Newburgh's and Ralph of Coggeshall's accounts of the Green Children, as well as some of William's other 'wonders'—although he omits William's discussion of the ability of 'demons' (or 'evil angels') to create 'illusions' and his conclusion that this demonic ability does *not*, in his view, suffice to explain the Green Children.

However, this chapter does *not* appear in this form in the 1604 edition of Malvenda's work—Plumtree cites it from the 1647 Lyons edition (Malvenda 1647: 2:91–92), by which time the work had been expanded from 'Libri XI' to 'Libri XIII'. Indeed, both passages are taken directly from Jean Picard's edition of William of Newburgh's work—the author credits the source under Picard's title *De rebus Anglicis*, and cites Picard's editorial notes for the text of Ralph of Coggeshall. And, as we have noted, Picard's edition was not published until 1610. Thus the references to the Green Children story must have been added later to Malvenda's original text of 1604, by Malvenda or another—and I can find no trace of an edition of the *De Antichristo* between 1604 and 1647, by which time Thomas Malvenda would have been dead for nearly twenty years. So it remains a moot point whether Malvenda himself would have considered the Green Children best defined as a diabolical miracle!

More indicative of 'enlightened' contemporary thought was perhaps the approach of philosopher Robert Burton (1577–1640), who included in his *Anatomy of Melancholy* (1621) a digression on the plurality of inhabited worlds, a much-debated theory at the time ('*per consequens*, the rest of the Planets are inhabited, as well as the Moone'). He suggested 'it may bee those two greene children, which *Nubrigensis* speakes of in his time, that fell from Heaven, came from thence' (Part.2 Sect.2 Memb.3 Subs.1; Burton 1990: 51–52). Burton had clearly read William of Newburgh—he refers elsewhere to his writings—although William gives no hint that the children had fallen from heaven. However, Burton was presumably unaware of, or deliberately ignored, Ralph of Coggeshall's account, for Ralph's description of the children's underground journey from their sunless home would be difficult to interpret as an aerial journey from another planet.

The Man in the Moone ...

... or a Discovrse of a Voyage Thither. ([Godwin] 1638)

A little later Burton's speculation may have inspired a friend of William Camden to develop further the idea that the Green Children had arrived from another planet. In 1590 Francis Godwin (1562–1633), later bishop of Llandaff and afterwards of Hereford, had accompanied Camden on an expedition to investigate the antiquities of Wales, for a second edition of the *Britannia* (Woolf 2004). And Lucian's *Vera Historia*, referred to by Camden, may have been part of the inspiration for Godwin's own venture into speculative fiction, which similarly describes an accidental journey to the moon and the strange civilization a traveller found there. Written probably between 1626 and 1629 (McColley 1937) but not published until 1638, five years after his death, Godwin's *The Man in the Moone: or a Discovrse of a Voyage Thither* ([Godwin] 1638) is famous as the earliest work of its kind in English and one of the most popular (Nicolson 1960: 71–85, 265F) (Fig. 2).

We learn from the personal account of the narrator, a Spanish traveller called Domingo Gonsales (carried to the moon in a home-made vehicle drawn by 'gansas' or wild swans), that the Lunar inhabitants, who are larger, longer-lived and in every way superior to those of Earth, have a short way with children who show early signs that they are likely to grow up 'of a wicked or imperfect disposition'—they dispatch them to Earth, and take away Earth children to replace them ([Godwin] 1638: 104–06; Clark 2006a, 212–15). The Lunars normally set their 'changelings' down on a high hill in North America, but Gonsales admits that 'they sometimes mistake their aime' and the children land in Christendom or in Asia or Africa. Gonsales claims that, though this seldom happens, there are reports to confirm it—notably 'one Chapter of *Guil. Neubrigensis, de reb. Angl.*: it is towards the end of his first booke, but the chapter I cannot particularly resigne [recall]'. The narrator's uncertain memory is a masterly touch—William of Newburgh's account of the Green Children does indeed appear towards the end of his first book, being the twenty-seventh of thirty-two chapters. One wonders whether it was Camden's likening of William of Newburgh's account to Lucian's earlier story of a lunar adventure

Fig. 2.   Domingo Gonsales carried to the moon by wild swans.
Illustration from Francis Godwin, *The Man in the Moone: or a Discovrse of a Voyage Thither, by Domingo Gonsales* (1638). © The British Library Board, C.58.c.2, plate 15.

that could have inspired his friend Godwin to incorporate them into his own similar tale.

Godwin's citation of William's work as '*de reb. Angl.*'—that is, *De rebus Anglicis*—indicates that it was the 1610 Paris printing that he made use of, for, as Lawton points out (1931: 39 note 2), that is the title carried by Picard's Paris edition. *The Man in the Moone*, however, was written in English, rather than in Latin, as a traveller's tale, apparently intended for the popular market. Most of Godwin's readers would not have read William of Newburgh, available only in Latin, and would not have heard of the Green Children of Woolpit. To most of them, the citation of 'one Chapter of *Guil. Neubrigensis, de reb. Angl.*' would be neither more nor less significant than the subsequent citations of two obscure or even fictitious Spanish authors, Inigo Mondejar and Joseph Desia de Carana, apparently also witnesses to the occasional misdirection of Lunar delinquent children.[7]

If he consulted the Picard edition of William's text, Godwin would also have known Ralph of Coggeshall's version, which, as we have noted, was printed alongside the Newburgh text in Picard's 1610 edition. And in spite of his claim that he (or rather his fictional narrator, Domingo Gonsales) cannot recall exactly which chapter the story appeared in, he made much greater use of it than is immediately apparent. There are a number of subtle allusions to it in his description of the moon and its people, all the more telling for any knowledgeable reader because Godwin avoids any overt reference to William, other than the one apparently off-hand comment that we have seen.

As might be expected, the description of the manner in which the Lunars dispose of delinquent children contains other hints of the story of the Green Children. Lunar children lose their original strange colour when on Earth, to become more like us in colour ([Godwin] 1638: 104–05)—at least like the inhabitants of North America! It is however the 'ayre' of Earth rather than (as both William and Ralph seem to suggest) the diet that brings about this change. And these children are exiled because they are, from birth, identified as having faults of character—'likely to be of a wicked or imperfect disposition'. This is surely a reflection of the green girl's disposition in later life as described by Ralph of Coggeshall: 'she remained very wanton and impudent' ('*nimium lasciva et petulans exstitit*'). Although William of Newburgh does not confirm this description, Godwin would have seen *Ralph's* words in Picard's notes to the 1610 edition of William's text that we know he consulted (above).

When Gonsales first meets the Lunars he is astounded not only by their size (most of them giants to our eyes) and their colour, but also by the nature and colour of their clothing. He had never seen, he says, any 'cloth, silke, or other stuffe to resemble the matter of that whereof their Clothes were made; neither [...] can I devise how to describe the colour of them' (ibid.: 71). The similarity to William of Newburgh's 'they were dressed in clothing of an unusual colour, made of unknown material' must be more than coincidental. Godwin/Gonsales expands on this unusual colour. Both the Lunars and their clothes are of 'a colour never seen in our earthly world'—as fruitless to attempt to describe it, he tells us, as to explain to a blind man the difference between blue and green. Their language, too, is incomprehensible (ibid.: 93–96).

Gonsales is also at some pains to describe the different forms of light that illuminate the moon—sunlight, earthlight, and the light (owing to 'the propin-quitie of the stares and other Planets') to be found on the side of the moon hidden from the earth, especially 'what manner of light there is in that world during the absence of the *Sunne*' (ibid.: 88–89). I am reminded of a question that William tells us was posed to the Green Children on whether the sun shone in their land, and their reply: 'Our land is scarcely illuminated by [the sun's] rays; it gets only the amount of light that among you precedes sunrise or follows sunset.'

But of all the Lunars' similarities to the Green Children, it is surely their attitude to St Martin that is most striking. For when Gonsales, trying to communicate with them, recites the names of a number of saints: 'at last reckoning among others *st. Martinus*, they all bowed their bodies, and held up hands in signe of great reverence: the reason whereof I learned to bee, that *martin* in their language signifieth God' (ibid.: 83). Moreover, we hear of an island called '*insula Martini*'—'the island of God'—where the people are particularly holy (ibid.: 90). There can surely be little doubt that this is inspired by the Green Children's claim, reported by William of Newburgh, 'We are people from the land of St Martin—who is held in particular veneration in the land of our birth.' Given the difficulty of explaining this special reverence for St Martin in the context of the Green Children's own time—as we shall discuss below—or in that of Godwin (although see Clark 2007 for the possible significance of the name 'Martin' to Godwin's readers), it seems unlikely to be a matter of independent inspiration.

Aside from Godwin's 'essay of Fancy', the story of the Green Children was used in scientific discussions, not of interplanetary travel, but of the possibility of the existence of a subterranean world (or worlds) within our own. William Poole, in his edition of *The Man in the Moone* (Godwin 2009: 22 note 1), draws attention to the fact that German philosopher Athanasius Kircher (1602–1680) quoted William of Newburgh's account as evidence for the existence of subter-ranean inhabited worlds: '*Mira historia de hominibus subterraneis, ex Guilielmo Neubrissensi Anglico scriptore decerpta*' (Kircher 1678: 2:120–22).

And the antiquary and biographer John Aubrey (1626–1697), responding in
the 1680s to a theory put forward by his friend the astronomer Edmond Halley
that the earth was hollow, containing within it two other concentric spheres
around a solid core, drew the Green Children into the discussion (Poole 2005:
201–02).[8]

> Eusebius Nieuwebrigensis So: Jesu speakes of a Country under
> Ground some where here in England out of which thrô a Cleft came
> some children as I remember, who related very strange things of a
> Territory there, & who had never seen the Sun, but had some light
> thrô certaine crannies &c: I have quite forgotten the particulars.
> (Bodleian MS Aubrey 1, fol. 88v)

Aubrey mistakenly attributes the story to 'Eusebius Nieuwebrigensis So:
Jesu'—the Spanish Jesuit and mystic Juan Eusebio Nieremberg, author of
Historia Naturae (1635) (Poole 2005: 209 note 46). He had presumably not
read William of Newburgh's work, but took his reference from either William
Camden or Robert Burton, both of whom, as we have seen, refer to the author
merely as 'Nubrigensis'—and Aubrey admits he had in any case 'quite forgotten
the particulars'!

In spite of these references to the Green Children in seventeenth-century
literature, there is no evidence that the story had survived independently in oral
or written tradition in Suffolk. Suffolk writers such as Robert Reyce, author
of *The Breviary of Suffolk* (1618), and the anonymous author of *The Chorography
of Suffolk* (c.1602) in the seventeenth century (Reyce 1902; MacCulloch 1976)
and John Kirby in the eighteenth century (Kirby 1735), even when describing
Woolpit, do not mention the Green Children.[9]

The nineteenth century and after

Among the more extraordinary attempts to 'explain' the Green Children is
that by Algernon Herbert in the first volume of his revisionist history of early
Britain, *Britannia after the Romans*, published (anonymously) in 1836, with a
second volume in 1841.[10] He attributes the story to William of 'Newbridge'.
After likening the Children's land of St Martin to the fairy realm visited by
the boy Elidurus, in the story related by Gerald of Wales that we shall discuss
below, and emphasizing the importance to the 'Druidic' Britons of painting
the body with woad, he concludes: 'The legend in my opinion relates to the
secret orgies of the "virides Britanni" ["green Britons"] and the mysteries of

Manogan and Brithan' ([Herbert] 1836–1841: 1:lx).[11] The full significance of these 'mysteries' and the sinister authority of St Martin of Tours in post-Roman Britain may perhaps become clear to those who persevere with the rest of Herbert's obscure and eccentric text—we shall return later to one element of it, Herbert's identification of St Martin with the Welsh Myrddin or Merlin.

But it seems after all to have been Thomas Keightley who popularized the story of the Green Children in 1850, when he included a translation of Ralph of Coggeshall's text in the second edition of his *Fairy Mythology* (Fig. 3)—the story does not appear in the first edition (1828). Keightley did not base his translation directly on an edition or manuscript of Ralph's *Chronicon Anglicanum*—he was, he says, unable to locate the passage in the eighteenth-century edition by Martène and Durand that he consulted: 'We could not find it in the Collection of Histories, etc., by Martens and Durand,—the only place where, to our knowledge, this chronicler's works are printed' (Keightley 1850: 281). Indeed, as we have already noted, the edition by Martène and Durand excludes not only the story of the Green Children but Ralph's other accounts of 'wonders'. Keightley tells us that instead he drew on the extensive quotation of Ralph's Latin text that Jean Picard included in his notes on William of Newburgh's alternative version of the story. As we have said, this was contained in Picard's early printed edition of William's works—the Paris edition of 1610 (William of Newburgh 1610: 704–06).

Furthermore, it is likely that Keightley found Picard's notes *not* in a copy of the 1610 printing but through their later inclusion in the edition of William of Newburgh published in Oxford by Thomas Hearne, based upon that by Picard (William of Newburgh 1719: 618–20)—for it is from *Hearne's* edition, not Picard's, that Keightley tells us he summarized *William's* story (Keightley 1850: 282–83). Amidst such a complex of borrowings, it is perhaps not surprising that a small but significant phrase in Ralph's original account has got lost in transmission by the time Keightley prints it (as noted by Paul Harris (1998: 83)). Missing is the reason that the girl later gave for the children's refusal to eat the food they were offered—that they thought it was 'inedible' (something to be discussed further below). The phrase '*quia omnia huiusmodi cibaria incomestibilia esse credebant*' ('because they believed all foodstuffs of this sort were inedible') was already absent from the Coggeshall text as Jean Picard printed it in the notes in his edition of William of Newburgh (1610: 705). Thomas Hearne (William of Newburgh 1719: 716–17), in his own supplementary notes to Picard's, draws attention to the omission; he refers for the fuller text to the manuscript of Ralph of Coggeshall then in the library of the Earl of Arundel (now London, College of Heralds (Arundel) MS 11—see Gransden

Fig. 3.   Frontispiece, by George Cruikshank,
for Thomas Keightley's *The Fairy Mythology* (1850).

1974: 323).[12] Another peculiarity of the Keightley version, which allow us to identify its long influence, is his reference to William of Newburgh as William of *Newbridge*.

Keightley's text seems to have become the standard form of the story, at least as it was to be known to folklorists. It was reprinted in Hartland's *English Fairy and Other Folk Tales* (Hartland [1890]: 132–34) and by Katharine Briggs in her *Dictionary of British Folk-Tales* (Briggs 1971: 1:262–63). Briggs takes the Coggeshall text from Keightley by way of Hartland. She adds to it a note summarizing the Newburgh version. This is also a quotation from Keightley (1850, 282–83)—apart from a final comment of Briggs's own very similar to something she had previously said in her *Fairies in English Tradition and Literature* (1967: 7–8): 'This is one of those curiously convincing and realistic fairy anecdotes which are occasionally to be found in the medieval chronicles.'

Thus her text incorporates Keightley and Hartland's attribution of the story to William 'of *Newbridge*'. Kevin Crossley-Holland (1966: unpaginated; 1982: 101; 1997: 207) quotes William's name in the same form—he presumably based his own retelling directly or indirectly on Keightley's version or Hartland's reprint of it. Indeed, in the earlier of his published versions he refers, like Briggs, to Richard de Calne as Richard de *Caine*—a form that seems first to have appeared in Hartland's *English Fairy and Other Folk Tales* ([1890]).

In a chapter entitled 'Fantasy' in a study of English prose style first published in 1928 and oft-reprinted, Herbert Read (later to rework the story in his own novel *The Green Child* (1935)) quoted Keightley's translation in full as his prime model of a folktale, 'the norm to which all types of Fantasy should conform' (1952a, 127–28). It also formed the basis of Enid Porter's account of the Green Children in her *Folklore of East Anglia* (Porter 1974: 76–77). It appeared again more recently in a book on *Fairies* by Janet Bord, in the context of 'real encounters with the little people' (1997: 126–28), and in Paul Harris's account of the Green Children in *Fortean Studies* (1998: 82–3).

Keightley, although he had access to William of Newburgh's account, chose to give the full text of Ralph's version and to refer to William only for additional details—thus failing to remark some essential inconsistencies between the two versions. Later commentators have followed his lead. Phrases such as 'William of Newburgh adds that …' or 'includes details not mentioned in Ralph's version' are ubiquitous (Patch 1950: 237; Briggs 1967: 8; Briggs 1976: 201; Westwood 1985: 174; Westwood and Simpson 2005: 707). Perhaps folklorists in particular are attracted by Ralph's fuller account of the children's subterranean wanderings, a familiar concept they can compare with other accounts of Otherworld journeys.

In 1861 William of Newburgh's *Historia* received the benefit of translation at the hands of the Rev. Joseph Stevenson. Thanks perhaps to this translation it was William's version of the story that, by way of a guidebook to East Anglia, came to be summarized in Lady Eveline Gurdon's compendium of Suffolk folklore from printed sources (Gurdon 1893: 33–34; quoting [King] 1875: 175–76). Later, William Dutt's popular guidebook to *Suffolk* (1904: 337)—still in print in its sixth edition as late as 1957—also summarized the Newburgh version (referring to the Rolls Series Latin edition of the *Historia* by Howlett), giving the story wide circulation as well as currency in Suffolk.

Most recent writers, even in Suffolk, seem to have derived their versions of the story from one or other of these published accounts. There is nothing to suggest the existence of a long-lived oral tradition. But there seems little doubt that once the story of the Green Children had appeared in print—perhaps particularly in local guidebooks—it re-entered local tradition, where it survives today.

Tea at the vicarage

'Well,' replied the Parson, 'I expect it is quite as good an explanation as you will find, so mind you put it in your book.' (Maxwell 1926: 108)

In what seems to have been a twentieth-century development of the story, the children have become identified with the 'Babes in the Wood', a story familiar in printed ballads and chapbooks since 1595, and in pantomimes more recently (Westwood 1985: 170–71; Westwood and Simpson 2005: 521–22). Two orphaned children, a boy and a girl, are left in the care of their wicked uncle. The uncle plots to steal their inheritance, and hires two ruffians to take them into the wood and kill them. One of the ruffians is reluctant, and kills the other to protect the children. He leaves the children in the wood, promising to return with food—but does not come back. The children starve to death, and robins covers their bodies with leaves (Fig. 4). The uncle later dies in poverty.

This morbid story was not in origin a folktale, though it bears some resemblance to the familiar stories of 'Snow White' and 'Hansel and Gretel'. The story was first printed (purportedly as an account of an actual event) by Norwich printer Thomas Millington, and registered at Stationers' Hall on 15 October 1595. From the start the story was located in Norfolk, and may

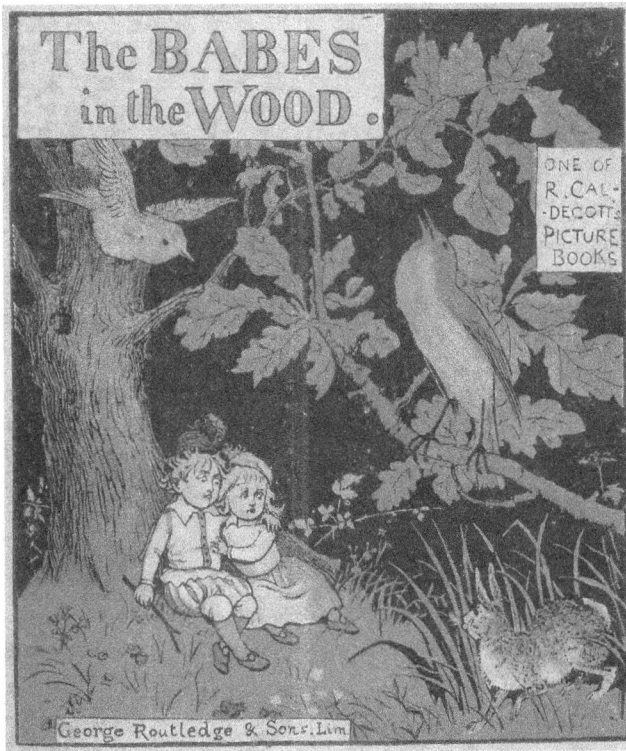

Fig. 4.   Cover of *The Babes in the Wood* by Randolph Caldecott (*c*.1880).

have been inspired by rumours about the de Grey family of Griston Old Hall, near Watton, west of Norwich. An eleven-year-old boy Thomas de Grey had died mysteriously; murder was suspected and suspicion fell on his uncle, Robert de Grey, who inherited his nephew's fortune, but later died in debt. Locally at least the wood where the children died was identified as Wayland Wood, near Watton, which became known as 'Wailing Wood' (Map 1). An oak tree reputed to be the tree under which the Babes had lain down to die was struck by lightning in 1879, attracting sightseers from all over Norfolk.

The potential association of the Babes in the Wood with the story of the Green Children seems first to have been recorded by artist and travel-writer Donald Maxwell (1877–1936), who in 1926 titled a chapter of his book *Unknown Suffolk* (1926: 103–12) 'The little green people of Woolpit'. Walking near Woolpit, Maxwell had met the vicar, who invited him back to tea in the vicarage. There the vicar (properly the rector) entertained his visitor with the tale of the Green Children. Asked if he believed it, the vicar said: 'I believe the story is too circumstantial to be entirely fictitious. I think there is no doubt two green children really did come up from out of the ground, but how they had got there and how they had become green is beyond me' (ibid.: 106–07). However, when pressed, he provided a prequel in the form of the story of the Babes on the Wood (ibid.: 108). The children's green coloration was due to arsenic administered by their wicked uncle; when this failed to kill them he had them taken to the Wailing Wood near Thetford and left for dead.[13] However, the uncle, fearing discovery, had returned to the wood later and removed the supposedly dead bodies, carried them to a distant place, and dumped them in a pit just outside Woolpit, where they revived and the villagers found them.

Sadly, it is clear from the tone and the context (at least as reported by Maxwell) that this story was not a popular local version that the vicar had heard from villagers, but an imaginative perhaps impromptu rendition of his own, providing the Green Children with a plausible backstory. Maxwell responds in like manner: '"A splendid story," I said, with enthusiasm, "and quite worthy of Brown, at his best."' In Maxwell's earlier chapters we have met the author's friend Brown—who has a talent for imaginative historical reconstructions and is 'always on the look out for historical romance'. '"Well," replied the Parson, "I expect it is quite as good an explanation as you will find, so mind you put it in your book."'

Although Maxwell does not give the name of his informant, the rector of St Mary's, Woolpit, at the time of his visit to the village was the Rev. Gerald Francis Homer Page (1882–1941).[14] Page was born in Woolpit, and both his father and his grandfather had been previous rectors of the parish—an older brother had been presented to the parish in 1902 but had died before he could take up the post. He himself was ordained priest in 1911, became rector of Woolpit in 1914 and served in that position until his death in May 1941 (*Bury Free Press* 1941). Maxwell could hardly have met anyone better placed to be knowledgeable about Woolpit and its history.

This version of the story—with some variation—was also known to folksinger and journalist Bob Roberts (1907–1982), who first moved to Suffolk in 1949. According to Roberts's version, printed in 1978, the Babes, green from arsenic poisoning, had fled from the wood where they were abandoned (perhaps, he thought, Thetford Forest?), and had stumbled into the pits at Woolpit (Roberts 1978: 84–85). It is unclear whether Roberts had found this story circulating locally or had simply taken it from Maxwell's book. However, he does seem to have had local contacts, for he concludes: 'I was told that there are still people in Woolpit who are "descended from the green children" but no one would tell me who they were.'

Mary Baine Campbell (2016: 123) provides another distracting Norfolk connection when she refers us to an article published in the *East Anglian Magazine* in 1952, where the author tells us:

> Pixies and elves, nixies and pishogues, leprechauns and gnomes—
> all of them were persistent nuisances, sometimes dangerous [...]
> The Green Children of Norfolk were a branch of this clan. I have
> heard it said that until quite recently there was a hole in a field
> beside the Swanton Morley-Bawdswell road. It was neither an old
> well nor a drain. It did not appear to have been used by fox, badger
> or rabbit. Surrounded by coarse clumps of grass and bracken and of
> unguessed depth, the hole remained a mystery. A whisper spread
> that it was an entrance to St. Martin's Land where it is always dusk
> and where the Green Children live. These pixies have always been
> a constant trouble to the people of East Anglia. The hole was filled
> in! (Tyler-Whittle 1952: 652–54)[15]

Swanton Morley and Bawdeswell (usually so spelt) lie in central Norfolk, about 35 miles (56 km) north of Woolpit. The identification of 'the Green Children' as the generic name for a race of East Anglian 'pixies' is eccentric, to say the least, and surely unfounded. Survival since the twelfth century so far from its origins of an oral tradition of St Martin's Land, complete with the knowledge of its 'dusk' or twilight illumination, seems most unlikely. The 'whisper' that spread about the significance of the hole in the field must surely have been started by someone who had recently come across an account of the Green Children of Woolpit, perhaps in a book about East Anglian folklore!

Woolpit itself, for a while best known as the home of Clarecraft Designs, manufacturers of highly collectible figures of characters from Terry Pratchett's Discworld (the company closed in 2005), is graced with a village sign, erected in 1977 for the Silver Jubilee of Queen Elizabeth II, that shows the Green Children (Fig. 5); they appear on a parish banner in the church; in 2012 Woolpit Museum opened an exhibition on the subject (Anon. 2022a) and sold a booklet (Cockayne n.d.); the story is recounted on the village's own website (Anon. 2022b); and in 2016 the annual Woolpit Festival included a perfor-mance of *The Green Children*, a children's opera composed by Andrew Wilson, with the Gelächter Wind Trio and children from Woolpit School.[16]

But the story is well known far beyond Woolpit. Most extraordinary of the developments undergone by the story of the Green Children in the twentieth century was the sudden appearance of an account of a similar event, said to have

Fig. 5.   Woolpit village sign. Photo: John Clark.

occurred in Spain in 1887. The story of 'The Green Children of Banjos' is now
widely known, thanks to its appearance on a number of websites. It was this
story, rather than that of the Green Children of Woolpit, that inspired a song
'Green Children' by the American folk-rock group 10,000 Maniacs, which was
included on their CD *Love Among the Ruins* (Geffen Records GEFD-25009: June
1997). The supposed events of 1887 in the Spanish village of 'Banjos' (there is
no such place recorded in a gazetteer of Spain, and perhaps we should read this
as an error for the common Spanish place-name 'Baños' ('baths' or 'spa')) were
popularized by Charles Berlitz in his book *Charles Berlitz's World of the Incredible
but True* in 1991. They seem to have their origin in a chapter headed 'Were these
children from another world?' in an American paperback on unsolved mysteries,
Strange Destinies, written by John Macklin ('internationally recognized expert
in psychic phenomena' according to the book cover) in 1965.

   I owe my introduction to Macklin's book to Garth Haslam's 'Anomalies'
website (Haslam 2002). As Haslam showed, Macklin's account (1965: 23–26)
is nothing more than a bogus updating and translocation to Spain of the
Woolpit story—complete with a local landowner called 'Ricardo de Calno' as
an Hispanic stand-in for Suffolk's Richard de Calne. For example, William of
Newburgh's comment on the story, 'I was so overwhelmed by the weight of so

many competent witnesses that I have been compelled to accept it' (*exactly* as it
had appeared in Joseph Stevenson's 1861 translation), is put into the mouth of
a priest who comes from Barcelona to investigate the occurrence.

We may enlarge on Haslam's conclusions and note that comparison of the
texts confirms that Macklin's story was modelled directly on Harold Wilkins's
version of the medieval Woolpit story (itself highly speculative, as we shall see),
which had appeared a few years earlier (Wilkins 1959: 187–91). The story
of the Green Children of Banjos is a hoax. It would be invidious to suggest
whether John Macklin originated it or whether he was misled by an informant.
Those who have recounted it since have made no attempt to find corroborative
evidence, but have simply copied and elaborated on their source—a common
practice among authors in this field.[17]

Retellings and reworkings

We have already noted that in the twentieth and twenty-first centuries many
authors have retold the story of the Green Children as fiction or incorporated
it into their works.[18] Most have been fairly straightforward retellings, usually
for children. Kevin Crossley-Holland has returned to the story on a number
of occasions (1966, reprinted in collections in (at least!) 1982, 1997 and 2018;
Crossley-Holland and Marks 1994, reprinted in Crossley-Holland 2005:
17–31). His original 1966 book won him and its illustrator Margaret Gordon
the Arts Council Prize for the Best Book for Young Children, 1966–68, and
in March 1968 it was featured in the BBC television afternoon story-time
programme for young children *Jackanory*, narrated by Ian Hendry and showing
some of Margaret Gordon's illustrations from the book.[19]

When Crossley-Holland's story first appeared in 1966, a collaboration on
an opera on the same theme was already being planned by composer Peter
Maxwell Davies (1934–2016) and Australian author Randolph Stow (1935–
2010) (Falkiner 2016: 465–66, 471–72, 502–03; Richards 2018: 32). Randolph
Stow had become fascinated by the story of the Green Children, which he was
later to weave into his own novel *The Girl Green as Elderflower* (1980), as we shall
see. He had first, he reported, come across the story in 'a trashy paperback
with a title like "Great Tales of the Unexplained"' while staying in a hotel in
Barrow (now Utqiagvik), the northernmost town in Alaska, in October 1965
(Falkiner 2016: 452–53).[20]

By a further coincidence a year later, Stow, by now in England and working
on the libretto of the planned opera, learnt at a party that librettist Eric
Crozier (1914–1994) had for years been trying to persuade Benjamin Britten

(1913–1976) to take up the same subject (Falkiner 2016: 502; Richards 2018: 32).[21] In fact, Britten had been considering the theme for an opera as early as 1950, while still working with Crozier on his opera *Billy Budd*, when a friend sent him translations of William of Newburgh's and Ralph of Coggeshall's accounts (Mitchell et al. 2004: 604–05). Sadly nothing came of either opera project, although by August 1969 Stow had completed a draft libretto (Falkiner 2016: 503).[22] He was later to incorporate some of the dialogue in *The Girl Green as Elderflower*. Kevin Crossley-Holland himself later wrote the libretto for a children's opera with music by Nicola LeFanu (LeFanu and Crossley-Holland 1990), first staged at the King's Lynn Festival in 1990.

I do not know when the Green Children first appeared on stage. However, in 1956 the amateur Buxhall Dramatic Class, based in the village of Buxhall just south of Woolpit, produced *The Green Children*, a pantomime by Mrs Lana Palin. It toured round local villages—complete with pantomime horse—and was seen by over 2,000 people in ten different villages (*Bury Free Press* 1956; *Diss Express* 1957). After its successful tour the author, Mrs Palin (not local herself, she had moved to the area five years earlier and became fascinated by the story), commented: 'well over two thousand people have heard this delightful legend, *many of them for the first time*' (my emphasis; *Diss Express* 1957). So presumably the story was not universally known in the Woolpit area or among local villagers in the 1950s.

Glyn Maxwell's verse play *Wolfpit* was first performed by the Cambridge University Amateur Dramatic Club at the Edinburgh Festival Fringe in 1996 (Maxwell 1996; Edinburgh Festival Fringe 1996: 40, 67). Another dramatization, this time in Suffolk dialect, by Shirley Bignell, appears as one of two *Suffolk Tales* on an audio CD, with notes for teachers and intended for classroom use (Bignell 2000). More recently American playwright Don Nigro (b. 1949) has written a short play *The Recollection of Green Rain*, included in his collection *Pirandello and Other Plays* (2021: 73–88).[23] It envisages that Walter Map (Welsh contemporary of William of Newburgh and Ralph of Coggeshall, whose book *De Nugis Curialium* was a collection of courtly gossip and tales of wonders, ghosts and fairies), had also set out to investigate the story of the Green Children. It is a two-hander, in which Map meets and interviews 'Agnes', the green girl herself.[24] During a debate about the nature of reality in which Map proposes various mundane explanations, she attempts to seduce him. He suggests that she made up the story as a child, even if she now believes it to be true.

Martin Robertson (1911–2004), formerly Lincoln Professor of Classical Archaeology and Art at Oxford, included a poem 'The Green Children of Woolpit' in his collection *A Hot Bath at Bedtime* (1977). The story also provided a title and an epigraph for the poem-sequence 'The Land of Saint Martin' (Prynne 1982) by modernist poet J.H. Prynne (b. 1936).[25] Jane Yolen (b. 1939), American writer of fantasy, science fiction, and children's books, first published a short but atmospheric poem 'The Green Children' in *Asimov's SF* magazine in 1993 (Yolen 1993).[26] And Marianne Burton's short poem 'The Green Girl's Husband' was published in the *Times Literary Supplement* in 2012 and included in her collection *She Inserts the Key* (2013: 15):

> She smelt as a pond when heat sets off weed,
> or wheat after rain when the heads swell and dampness forces the
>   husks apart.

In 2015 *The Green Children*, a poem by Essex musician/poet Martin Newell, was published in a hand-printed limited edition by Jardine Press, with a cover illustration by James Dodds; he later recorded it with accompanying music by The Hosepipe Band.[27] In Newell's poem, the girl is named Agnes, and eventually marries Richard Barre—names that demonstrate the pervasive (dare one suggest pernicious?) influence of Duncan Lunan's reconstruction of events that we discuss later in the section 'Who was Agnes Barre?' (Chapter 6).

Most of these new versions have elaborated on the bare bones of the story as told by Ralph and William, for example by giving names to the villagers and to the children and providing dialogue. Judith Stinton's *Tom's Tale* (1983) is typical. It is a short book for young readers with illustrations by Janet Duchesne: 'When Tom goes to the forest to look at the wolf-pit, it isn't wolves he finds there, but something much, much stranger: two children, green from head to toe' (Stinton 1983: back cover).[28] The children in this version are given the names Griselda and Martin. Stinton expresses the totality of the children's 'greenness':

> [Tom's mother and sister] gazed at the green hair, the green teeth,
> the green hands. Even the children's toe-nails were green. (Ibid.: 19)

The LeFanu/Crossley-Holland opera of 1990 includes snatches of the children's own language (in which the children name themselves as Erha and Imho—the scrambled letters of 'her' and 'him' provide the clue to the interpretation of the language), as well as an enchanting May morning round that Crossley-Holland reprints in his 1994 book. Crossley-Holland's 1994 version, perhaps inspired by his libretto for the opera, is told in the first person by the green girl. It is essentially a love story, in which the green girl 'Airha' becomes betrothed to Guy, the steward's son, and concludes 'My country and your country, they can both be my home.' Alan Marks's illustrations are perhaps the most evocative and romantic to be found in any published version of the story (Fig. 6).

Adrian Mitchell (1932–2008) set *Maudie and the Green Children* (1996) in the year 1499, and provided a new ending, in which the green girl leaves her husband in Lynn and, with her young green baby, returns to her home in what the narrator calls 'Merlin Land'. The story is told by a village girl, Maudie Hessett ('Some call me simple. That's all right. Simple folk are lucky folk'), and enlivened by cartoon-like illustrations by Sigune Hamann. *The Green Children of the Woods* by James Lloyd Carr (1912–1994; better known for his prize-winning novel *A Month in the Country* (1980)) though patently inspired by the Woolpit tale, tells a rather different story set in Essex and London in 1666 (Carr 1976). Richmond Warner's *The Green Children* (2019) is an updated story set around the preserved Foxfield Railway in Staffordshire, relocating the events to the heyday of that railway in the early twentieth century. Elsewhere, the Green Children's 'St Martin's Land' made a fleeting appearance as an alternative name of the

Fig. 6.   Woolpit village children discover the Green Children.
Illustration by Alan Marks (detail) for *The Green Children*
(Crossley-Holland and Marks 1994, cover). © Alan Marks.

Otherworld reached through a tunnel under King's Cross railway station in the children's story by Eva Ibbotson (1925–2010) *The Secret of Platform 13* (Ibbotson 1994). 'The Green Children of Woolpit' trilogy by Mark Bartholomew, a history teacher at Stowmarket Middle School (*Whispers in the Woods* (Bartholomew 2006a), *Chaos in the Cathedral* (2006b) and *Swords in the Summer* (2007)), follows the adventures of the Green Children as they search for their father, and their meetings with legendary figures such as the Green Man, Robin Hood and the Green Knight. The most recent retelling of the story for children that I am aware of is American author J. Anderson Coats's *The Green Children of Woolpit* (2019), aimed at 'middle grade' children (ages 8 to 12), an extraordinary elaboration upon the original story with an imaginative (and disturbing) vision of 'Those Good People' and their Otherworld. It is described as 'An eerie, spine-tingling fantasy about a young girl who discovers two Otherworldly children—and an ancient bargain that threatens to destroy them all'.[29]

Equally eerie, but for adults, is Edward Carey's recent 'These our monsters', the title story in an anthology of 'new' folktales and legends each inspired by an English Heritage site—in this case Bury St Edmunds Abbey (Carey 2019).

And this perhaps leads us into consideration of those other authors who have been inspired to rework or reimagine the story for an adult readership.

The short story 'The Green Child' by John Crowley (b. 1942), which first appeared in 1981 in an anthology of fantasy stories, seems at first a rather pedestrian retelling. The opening 'This story is recorded by Ralph of Coggeshall and William of Newburgh, both of whom say it took place in their own time' suggests that we should expect a faithful reflection of what Ralph and William wrote. Instead, Crowley makes a number of unacknowledged changes to the story. A kindly village woman, rather than the harvesters, finds the Green Children at one of the wolf-pits. Absent, just as in William of Newburgh's version, are Sir Richard de Calne and his family and the manor of Wykes. But also absent are the mystery of why the children refused food for several days and the accidental discovery that they would eat beans. On the very first evening the village wise man (reputedly a 'fairy doctor') says 'Give them beans [...] Beans are the fairy food' (a debatable claim, in any case!) (Crowley 1981: 2). An addition, not found in the original, is the green girl's claim that the people of St Martin's Land. although Christian, worshipped 'on Saturdays like the Jews' (ibid.: 5). These and other unexplained changes add little to our appreciation of the strange interplay of the realistic and the fantastic that imbues the original.

However, one of Crowley's additions is notable—and perceptive. Both children having refused all food but beans, the girl at last accepts a bowl of milk from the woman who has taken them in.

She took it now, with a kind of reverent fear, and as carefully as though it were mass-wine, she drank some. She gave the bowl back to the woman, wiping her mouth with the back of her hand, her face frightened yet resolute, as though she had drunk poison on purpose. [...] Years later the woman would look back and try to remember if the girl had ever cried again; and did not remember that she ever had. (Crowley 1981: 3–4)

This is surely a rite of passage, and it is treated with appropriate solemnity and ceremony. By partaking of ordinary human food, the girl commits herself to the human world and abandons hope of returning to her own land. As we shall see, the well-known belief that mortals who eat Otherworld food are condemned to dwell forever in that Otherworld has as a corollary an understanding that human food holds similar dangers for fairies. Stith Thompson's *Motif-Index of Folk-Literature* (1955–1958) includes Motif C211.3.2 (or C212.1 according to Cross 1952) 'Tabu on fairies eating mortal food'. Related is Motif C661 'Girl from elfland must eat earthly food in order to remain'. Though we can read this element into the original story (and we shall discuss its significance below), Crowley seems alone among recent rewriters to have recognized it and made it explicit.

Crowley does not acknowledge his immediate source. However, a number of internal clues indicate that his ultimate inspiration was once again Keightley's 1850 publication (probably at several removes, for we have seen how often that version was reprinted). Several phrases in Crowley's story echo Keightley closely—for example, Crowley's final paragraph 'William of Newburgh says these events took place in the reign of King Stephen, and that at first he didn't believe the story, but that later the general testimony compelled him to believe it to be true' surely reflects Keightley's comment 'The story is also told by William of [Newbridge], who places it in the reign of King Stephen. He says he long hesitated to believe it, but was at length overcome by the weight of evidence.' (Keightley's second sentence more closely reflects William's actual words—Crowley's text reads like a further paraphrase of Keightley.) Like Keightley, Crowley never gives the modern name of the village of Woolpit, and, like Keightley, places the green girl's marriage at 'Lenna'—perhaps Keightley had failed to recognize the name of [King's] Lynn in its medieval Latin guise.

The literary works discussed so far have been, for the most part, retellings or straightforward reworkings of the original. Other authors have been inspired to produce variations on the theme or incorporate elements of it in new contexts. For example, in 'Elphenor and Weasel' (one of a collection of stories of fairy-folk, originally published in *The New Yorker* magazine) poet and novelist Sylvia Townsend Warner (1893–1978) introduces a green fairy who lives with her people under a hill in Suffolk—presumably one of the fairy-race from which the Green Children originated (Warner 1979: 23–37). And in a most unexpected setting, in Marly Youmans's novel of the American Civil War, *The Wolf Pit* (2001), the Green Children and the wolf pit from which they emerged provide a central motif, as well as the title, as a young Confederate soldier muses in the midst of war on the fate of the two strange children he has read about in a book of folktales.

A more complex development is that found in *The Moon is Feminine* (1938) by Clemence Dane (the pen-name of Winifred Ashton (1888–1965)). This novel weaves a fictional story around Henry Cope, a real-life Brighton eccentric of the Regency period known locally as 'the Green Man' (Caufield 1981: 53–54). It suggests that he was a descendant of Woolpit's green girl—whose story Dane summarizes (especially pp. 38–40, with a presumed misprint that has the children living on 'baked beans' instead of the 'naked beans' (*'fabas nudas'*) of Ralph of Coggeshall's account).

Perhaps the most unusual, but best known, reworking is the sole novel by the eminent literary critic and poet (Sir) Herbert Read (1893–1968), *The Green Child*, first published in 1935 (King 1990: 133–38; Melville 1944). As we have seen above, Read was familiar with Keightley's translation of Ralph of Coggeshall's text and quoted it as an example of a typical folktale in his 1928 study of English prose style. In his only novel, 'a romance' (as it was originally subtitled), Read sets the story of two mysterious Green Children in about 1830 (although anachronistic references to a clockwork toy train suggest a rather later Victorian setting) and in a more northerly landscape than Suffolk, apparently that of his own boyhood home in Yorkshire (Graham Greene in Read 1947: vi). The two children, aged about four, come walking into the unnamed village from the direction of the moors. They 'could not speak any known language, or explain their origin'.

> Moreover, these children, who were lightly clothed in a green web-like material of obscure manufacture, were further distinguished by the extraordinary quality of their flesh, which was of a green, semi-translucent texture, perhaps more like the flesh of a cactus plant than anything else, but of course much more delicate and sensitive. (Ibid.: 26)

The boy dies before he can be baptized—indeed just as he is being taken into the church for baptism (ibid.: 33), but the girl, Sally or Siloën, the Green

Child of the title, eventually marries the local miller, the ignorant and brutish Kneeshaw. Her subsequent story is entwined with that of Oliver/Olivero, an English-born adventurer who, after establishing a utopian state (a benign dictatorship) in South America, fakes his own death and returns to his native village thirty years after the appearance there of the Green Children. There he fights and accidentally kills Kneeshaw, and frees the Green Child Siloën. Together he and Siloën rediscover the route to her homeland, a cavernous twilight realm filled with the sound of crystal bells, a cold intellectual utopia that surely many of the book's readers may find as ultimately unsatisfying as I do. The last chapter describes Oliver's life there and his final union with Siloën in death.

The many commentators have found great difficulty in placing and interpreting Read's work. A reviewer (Rosenthal 1969) wrote of the 1969 reprint 'The Green Child is a finely wrought, visionary, marvellously written work of the imagination [...] it is also unclassifiable, being part romance, part political tract, part philosophical treatise.' D.S. Savage (1978: 205) defined it as 'a minor classic in its own genre, that of the romantic fantasy or fantastic romance'. However, on the basis of this novel, Read earned an entry in The Encyclopedia of Science Fiction, and with its two utopian settings, one the South-American political utopia, the other the mystical underworld utopia of the Green Child's home, it certainly embodies features familiar in the genre of science fiction (Clute and Nicholls 1993: 993). One recent commentator, discussing the Green Children of Woolpit in the context of the possibilities of 'medieval science fiction' and the way in which their story had influenced not only Francis Godwin's The Man in the Moone but (perhaps) the modern concept of science-fictional 'little green men', concluded that Read's novel was science fiction not only in its own right but because

> In the context provided here of anticipations in the earlier history,
> chorography and narrative fiction sprung from the appearance of
> the Green Children in medieval Woolpit, it is also, and fascinat
> ingly, science fiction by its temporal and formal DNA. (Campbell
> 2016: 129)[30]

Read later said that his story was, apart from research for the South American scenes, 'merely the spontaneous elaboration of an old English legend' (quoted by Barker 1977: 456). Others have claimed to recognize its dependence on Plato's Phaedo (Barker 1980) and on works by W.H. Hudson such as Green Mansions and A Crystal Age (King 1990: 135). There have been both Jungian and Freudian interpretations (Harder 1973: 723; Savage 1978: 213)—one notes in particular (and with some bewilderment at his confidence) Savage's conclusion that 'There is no possible doubt that the poetic-symbolic core of *The Green Child* is a myth of incestuous regression to the mother, earth and death' (Savage 1978: 221).

The Green Child was reissued in 1945, with four compelling illustrations by New Zealander Felix Kelly (1914–1994). It has been reprinted several times since, and has been translated into (at least) Italian (Read 1952b), Spanish (Read 1979; 2010) and Russian (Read 2004). The Roman Catholic theologian John S. Dunne (1929–2013) devised a 'musical interpretation' of *The Green Child* whose opening lyrics 'Once upon a time of loss I set out on a mystic road of love' provided the title for one of his books (1999: 1).

The Australian writer Randolph Stow (1935–2010) skilfully wove the Green Children into his novel *The Girl Green as Elderflower* (1980). Stow, as we have seen, had been fascinated by the story ever since he came across it in 'a trashy paperback with a title like "Great Tales of the Unexplained"' in 1965 (Falkiner 2016: 452–53). His planned opera, with music by Peter Maxwell Davies, had come to nothing, but Stow was able to use dialogue from his abandoned libretto in his new novel. His story is set in modern Suffolk, where his protagonist, Crispin Clare, brought near to death by illness and stress in a tropical country, finds renewal in writing fresh versions of Ralph of Coggeshall's tales of wonders—the Green Children, the fairy child Malekin of Dagworth and the wild man of the sea of Orford—that incorporate family and neighbours from the Suffolk village where he is convalescing (Stow 1980; Hassall 1986: 147–64; Duckworth 2011; Falkiner 2016: 594–98). Stow said he 'wanted to recreate the mental state of the twelfth century and did a lot of research on the chronicles [...] Because they all firmly believed that these fantastic things they were telling were true. And I wanted to see what sort of world they thought they lived in, if they thought they could be true' (Falkiner 2016: 595–96). References to other medieval beliefs and Suffolk folklore contribute to this merging of past and present, as the 'girl green as elderflower' of the title blends with the unusual child Amabel and a mysterious stranger, possibly a Scandinavian au pair (or possibly Welsh—but certainly 'very wanton' as described by Ralph of Coggeshall). In an appendix Stow provides his own translations from Ralph of Coggeshall and William of Newburgh.[31]

Terri Windling (b. 1958) had published John Crowley's 'The Green Child' in an anthology she edited in 1981. Elsewhere she calls it 'a simple, elegant retelling of a curious English legend' (Zipes 2000: 115). In 1995 she returned to the theme, and included her own more complex retelling in a new anthology called *The Armless Maiden*. This collection of rather dark reworkings of fairy tales brings out some of the more sinister aspects of familiar stories, and their apparent portrayal of themes of child abuse and incest. It is dedicated to children at risk and to adult survivors of childhood abuse (Windling 1995: 16). Echoing Windling's own statement of the purpose of the book, the British Library and the Library of Congress both catalogue it under 'Fantasy—therapeutic use'. And we shall note below Catherine Clarke's assessment of William of Newburgh's account as itself an example of the 'literature of trauma', a literary response to traumatic events (Clarke 2009).

Windling introduces her story 'The Green Children' (1995: 269–74) as based on 'an English fairy story recorded as historical fact in the medieval chronicles of both Ralph of Coggeshall and William of Newbridge' (the 'Newbridge' reflecting her ultimate dependence on Keightley's translation). Her retelling is set in Arizona, where the narrator Emily is living with her mother and her brothers in a trailer park. We learn that Emily had been abused by someone she calls only 'That Man'. Her mother has killed him while protecting Emily, and has fled with her children. The Green Children appear to the family one Sunday in the Rincon Mountains and are taken in by Emily's momma. The origin of the Green Children is never explained—the girl is too young to remember their home clearly and the boy never speaks. Emily believes that their mother, unable to provide for them, had deliberately abandoned them where they would be found and brought up by a kindly family. The boy dies; the girl grows up and loses her green colour and 'this spring she's set to be married. She don't talk about the green country no more.'

In a poignant ending (ibid.: 274), Emily reveals that on Sundays she herself now sits alone on the rocks by the falls where the Green Children had first appeared: 'Maybe somebody in that green country will hear me. Maybe somebody will let me in.'

Another literary treatment of the Green Children was in a chapter in the well-received first novel by American Kevin Brockmeier (b. 1972) *The Truth about Celia*, published in 2003. The Celia of the title is a seven-year old girl who has disappeared mysteriously and without trace, while playing in the yard of her parents' house. Her father, like Brockmeier himself a writer of science fiction and fantasy stories, attempts to come to terms with his grief through his writing (rather like the protagonist of Randolph Stow's novel, and mirroring the 'Fantasy—therapeutic use' of Terri Windling's anthology). He composes a series of short stories about Celia, what might have happened to her, how she might have grown up, the effects of her disappearance on family and neighbours.

These stories, in various narrative voices, make up the book. One chapter, perhaps the strangest, is 'The Green Children' (Brockmeier 2003: 55–76). The fictive author imagines Celia transported back to the Middle Ages, her skin somehow turned green ('the pale flat green of wilting grass'), and appearing along with an otherwise unknown little boy in the wolf-pits outside Woolpit. The narrator of this story within a story is a strange local character, Curran, who, like St Christopher, carries people across the river on his back. He sees the children when they are first discovered; he is the last in Woolpit to speak to 'Seel-ya' when ten years later she runs away from Richard de Calne (who wishes to marry her) and leaves Woolpit for good—possibly to find a husband in King's Lynn.

Brockmeier presents a number of interesting variations on the original theme. He seems to have been the first author to consider, through the context of Celia's father and his writing, the potential reactions of the Green Children's *parents* to the disappearance of the children from their own world.

Brockmeier's chapter 'The Green Children' was subsequently selected and abstracted from his novel for inclusion in *The Year's Best Fantasy and Horror* of 2003 (Datlow et al. 2003: 454–64). As in the reworkings of the story by Terri Windling and Randolph Stow, it is the reflection of the mystery of the Green Children in the 'real' world that lies at the core of Brockmeier's book.

More recently Polish Nobel Prizewinning author Olga Tokarczuk (b. 1962) published a short story 'Zielone Dzieci' ('Green Children'), which clearly takes its inspiration from the Green Children of Woolpit—two mysterious green children are discovered, they refuse food, they are baptized but the boy dies, the girl tells about her homeland—but Tokarczuk places the story in a very different setting (Tokarczuk 2018).[32] It is set in 1656; the narrator is William Davisson, a Scottish physician in the service of King John II Casimir of Poland, caught up in the war with Swedes and Russians in eastern Europe. In what is now western Ukraine, the royal party take refuge in the manor house of Kurcewicz, the chamberlain of Łuck (now Lutsk), in a village surrounded by marshes. Soldiers bring in two waifs they have found in the marshes, who are green ('between celadon green and olive green'). 'It could be we have captured some Polish elves,' jokes Dr Davisson.

The doctor discovers that the children's hair is like moss or lichen; their skin seems vegetable-like and apparently absorbs the sunlight. Because of an accidental injury, Davisson is left behind at the Kurcewicz house when the king and his entourage move on. The boy dies soon after baptism (proving his diabolical nature, say the household servants). Examining the body, Davisson can see 'just a child, not a curiosity' and wonders about the whereabouts of his parents and their reaction to the loss of their children. Later the girl reveals to Davisson's servant boy Opaliński that she comes from a land in the forests beyond the marshes, where the moon shines brighter than the sun does here. The people get most of their sustenance from the moonlight, and need eat only a few berries, nuts or fungi. They live in harmony with nature and with the trees in whose branches they sleep. In the distance they see not the 'bright land' reported by Woolpit's green girl, but a world ravaged by war, with homes and villages in flames. Finally, one night, all the children in the Kurcewicz house and the village disappear, along with the green girl and Davisson's servant Opaliński. Nothing is explained—although we may surmise the children have gone to join the green girl's people in the forest—and Davisson leaves to join the king.

In 2020, introducing *Hag*, a volume of 'forgotten folktales retold', originally commissioned as a series of podcasts with a strong feminist slant, Carolyne Larrington noted:

> Many of the stories in *Hag* are in dialogue with 'folk-horror' or the 'new weird', a cultural trend that emerged in the 1970s in films such as *The Wicker Man* and is still being revived today with hit films like 2019's *Midsommar*. The past re-emerges into the present—or is revealed never quite to have gone away—violently and disruptively; the contemporary characters do not necessarily understand what they are dealing with or how to combat the forces that have been aroused. (Larrington 2020: 12–13)[33]

This is certainly true of Daisy Johnson's contribution to the retellings, disarmingly titled 'A Retelling' (Johnson 2020).[34] Johnson (b. 1990) self-references as the narrator, an author commissioned to write a retelling of the Green Children story. She visits Woolpit and the mysterious Lady's Well (to which we shall return) and apparently brings back some uncanny influence or contagion to her London flat. Her eyesight is affected, she has bad dreams. An intruder, apparently the green girl, arrives and takes up residence. The intruder takes constant baths and will eat nothing but beans (baked beans from a can!). The flat becomes damp and overgrown with mould. The pair return to Woolpit and the Lady's Well, where they dig a pit in which the narrator is buried alive:

> but the earth is moving and there are seams of light and I take in a breath big enough for a lifetime. (Johnson 2020: 36)

Sonia Overall's short but effective retelling 'Green is the colour' appeared in a literary magazine in 2021. It is allusive—there is no mention of Woolpit, no introduction or postscript to advise the reader of the story's origin. Perhaps, at least among readers of literary magazines, the story is so well known now as to require no explanation. It relates events from the green girl's point of view, but addressed as 'you' and in the present tense.

> Tell those who will listen tales of how you came to be here. Change the story a little with each telling. Do not tell them, your husband, your children, that you are just passing the time, waiting it out until you can once more lie beneath the sweet green knots of grass. (Overall 2021: 41)

Some of these retellings and reworkings have uncovered (or created anew) great depths of meaning in the story; several recent reworkings, such as those by J. Anderson Coats and Daisy Johnson, have emphasized the uncanny, perhaps sinister, nature of the Green Children. These are not the weeping innocents of the original story.

All the authors, sometimes explicitly, seem to have accepted the original as a folktale, a traditional narrative that can be recast without doing violence to any historical truth. The most effective treatments of the story surely remain those by writers such as Kevin Crossley-Holland, Randolph Stow and Terri Windling who have left its mystery intact, who have not tried to explain, or to explain away, the Green Children or St Martin's Land. Writing for children or in the field of fantasy or perhaps most recently 'folk horror', these writers have been less bound by the traditions of genres that require a strict separation of mundane fact from fantasy. Indeed, in their treatment of the story they have heeded Diane Purkiss's advice: 'leave it alone in its Borgesian glory' (2000: 63). 'God needs secrets just like you and me' says Emily in Windling's story (1995: 274). To quote Diane Purkiss further: 'The power of the story comes in the end from our pity for these ultimate strangers in a strange land, these small, vulnerable ETs.' To explain their origin would be to destroy that power.

Kevin Crossley-Holland, Randolph Stow and these other modern authors have clearly found a strange fascination in the story of Woolpit's Green Children. Since its rediscovery by Keightley, the story has reappeared in an extraordinary variety of forms and contexts, and its popularity is undoubted. There have been equally wide-ranging approaches to the interpretation of the story and the assessment of its significance.

Note: An earlier, and considerably shorter, version of this chapter was published in *Science Fiction Studies* (Clark 2006a).

CHAPTER FOUR

Interpretations

Folklore

> But for hundreds of years [...] [the story] was passed by word of
> mouth from grandfather to father to son—and no-one would
> care to say how, or where, it all began. (Crossley-Holland 1966:
> unpaginated)

Some commentators have discussed the story of the Green Children in the
context of twelfth-century literary accounts of visits to a usually subterranean Otherworld (Oman 1944: 10–12; Patch 1950: 237). Others have
had no hesitation in identifying it as a 'folktale' and the Green Children as
'fairies'. To Keightley it was an aspect of *The Fairy Mythology*, and John Murray's
guidebook to East Anglia borrowed the same phrase and identified the story
as embodying elements of the 'true old "fairy mythology"' ([King] 1875:
176). Lady Gurdon (1893: 33–34) included the story alongside accounts of
eighteenth- and nineteenth-century encounters with fairies in the Stowmarket
area and elsewhere in Suffolk, and Edwin Hartland included the story in his
collection of *English Fairy and Other Folk Tales* (1890: 132–34). Katharine Briggs
accorded the children a place in her *Dictionary of Fairies, Hobgoblins, Brownies,
Bogies and Other Supernatural Creatures* (1976: 200–01).

In the postscript on 'sources' in his own retellings of the story, Kevin
Crossley-Holland reiterated his conviction that, although it was set shortly
before their own times by William of Newburgh and Ralph of Coggeshall, it
was a much older, traditional story: 'But for hundreds of years before that, it
was passed by word of mouth from grandfather to father to son—and no-one
would care to say how, or where, it all began' (Crossley-Holland 1966: unpaginated; repeated in Crossley-Holland 1982: 101; 1997: 207). His confidence
is impressive (as is his apparent conviction that such stories passed down
through the male line!), but there is no evidence for the existence of such a
tradition predating William and Ralph's time. Similarly, as we have already

noted, Herbert Read regarded it as a folktale—a judgement he made solely on stylistic and formal grounds: it shows, he claims, 'a clear objective narrative, but a narrative encumbered with odd inconsequential but startlingly vivid and concrete details', which he takes to be typical of traditional storytelling (Read 1952a, 127–28).

As an example of how a folklorist might interpret the story as folklore— in accordance with folkloristic 'best practice' of his time—we may consider an article on 'Suffolk Fairies' that appeared in the *East Anglian Daily Times* in 1909, cited by Francis Young (2019: 44).[1] After lamenting the scarcity of tales of fairies in Suffolk (had he not read the Rev. Arthur Hollingsworth or Lady Gurdon on the fairies of the Stowmarket area?), the author relates 'the classic Suffolk fairy tale'—that of the Green Children of Woolpit (Dutt 1909). He then notes the significance of the children's appearance out of the ground: 'The interest this Woolpit story has for the ethnologist and folklorist lies in the assertion that the children or fairies appeared out of some artificial pits or trenches'. He continues:

> At the present time, folklorists are practically agreed that many of our old fairy tales, especially those recording the mysterious appearances and mischievous antics of the "little folk," originated at a time when the survivors of a comparatively dwarfish race of people inhabited this country contemporaneously with a stronger and taller race. The dwarf race, which dwelt in beehive huts and, in some parts of the country, subterranean dwellings, is believed to have been a Stone Age people, with, perhaps, Lappish affinities, and these dwarfs were in occupation of the country when the earliest Celts arrived and conquered it.

Dutt is referring to what became known as the 'pygmy theory' of fairy origins (Silver 1999: 47–50; Purkiss 2000: 5–7). George Laurence Gomme had argued, in his introduction to a collection of excerpts from the *Gentleman's Magazine* on *English Traditional Lore* (1885: vi), that fairies had existed: they were a pygmy race, a short, dark, aboriginal people who had lived in Europe before the coming of the Aryan race. The concept was developed and popularized by David MacRitchie in his books *The Testimony of Tradition* (1890) and *Fians, Fairies and Picts* (1895). These earlier people were Finno-Ugrian—indeed they had 'Lappish affinities' as in Dutt's account. They built and inhabited underground 'earth houses', later known as fairy hills, but were driven into remote and wilder parts of the country by incoming Aryan (or Celtic) settlers. They had, however, according to MacRitchie, survived in some remote places alongside these later people until at least the eleventh century CE (Silver 1999: 48).

Dutt was perhaps optimistic in suggesting that 'folklorists are practically agreed' on this theory. Leading contemporary folklorists such as Andrew Lang, Alfred Nutt and Edwin Sidney Hartland were unconvinced. Hartland was forthright in his condemnation of MacRitchie's theories in his own book on *The Science of Fairy Tales*: 'however ingenious his guesses, however amusing his philology, however delightfully wild his literary and historical arguments, he will not succeed in convincing any serious student' (Hartland 1891: 351). However, many other folklorists accepted and developed the argument further. The theory was clearly prevalent enough when Dutt was writing for him to adopt it in explanation of the story of the Green Children. Thus, Dutt concludes that the events recorded by our two medieval chroniclers did *not* occur in Woolpit in the twelfth century as they claimed. Instead:

> It seems clear that we have here an instance of certain real occurrences, which happened in a remote period, being so impressed upon folk-memory as to be retained long after their true significance has been forgotten. (Dutt 1909)

A 'folk memory', then, of a meeting and interaction between Celtic farmers and the diminutive earlier Stone Age inhabitants of this land.

Dutt was writing long before the publication in 1955–1958 of Stith Thompson's *Motif-Index of Folk-Literature*, which supplied another perhaps more objective means of identifying—or at least analysing—a 'traditional' narrative. Katharine Briggs identified two traditional narrative elements in the story of the Green Children (Briggs 1971: 1:262–63)—Thompson's own Motif F233.1 'Green fairy' and E.W. Baughman's additional Motif F103.1 'Inhabitants of lower world ("Green Children") visit mortals, and continue to live with them' (Baughman 1966: 203). As his summary implies, Baughman seems to have based this particular motif, F103.1, solely on the story of the Green Children of Woolpit—he cites no other occurrence and there is nothing like it in Thompson independent of Baughman's citation. One wonders how far one is justified in treating as 'traditional' a motif that is apparently recorded only once![2]

However, one can also note the several other motifs to be found in the story to which Briggs does not refer—for example, the fate of the boy is encapsulated in Motif F329.4.2 'Lost fairy child found by mortals but it pines away', while the girl's marriage to a man from Lynn seems reflected in Motifs F300 'Marriage or liaison with fairy' and F302.2 'Man marries fairy and takes her to his home'.

The historians' approach

Outside the field of folklore, academic historians have taken a different approach. Writers on the development of history and historical writing have seen significance in the manner in which twelfth-century historians incorporated apparent 'fictions' into their texts. The works of William of Newburgh in particular were studied in this context by Nancy Partner (1977) and Monika Otter (1996). A concern solely with the methods and purposes of medieval historical writers may lead to conclusions such as that of Nancy Partner:

> I again want to admit quite fully and frankly that I consider the process of worrying over the suggestive details of these wonderfully pointless miracles in an effort to find natural or psychological explanations of what 'really', if anything, happened, to be useless to the study of William of Newburgh or, for that matter, of the Middle Ages. (Partner 1977: 122)[3]

Similarly, Elizabeth Freeman (2000; 2002: 179–213) has considered the work of Ralph of Coggeshall as a Cistercian author, noting his practice of incorporating anecdotes, usually based on oral testimony, at appropriate points in his narrative:

> When Ralph took the opportunity to include extra stories in the stream of history he did not choose more anecdotes about the king or about bishops. Instead he turned to local stories which contained strong overtones of all the interpersonal qualities that Cistercians sought to emulate—simplicity of speech, humility, the sharing of visions and news with one's fellow brethren, and hospitality. (Freeman 2002: 193)

She discussed the context and significance of the 'wonders' described in Ralph's writings, and saw them as representing a common theme: 'the threat posed by outsiders to the unity of the Christian community' (2000: 143; 2002: 212), and thus relevant to the narrative of the Fourth Crusade which enfolds them.

Jeffrey Jerome Cohen (2008) has interpreted William of Newburgh's treatment of the story of the Green Children in the context of the relationships between the different 'races' of Norman Britain—the English (of whom William was proud to declare himself one: 'our race, that is the English' (Cohen 2008: 85)), the Francophone Normans, who, Cohen tells us, had become naturalized as 'English', and the 'barbaric' Welsh, Irish and Scots, either wholly subordinated or banished to wild and distant regions.

> In the twelfth century the Welsh, Irish, and Scots found themselves trapped in a suffocating English circumscription of their identity: inferior, feral, barbarian. The Normans, meanwhile, took advantage of a flexibility within Englishness to disappear into that powerfully ascendant term. (Ibid.: 76)

William, Cohen suggests, is reluctant to admit the Green Children to his narrative: 'The power they exert, I would argue, derives from the fact that the narrative William grants them resonates [...] with the anxieties about conversion, assimilation, and continuity that trouble his *History* throughout its unfolding' (ibid.: 84). He concludes (as I understand it) that William is disturbed when he has to concede the existence of an 'otherness' in the heart of a unified and homogeneous 'England', rather than one safely excluded, placed beyond the bounds, in Wales, Ireland or Scotland:

> The panorama that he opens trades all-encompassing and seemingly homogeneous identities for hybrid expanses when Englishness combines with differences at once distant and intimate, middle spaces as yet unmapped that begin suddenly to expand. (Ibid.: 91)

Of Cohen's and Freeman's opinions, Michael Staunton recently concluded:

> If I were to choose between the two, I would see Freeman's as the more convincing. In my reading, Newburgh's *Historia* seems little troubled by 'anxieties about conversion, assimilation and continuity', as Cohen claims. Such concerns are largely confined to the opening chapters, and are certainly not prominent enough to suggest that Newburgh would include an elaborate story of green children because, despite himself, he is troubled by the continuing presence of the Britons and Normans. On the other hand, there is no doubt that a Cistercian like Ralph of Coggeshall would have been concerned with heresy, nor that heresy was commonly associated with the transformation of the body. (Staunton 2017: 123)

Meanwhile, Catherine Clarke (2009) has considered William of Newburgh's account of the Green Children (alongside other 'marvels and prodigies' he describes) in the context of current interest in 'literatures of trauma'—a style of writing that seems to respond, sometimes through metaphor, fantasy or use of folklore models, to periods of trauma affecting individuals or communities (ibid.: 59–60). She considers the Anarchy of the period 1135 to 1154, in the reign of King Stephen, as 'an historical context of extreme social disorder, violence, atrocity and suffering' (ibid.: 55) and seeks to identify responses to it in the writings of John of Worcester (d. *c.*1140), in the continuation of the Peterborough Chronicle (1122–1154) and in William of Newburgh's *Historia*.

She states:

> I do not argue that these narratives in William's *History* represent a deliberate attempt or intention to write trauma, but rather that they reflect an unconscious, troubled engagement with the difficulties of recent memory and history. (Ibid.: 66)

Clarke discusses (ibid.: 69–74) William's account of the Green Children and his reports in the following chapter of two marvellous discoveries—two hollow stones which, broken open, revealed in one instance a toad with a gold necklace, and in the other a brace of greyhounds—and of a local version of a widely known story about the theft of a cup from a fairy hill (William of Newburgh 1988: 118–21). She notes the location of these chapters, framed by chapters dealing with the unhappy reign of King Stephen, and concludes that 'these stories all generate a sense of disturbing, bewildering experience suppressed or imperfectly contained'. In terms of content and style, she remarks: 'these twelfth-century texts resonate profoundly with twentieth-century trauma theory' (Clarke 2009: 74).

Clarke refers us to the work of scholar and critic Kali Tal, who wrote: 'The writings of trauma survivors comprise a distinct "literature of trauma"' (Tal 1996: 17). Perhaps, while interpreting William of Newburgh's stories as a reaction to the communal trauma of the Anarchy, Clarke might have also considered the implications of the Green Children's own account of their homeland—they were themselves 'trauma survivors' whose own story of their lost home and their ordeal, at least as reported, seems to have been one of fantasy rather than fact. Clarke (2009: 72) quotes further from Tal: 'As Kali Tal remarks, "Traumatic events are written and rewritten until they become codified and narrative form gradually replaces content as the focus of attention"' (Tal 1996: 6). And as we shall see, it is likely that Ralph of Coggeshall himself recast the children's own story of their home and how they came to Woolpit in terms of a typical medieval Otherworld adventure.

Thus to all these academic authors the 'truth' or otherwise of the reports is irrelevant. Such students of historiography and of the motives of historical writers avoid any attempt to explain what 'really' happened. Indeed, Cohen, like Partner, explicitly dismisses such an approach to the story of the Green Children as told by William of Newburgh (Cohen 2008: 84) and relegates to a final footnote the existence of a second apparently corroborative account of the same events (although he wrongly—as we shall argue—describes it as 'independent') in the writings of Ralph of Coggeshall (ibid.: 94, note 26).

Michael Staunton, in a recent study entitled *The Historians of Angevin England*, has questioned this approach, commenting that in recent decades 'the exotic and bizarre—the green children and talking werewolves—common to most of our writers, take on an inordinate importance as a key to the writers' works as a whole' (Staunton 2017: 7). He devotes several pages to discussion of the Green Children story and its treatment by William of Newburgh and Ralph of Coggeshall (ibid.: 120–27). He takes issue with both Cohen and Freeman's interpretations of the authors' intentions (ibid.: 122–24), and asks:

> Can we accept the assumption underlying both interpretations, that such writers as Ralph of Coggeshall and William of Newburgh included seemingly isolated stories of strange phenomena with the expectation that some of their readers at least would take them as reflecting on other apparently unrelated sections, or on the work as a whole?

He notes (ibid.: 127) 'In recent decades it has become commonplace to see metaphorical meanings in supernatural stories in twelfth-century English historiography'—and that this tendency can lead to the over-interpretation of medieval historical writing. He concludes:

> [B]y reducing the stories of the supernatural to metaphors, or mirrors of the text, their very strangeness can be lost. The evidence suggests that most of our writers really did believe that mermen could be caught in the sea, that witches could fly into the air and werewolves speak to humans. These are among the remarkable things that had occurred in their days, and if they sometimes harboured doubts about what had happened, or expected that others would, that did not diminish their belief that wonderful things did happen. [...] Perhaps Newburgh's approach is the best one to follow. All such stories may hold hidden meanings, and some

we may identify, but some cannot be explained. And no one yet has succeeded in explaining the story of the green children.

Hence, by default, the historical study of 'what, if anything, really happened', ignored by academic historians with the skills, knowledge and experience to interpret the medieval chroniclers' accounts, has been left to the 'amateur' historians writing in the field of fortean studies.[4] And it is to their attempts to 'explain' the Green Children we must now turn our attention. Not surprisingly their explanations have not attracted the attention of academic historians. Even Duncan Lunan's rewriting of elements of twelfth-century English history, drawing on a wide range of authoritative medieval sources (1996; 2012), and his identification of a descendant of the green girl seated in the House of Lords, seem to have been of no concern to those qualified to comment—no review in the academic press as far as I am aware. Presumably most academic historians were unaware of what was being offered in the name of historical research. As a result, Lunan's views have gone unchallenged in the popular accounts of the Green Children found online, and his identification of the green girl as 'Agnes Barre' seems to have achieved canonical status![5]

From mundane to extraterrestrial

[I]t should be clear from the context which accounts in this chapter are factual and which are legendary. (Bord 1997: 122)

In a very different approach to Partner and Cohen, some commentators have taken the story more or less at its face value, or accepted that there existed a rational core of 'truth'. Charles Oman thought 'some story of drugging and kidnapping' lay behind it (Oman 1944: 11–12). Nicholas Orme suggests that the Green Children had been 'brought up half-wild upon some East Anglian moorland or woodland' and that 'Our own instinct may be to rationalize the children as orphans from the backwoods, anaemic through lack of a proper diet' (Orme 2001: 92)—although he goes on to admit that 'Starved and deprived though they were, there must have been something special about them to spark such a marvellous tale.' But such straightforward claims do not attempt to explain every strange detail of the story as it was recorded by William of Newburgh and Ralph of Coggeshall. To do that, others have gone much further along the path of rationalization.

We have already seen attempts to explain the children's green colour as the result of arsenic poisoning (Maxwell 1926: 108; Roberts 1978: 84–85), and Paul Harris has argued for a 'down-to-earth' explanation of the occurrence in the context of national events in the 1170s. By dismissing some of the more apparent 'folkloric' elements as conscious or unconscious elaborations, he attempts to reduce the story to a core of historical 'truth' (Harris 1998 and 1999—but see the comments by Clark 1999). Thus he identifies the children as members of a family of Flemish immigrants, perhaps made homeless by local violence against Flemish settlers after Flemish mercenaries had supported the rebellion of Robert, Earl of Leicester in 1173 (or possibly following anti-Flemish legislation in 1154) (Harris 1998: 90–92). Their incomprehensible language was Flemish, their strangely coloured clothing the product of the well-known weaving and dyeing skills of the Flemings. Their home, 'St Martin's Land', was possibly the village of Fornham St Martin (ibid.: 93), just north of Bury St Edmunds and only 8 miles (13 km) from Woolpit (Map 2) (although, rather confusingly, he also comments that St Martin is the patron saint of children in Belgium, and thus would have been familiar to Flemish children (ibid.: 87; 1999: 267)). To the suggestion that these identifications must have been equally obvious to a man such as Richard de Calne, Harris can only respond that Richard may have kept his suspicions to himself in order to protect the girl from persecution (1994: 94).

The children's strange coloration, Harris suggests, was the result of the medical condition known as chlorosis (ibid.: 89)—a diagnosis which, as we shall see, is more familiar from Victorian medical treatises on the ills of adolescent females (Humphreys 1997). Harris concludes that various 'elements of folklore' identifiable in the story were the result either of coincidence or of 'the conscious or unconscious "working in" to the story of these themes by the chroniclers'—and he finds these elements more in Ralph's version than William's (Harris 1998: 87), as we would agree.

Though Harris presents a feasible scenario at first sight, his arguments are not convincing. Our confidence is further shaken when he later returns to the subject and suggests an alternative identification of St Martin's Land— St Martin's Hundred in Romney Marsh in Kent (1999). As he himself disarm- ingly points out, his alternative explanations of St Martin's Land cannot both be true (1999: 269). A representative response is that of Brian Haughton, American author of books on ancient civilizations and historic mysteries. Haughton concludes that Harris's hypothesis is 'the most widely accepted explanation at present' and 'certainly suggests plausible answers to many of the riddles of the Woolpit mystery', but that 'the theory of displaced Flemish orphans […] does not stand up in many respects' (Haughton 2007: 237–38).

Attractive though this 'reductionist' approach may be, simply to accept those elements of the story that seem to have 'down-to-earth' (though convoluted) explanations and to explain away the rest as 'contamination' by folklore is surely not sound practice, even among fortean investigators. Some things that might seem to have obvious mundane explanations could just as easily be found in traditional tales—or be totally fictitious.

Other writers have been prepared to accept the story as simply 'inexplicable' and have cited it in books on 'The Unexplained'. The writers of such books have usually found inspiration in the work of the American Charles Fort (1874–1932), whose accounts of anomalous phenomena, published between 1919 and 1932, we have already highlighted. We have noted how 'Fortean' (or 'fortean') has come to be used both to describe such phenomena and to identify those who investigate them (Gardner 1957: 43; Simpson and Roud 2000: 134).

Fort himself gives no account of the Green Children—most of his reports were taken from nineteenth- and twentieth-century sources—but it is evident where he might have included the story (if he had been interested in such early accounts): around page 700 of the collected edition of his works (1974), between the Indian feral 'wolf children' and Kaspar Hauser.

As we have noted, recent publications on 'The Unexplained' have included three encyclopedias and a dictionary. In general, writers on 'The Unexplained' have treated the Green Children as another such mystery. For example, John Michell and Bob Rickard included the story in a chapter on 'Wild people' in their *Book of Wonders* (1977: 111), while Lionel and Patricia Fanthorpe included the Green Children among *The World's Greatest Unsolved Mysteries* in their book of that title (1997: 126–35).

In a perceptive article, Michel Meurger has pointed out that Bishop Godwin, in his *fictional* use of the story of the Green Children in *The Man in the Moone*, is a precursor of those many later authors who have found in both folklore and early historical sources reflections of phenomena that, when they have been reported in more recent times, have been identified as interventions by extraterrestrials in human affairs, such as UFOs and alien abductions (Meurger 1996: 308–09). Thus the 'flying ships' of folktales and medieval chronicles can be interpreted as alien spacecraft, the loss of time experienced by those who entered fairy mounds equated to that reported by 'abductees'.

Some authors, such as Harold Wilkins (1959), have seen in such medieval accounts simply the misinterpretation by deeply superstitious people of phenomena for which with our more advanced perceptions we find 'scientific' explanations in alien visitations and physical spacecraft.

Thus the Green Children have been called to testify in support of a variety of 'extraterrestrial' concepts or theories—the children were 'teleported' through a vortex in space from a parallel universe or a subterranean existence on another planet, perhaps Mars (Wilkins 1959: 187–91), or they wandered through tunnels from an inhabited world within our own, the base from which 'flying saucers' also emerge (Trench 1974: 121–23). More recently, Duncan Lunan completed a painstaking study of medieval documentary sources, first summarized in an article in the magazine *Analog: Science Fiction, Science Fact* (Lunan 1996) and since published as a book (Lunan 2012), to reconstruct the family history and connections of Richard de Calne of Wykes, who took the children in (he concludes that the green girl was christened 'Agnes' and later married the royal justice and ecclesiastic Richard Barre), the political activities of kings and royal servants, and the significance of various signs and wonders reported by medieval writers. He combined his historical study with speculations about humans abducted by aliens and established as a colony on a distant planet, a 'matter transmitter' linking that planet to earth, and the involvement of King Henry II and the Templar knights in dealings with extra-terrestrial entities, to create what he advisedly calls 'A Speculative Treatment of a Medieval Mystery' (Lunan 2012).[6]

In her book *Fairies: Real Encounters with the Little People* (1997), Janet Bord set the story of the Green Children and other early accounts of 'fairy folk' alongside modern reports of both fairies (some reports supported by photo-graphic evidence) and the diminutive aliens usually associated with UFOs (Bord 1997: 126–28). Her contention that 'it should be clear from the context which accounts in this chapter are factual and which are legendary' (ibid.: 122) is, I would suggest, optimistic! Her preferred conclusion is that the evidence 'seems to point to a multiplicity of beings living in a variety of "other worlds" located not far away from ours but to which we do not yet have easy access'—although she is also ready to accept the alternative that 'it is probably all in the minds of the witnesses' (ibid.: 151).

A more questioning approach to the relationship between folklore and such speculation was that adopted memorably by the astronomer Jacques Vallée in his book *Passport to Magonia: From Folklore to Flying Saucers* (1970). Vallée noted that 'beliefs identical to those held today have recurred throughout recorded history and under forms best adapted to the believer's country, race, and social regime' (1970: viii). In contrast to Harold Wilkins, who felt justified in finding 'scientific' explanations for medieval folktales, Vallée drew no conclusions about the 'reality' of flying saucers. He suggested only that 'the mechanisms that have generated these various beliefs are identical' and 'it has little to do with the problem of knowing whether UFO's are physical objects or not' (ibid.: 149). Thus phenomena perceived as fairy-folk in the twelfth century and as extraterrestrials in the twentieth or twenty-first century are the same, interpreted within a contemporary framework of belief and knowledge—but neither interpretation is necessarily the 'true' one.

The title of Jacques Vallée's book recalls *Magonia*, the supposed home-port of flying ships that reputedly plundered the region of Lyons in the time of Archbishop Agobard (779–840). In a more recent paper in the occasional publication *Fortean Studies*, Jean-Louis Brodu (1995) adopted a critical approach to 'ufological' treatments of Agobard's account of Magonia, stressing the need to interpret such accounts in the context of their own time.

We should recognize an important difference between these modern 'fortean' writers, particularly many of the contributors to *Fortean Studies* and the associated long-running magazine *Fortean Times*, and Charles Fort himself. As we have noted, Fort's approach entailed the acceptance of even the most unlikely account of inexplicable events. Many forteans now treat the evidence with caution, and readily accept that accounts of anomalous phenomena are shaped and even inspired by contemporary culture.

Science fiction?

Looking for little green men. (Trudel 2005)

In a paper published in *Science Fiction Studies*, a journal devoted to the critical study of science fiction (sf or SF) and its historical development, I considered the ways in which the story of the Green Children has been retold and reworked by later authors, from Francis Godwin's *The Man in the Moone* to modern times (Clark 2006a—and see 'Retellings and reworkings' above). I concluded:

> Francis Godwin's *Man in the Moone* was science fiction—'the first work which can properly be called such' (Philmus 1996: 260)—and Herbert Read's interpretation of the Green Children's homeland is surely science fiction. Other than these works, the genre of science fiction does not seem to have made much use of the tale. (Clark 2006a, 224)

While that paper was already in the press, an essay 'Looking for little green men' by the Canadian science fiction author and critic Jean-Louis

Trudel (b. 1967) appeared in the *New York Review of Science Fiction*.[7] In this he discussed the Green Children in the course of a survey of the possible origins of the familiar concept of green-skinned extraterrestrial aliens, such as Edgar Rice Burroughs's 'Tharks' of Mars and the 'little green men' who reportedly piloted flying saucers (Trudel 2005).[8] Summarizing the story of the Green Children, and noting the uses made of it by Burton and Godwin, he saw them as precursors of these later fictional aliens, alongside green fairies and the 'Green Man' (ibid.: 6–8).[9]

Neither of these two essays argued that the story of the Green Children was in itself science fiction. But it has since been discussed by contributors to a volume titled *Medieval Science Fiction* (Kears and Paz 2016a). In their introductory chapter, the editors of this volume consider the significance of this provocative title (Kears and Paz 2016b). Did 'science' exist in the Middle Ages, or was the whole period 'fundamentally unscientific'? How did medieval writers portray and interpret the 'alien'? How are the Middle Ages (either our own medieval period visited by a time traveller or a 'medieval' culture encountered on a distant planet or in the distant future) represented in science fiction?[10] Their instructions to their contributors included: 'Consider where, how and why "science" and "fiction" intersect in the medieval period' (ibid.: 26).

In the title of her contribution to the volume (Campbell 2016), Mary Baine Campbell quotes from Robert Burton's reference to the Green Children: 'Those two green children which Nubrigensis speaks of in his time, that fell from heaven'. She questions whether the story of the Green Children might indeed be identified as 'a kind of science fiction' (ibid.: 118).[11]

> The crucial distinction between the demons, monsters and spirits of poetry, prose romance and folklore, and the Green Children of Woolpit is the insistence of both the credulous Ralph and especially the incredulous William on eye-witness testimony, including direct quotation from the alien beings in question about their experiences elsewhere, beyond the lands of 'our people'. (Ibid.: 120)

Not only do the children and their testimony 'belong to the realm of science or *ratio*', but 'The magic, or at least the charm, of modern science fiction is in that precise combination of *ratio* with news from someplace and someone fundamentally, ontologically elsewhere—whether in space, time, scale or other dimensions' (ibid.: 120–21).

Campbell considers the views of Partner (1977) and Cohen (2008), mentioned above, and the discussion by Gautier Dalché (1989) of 'the land of the Antipodes', which we shall return to later (Campbell 2016: 124–26). She traces the influences of the story of the Green Children through Burton and Godwin to the 'little green men' discussed by Trudel and to Herbert Read's *The Green Child*, linked to the Green Children of Woolpit by 'a sort of temporal and formal DNA' (ibid.: 129). She concludes:

> I am aware that this remark makes one grand tautology of my essay, which seems to claim that the emergence of little green men in William of Newburgh's account of 'The Anarchy' in Yorkshire (and East Anglia) under Stephen is science fiction because a chain links it with the little green men of modern science fiction and the inhabited planets of seventeenth-century science fiction, while the 'science fictionality' of Read's *The Green Child* inheres in its own temporal confusion with the places and period of William's and Ralph's histories. (Ibid.: 129)

In his chapter 'The riddle of medieval technology' in the same volume (Sawyer 2016), Andy Sawyer sees parallels that can link Gervase of Tilbury's reports of 'ships in the air' as well as the story of the Green Children not only with phenomena collected by Charles Fort but with 'the plausibility offered by hard science fiction' (ibid.: 156–57).

> In other words, these may be stories which, to the sophisticated re-teller at least (and to the audiences of Gervase or Ralph's books), are told because they are mysteries with the illusion of truth, which speculate about the nature of the reader's world without necessarily becoming a definite explanation. They may, in other words, be closer to SF than to pseudo-science in that they are seen as fictions (or at least 'tall tales') which corroborate in some way the worldview of those who pass them on.

In considering tales that might serve to corroborate the narrator's 'worldview' Sawyer might also have directed our attention to the well-known story told by Gervase of Tilbury of the swineherd who in midwinter ventured through Peak Cavern in Derbyshire in search of a lost pig, only to emerge in the summer harvest fields of a strange land (Gervase of Tilbury 2002: 642–45), a story that we shall discuss in detail later—for Gervase concluded, on the basis of the swineherd's report that he had found the seasons reversed, that he had arrived in the lands of the Antipodes, a perfectly acceptable conclusion in the light of medieval science and medieval understanding of geography (see 'The land of the Antipodes' in Chapter 7; and see also Gautier Dalché 1989).

But do similarities in style and tone between these medieval accounts and modern science fiction with its underlying basis of 'hard science' sufficiently qualify them as 'science fiction' themselves? Today, we are used to a handy distinction between 'fiction' and 'non-fiction' in libraries or bookshops. Yet it is clear that these stories were *not* considered to be fiction (that is, 'untrue, nonfactual stories') by the authors who reported them—nor, presumably, did readers interpret them as such. Whether a distinction between 'fiction' and 'non-fiction' can properly be made when discussing medieval literature is admittedly debatable. Campbell cites her own work (Campbell 1999) and that of Lennard Davis (1983) for the development of the 'novel' form from 'early prose fictions of a certain length [which] were usually called histories ("true histories"), when not called "travels"'—and the difficulty contemporary critics had in distinguishing between 'true history' and 'hoax' and 'fiction' (Campbell 2016: 126 and note 17).[12] She herself considers *Robinson Crusoe* ('the first English novel'—published of course as if autobiography, an apparently 'true' self-penned memoir of the title character's life and adventures) to be an early example of science fiction (ibid.: 127).[13]

However, William of Newburgh himself famously cast doubts on the 'truth' or 'factuality' of Geoffrey of Monmouth's *History of the Kings of Britain*, making a distinction between 'figments' or 'fictions' on the one hand and 'histories' on the other, when he accused Geoffrey of taking the stories or fables (*'fabulae'*) of King Arthur 'from the old fictitious accounts of the Britons [*ex priscis Britonum figmentis*]' and cloaking them with 'the honourable title of history [*honesto historie nomine*]' (William of Newburgh 1988: 28–29).

Indeed, in the case of the Green Children of Woolpit, William took great pains to investigate the truth of the accounts that he had heard <W1>:

> Certainly I long hesitated about this matter, although it is spoken of
> by many people. It seemed to me ridiculous to take on trust a story
> that had either no rational basis or a very obscure one. At last I was
> overcome by the evidence of so many witnesses of such weight; so
> that I was forced to believe it.[14]

Though he perhaps had remaining doubts, he seems to accept the story of the Green Children as a matter of '*historia*'—unlike the '*fabulae*' of King Arthur— as close as one can get perhaps to the modern dichotomy of 'fact' and 'fiction'.

But one may argue that he recounts this event and other similar 'marvels' *not* because they 'corroborate' his world view and those of his readers (as suggested by Sawyer (2016: 156–57)) but because they *challenge* those same world views. Moreover, in a postscript <W28>, William adds that many wonders are illusions, the result of the machinations of demons or 'evil angels'—but he refuses to adopt this explanation (which would surely be respectable in terms of the medieval understanding of the world, in which demons had their proper place) in the case of the Green Children—*'abstrusior ratio est'* ('the scientific explanation is more puzzling')—he concludes: there must be a rational explanation. Perhaps the Green Children were in modern terms not 'science fiction' but were simply accepted as 'science fact' (although it was a puzzling fact).[15]

CHAPTER FIVE

The Chroniclers and the Texts

The chroniclers

Since Keightley's publication of the story in 1850 there have been many different approaches to the Green Children. Folklorists, historiographers, historians of science fiction, forteans and ufologists, all have made use of the story, and have studied it employing the methods of their own disciplines and in the light of their own preconceptions—and seemingly largely in ignorance of each other's work and concerns. Many of their interpretations have in common a reliance on secondary sources, a failure to recognize the significant differences between the two surviving versions and a lack of any attempt to analyse the story in detail. The purpose of this book is to remedy this situation and to put the study of this strange story on a sounder footing, and to review critically some of the many interpretations. It does not attempt an 'explanation'.

Our starting point must be with the two medieval historians who provide our only primary versions of the story. The first, William of Newburgh (*c.*1136–1198), was born in east Yorkshire—not far, he tells us, from the stream known as the Gypsey Race and a celebrated 'fairy hill' usually identified as the Neolithic mound called Willy Howe, close to Wold Newton, in the Yorkshire Wolds west of Bridlington (William of Newburgh 1988: 118–19; Grinsell 1976: 168–71). He was educated in the Augustinian priory of Newburgh, near Coxwold, north Yorkshire (Gransden 1974: 263–68; William of Newburgh 1988: 1–5). He became a canon there, and in about 1196 or 1197 began writing a history at the request of Ernald, abbot of nearby Rievaulx Abbey, the earliest Cistercian abbey to be established in northern England. William's *History of English Affairs* (*Historia Rerum Anglicarum*) begins in 1066 and ends abruptly in 1198, when it is assumed that he died with his work unfinished. He relied upon earlier historians such as Henry of Huntingdon, paraphrasing his sources (usually without crediting them) but adding a great deal of new information. For events 'within living memory' he drew also on eyewitness accounts.

And it is clear what sort of witness he trusted: he credits accounts to 'the venerable archdeacon of the area', 'an aged monk who was well-known in that

Fig. 7.   Coggeshall Abbey, Essex—the chapel of St Nicholas at the
abbey gate, *c.*1220. Photo © Gary Woods/Alamy Stock Photo.

area', 'certain people of noble birth who were there' or 'a person born in the
locality'—his preferred sources were people of repute with local knowledge
(Partner 1977: 116–18). The approach is also that of most of his contemporaries. As Carl Watkins puts it: 'Clearly in the mind of the chronicler the status
of the witness and their vocation were intimately bound up with the weight that
was to be attached to their evidence' (Watkins 2001: 96). Nor were William's
sources solely local eyewitnesses. He was willing to credit accounts transmitted
and vouched for by people he trusted. He acquired detailed information on
events elsewhere, perhaps through contacts with other Augustinian houses,
particularly in London and East Anglia (Gransden 1974: 267).[1]

Much less is known of Ralph, beyond the bare facts that he was a monk at
Coggeshall (a small Cistercian monastery between Braintree and Colchester
in north Essex—Map 1; Fig. 7), becoming abbot in 1207 and resigning that
post because of ill health in 1218 (ibid.: 322–31). He may have died in about
1226 or 1227. His *English Chronicle* (*Chronicon Anglicanum*) covers the period
from 1066 to 1224—although it is not certain how much of it is Ralph's own
work. The earliest surviving manuscript, now in the British Library, seems to
be a draft, with changes, erasures and corrections. Freeman (2002: 179–81)
identifies three sections: brief annals from 1066 to 1186, copied by Ralph
from a pre-existing set of annals; a more elaborate account of the years 1187

to 1205, drawing on new written sources and oral testimony, the core of the volume and Ralph's self-proclaimed work; and a final section to the year 1224, apparently the work of a number of hands and betraying different interests.[2] The Cistercian network provided news, and Ralph seems also to have acquired information from the frequent visitors, both ecclesiastic and lay, who passed through Coggeshall.

Ralph has also been credited with the writing of *Visio Thurkilli*, a report of the vision or dream of an Essex peasant called Thurkill. Thurkill described how, while his body lay in a coma for two days, his spirit had journeyed through the world of the afterlife, and had seen Purgatory and the regions of the damned and the blessed. This had happened in October 1206 at Stisted, where Thurkill lived (less than 4 miles (6 km) from Coggeshall—Map 1) (Ward 1875; Ralph of Coggeshall 1978; Schmidt 1978). It was H.L.D. Ward who first attributed this work to Ralph in 1875. Although the evidence is circumstantial the attribution seems to be generally accepted (Ralph of Coggeshall 1978: v– vi; Gurevich 1984: 54; Zaleski 1987: 81–82; Carozzi 1994: 514–15; Watkins 2002: 18; Staunton 2017: 122).[3] H.R. Patch discussed a number of accounts of similar 'visions' (although usually experienced by monks or other churchmen) in his study of medieval Otherworlds (Patch 1950: 80–133). The afterlife they describe is very different from the Otherworld of the Green Children, but, as we shall see, there are similarities and perhaps mutual influences that link the Otherworlds of folklore and such visions of the afterlife.[4]

Tales of wonder

> Another wonder also, not unlike the previous one, happened in Suffolk at St Mary of the Wolfpits. (Ralph of Coggeshall)

Both William and Ralph seem to have enjoyed a good story, particularly one about what we would call the supernatural. William's stories of ghosts—or rather of vampire-like 'revenants'—are especially notable and have been much discussed (Howlett 1885: 474–82; Partner 1977: 134–40; Joynes 2001: 87–90, 97; Simpson 2003: 390–94; Watkins 2007: 185–89; Ruch 2013). The story of the Green Children remains unique in that essentially the same story is told by two authors. Although, as we shall see, their accounts are not totally independent, they provide two separate versions we can compare—as well as a basis for comparison with other contemporary tales of Otherworld visits or visitors.

Towards the end of several of the books of his *History* William introduces a chapter or so of 'marvels and prodigies'—'*mira et prodigiosa*' (William of Newburgh 1988: 14). It is in this context that he includes the story of the Green Children, as Chapter 27 of his first book, following accounts of the woes of England in the reign of King Stephen (1135–1154) in Chapter 22, events in Scotland under King David I (1124–1153) and the accession of Malcolm IV (1153–1165) (Chapters 23–25), and successions to the bishoprics of York and Durham in 1153–1154 (Chapter 26). Chapter 27 is devoted to the Green Children, and, as we have already noted, Chapter 28 tells us of marvellous discoveries of a toad and two dogs embedded in stone, yet alive, and the theft from a fairy hill of a cup later given to Henry II (William of Newburgh 1988: 114–21). These episodes are clearly marked as a digression from the main flow of William's *History*: 'when he is finished William explicitly returns to the *series temporum* ("*ut autem iam ad seriem historiae narrationis redeam*")'—'I now return to the chain of historical narrative' (Otter 1996: 103; William of Newburgh 1988: 122–23). Thus in Chapters 29 and 30 he recounts the arrival in England in 1153 of Henry, son of the Empress Matilda, his eventual acceptance by King Stephen as his chosen successor. The marriage of Henry 'the future king of England' to Eleanor of Aquitaine is recorded in Chapter 31, and the death of Stephen in 1154 in Chapter 32, the last in this first book of the *History* (William of Newburgh 1988: 122–33).

However, as we have seen, Catherine Clarke regards these chapters of 'marvels and prodigies' not as digressions, but as integral reflections of William's response to the horrors of Stephen's reign, a twelfth-century example of the 'literature of trauma' (Clarke 2009).

Yet Ralph of Coggeshall also interrupts his narrative with tales of wonder, but at what seems to be a rather less traumatic point in his history. Following his account of the preparations for the Fourth Crusade in 1199, he gives us, in successive chapters, not only the story of the Green Children but also other Suffolk tales of the wild man of Orford (Ralph of Coggeshall 1875: 117–18) and the 'fairy' child Malekin of Dagworth (ibid.: 120–21), as well as several reports of evidence of the existence of giants elsewhere in England and Wales (ibid.: 120), and stories of heresy, witchcraft and miracles in France (ibid.: 121–29). He then, like William, returns to his interrupted historical narrative.

We have already noticed how commentators on the writing of history in the twelfth century, such as Jeffrey Jerome Cohen and Elizabeth Freeman, have interpreted these stories of 'marvels' as being deliberately inserted by the historians as reflections of or metaphors for the historical narrative that surrounds them. Yet, for our purposes, we may surely accept Michael Staunton's assessment of our authors' attitude: 'These are among the remarkable things that had occurred in their days, and if they sometimes harboured doubts about what had happened, or expected that others would, that did not diminish their belief that wonderful things did happen' (Staunton 2017: 127).

The fact that these events were 'marvels' did not make them incredible. Wonders, miracles and portents were very much part of the medieval view of the world. However, William and Ralph's contemporary Gervase of Tilbury makes a clear distinction between miracles, '*miracula*'—which are supernatural occurrences to be ascribed to divine power—and marvels, '*mirabilia*'—which are natural but cannot be explained by human intellect: '*Mirabilia uero dicimus que nostri cognicioni non subiacent, etiam cum sunt naturalia*' (Gervase of Tilbury 2002: lvii, 558). Similarly William of Newburgh defines '*mira*' as things for which the explanation is hidden—'*occultam habent rationem*'—while admitting that magicians ('*magi*') and 'evil angels' can create strange visions, objects and appearances, thus perhaps allowing a broader definition of '*mira*' than Gervase's '*mirabilia*' (William of Newburgh 1988: 118–21).

William seems to devote at least as much effort to investigating reports of such things and satisfying himself that the witnesses were bona fide as he does in the case of more natural events. He was not alone in this. Carl Watkins (2001: 94–99) discusses the great efforts made by medieval chroniclers to evaluate the trustworthiness of reports of wonders. He concludes:

> When describing a wonder, they invariably included information about who had told them about it, assuring the reader or hearer that the source was trustworthy. [...] When confronted by wonderful accounts that defied these patterns [the customary course of nature], the chronicler expected his public to be sceptical, and so deployed the full credentials of his witnesses to convince his audience of the report. (Ibid.:107)

On the other hand, in a study of twelfth-century historiography, Monika Otter places William among a small group of historians who

> test the limits of referentiality and historicity by inviting in phenomena and episodes that strain belief, often, it seems, for the sole purpose of raising the question of what should be done with such troublesome intruders. (Otter 1996: 94)[5]

However, William is concerned to make it clear that the events he relates were well attested by eyewitnesses. Moreover, he attempts to find explanations, seeing many wonders as being merely illusions, the result of the machinations of demons or 'evil angels' (William of Newburgh 1988: 120–21)—although he admits defeat in the case of the Green Children.

Ralph of Coggeshall, though equally careful to name witnesses, seems less concerned to seek explanations. Apart from frequent references to freakish weather, famines and pestilences, earthquakes and extraordinary appearances in the heavens (Ralph of Coggeshall 1875: xv–xvi), he records a number of other unusual events, such as the strange affair of the visit paid to Coggeshall Abbey in the days of Abbot Peter (1176–1194) by a group of men dressed like Templars, who appeared to one man only, then vanished (ibid.: 134–35; Freeman 2002: 192–93). He does not attempt to explain this event ('Who these men were, or how they came, or where they went, remains unknown to the present day'). But he is at pains, like William, to confirm the trust-worthiness of a witness, in this case the sole eyewitness, lay brother Robert: 'we who knew his way of life and his conscientiousness (*conscientia*) don't doubt his story'. Brother Robert was, notes Elizabeth Freeman, an exemplary Cistercian, for the order were 'strong admirers of simplicity in thought and words' (2002: 192–93). He was a humble and plain-spoken man, who repeated his story in a straightforward manner on numerous occasions, even when he was nearing death. All this, to his audience, added to the credibility of what he said (Watkins 2001: 102).[6]

But both William and Ralph were storytellers as well as historians (if the distinction is meaningful—as Freeman (2002: 212) puts it, 'medieval writers of history conceived of the past in terms of narrativity'). Postmodernists might argue, according to Otter (1996: 10), 'that history is nothing but discourse, that there is no reality outside the text'. While not espousing this extreme view, Otter emphasizes the fact that 'history [...] must translate [reality] into narrative, a more or less orderly sequence, one or just a few causal chains, a beginning, middle, and end'. We can expect, when comparing the two extant versions of the story of the Green Children, to see the results of this process— Ralph and William will have selected and ordered their material into coherent narratives. And since the narrator of any tale would do the same, we should not perhaps be surprised if the resulting 'history' resembles a folktale—or at least a folktale in the developed *written* form in which it is generally known to a modern literate audience. And indeed, in considering the works of their contemporary, Gerald of Wales, Elissa Henken has noted how often his accounts of 'wonders' resemble in approach and style modern 'contemporary legends' known from oral sources (Henken 2001).

The two writers' accounts of the Green Children seem, at first sight, independent of each other. As the Latin texts show (Appendix), there is no obvious use of identical wording or phraseology, no point at which we can say Ralph is quoting William, or vice versa. On the surface, the two historians seem to have composed their accounts independently, drawing on different sources of information. Ralph acknowledges a single source, the same Richard de Calne and his family who had given the children refuge when they were first found. Although he credits Richard de Calne and his household directly only for the account of the green girl's later life, in the circumstances he surely heard from them the full story of the original discovery of the children. Sir Richard must have enjoyed entertaining his friends with the tale. Ralph claims to have heard about the girl many times from Sir Richard and members of his household (*'sicut ab eodem milite et eius familia frequenter audivimus'*). As in the case of Brother Robert and his tale of the vanishing Templars, Ralph and his contemporaries took frequent and consistent repetition of a story as *prima-facie* evidence of its truth. As Carl Watkins put it: 'Chroniclers were therefore conscious that the accuracy of testimony turned on the witnesses' powers of memory and their inclination to remember and repeat a story accurately' (Watkins 2001: 102). William of Newburgh, on the other hand, seems convinced not by the repetition of a single version but by the number of sources from which he heard it. He comments 'it was reported by many people' (*'a multis praediceretur'*) and seems to have been overwhelmed 'by the evidence of so many witnesses of such weight'.

However, here we face a problem: William is known for his practice of paraphrasing his written sources and neglecting to credit them (Gransden 1974: 264)—as his Victorian editor Richard Howlett put it, 'his style and his habit of recasting borrowed passages [render] it exceedingly difficult to detect his mode of building up his history' (Howlett 1884: x–xi). As we shall see, the apparent independence of our two basic texts is illusory.

Yet the very existence of two accounts is of some comfort to the student. For most twelfth-century 'marvels' we have the evidence of only a single contemporary authority, and where there are similarities to other tales they seem to reflect a common origin in folk tradition. But in this case there is no doubt that the two historians are describing a single event that they both believe actually occurred. We can legitimately look for similarities and discrepancies in their accounts.

Although, as we shall see, there is reason to think that Ralph and William derived some at least of their knowledge of the Green Children from the same source, both writers had many independent sources of information.

Just as Ralph, abbot of a small Cistercian abbey, seems to have kept himself well informed on national events through links with other Cistercian houses (Gransden 1974: 324–25), William of Newburgh had contacts with other Augustinians. Gransden (ibid.: 267) suggests that his extensive knowledge of events in East Anglia may have come by way of the Augustinian priory at Thetford, 15 miles (24 km) from Bury St Edmunds and little further from Woolpit. Even closer to Woolpit, as Harris points out (1998: 83), was the Augustinian priory of Ixworth (Page 1907: 105–07), a few miles from the house of Richard de Calne at Wykes to which, Ralph of Coggeshall tells us, the villagers first took the children (Map 2).[7] And we also remember that William was originally prompted to write his history by Abbot Ernald of Cistercian Rievaulx—was he therefore able to draw on the Cistercian information network?

CHAPTER SIX

The Framing Narrative

Analysing the texts

There are clearly two elements in the story of the Green Children as transmitted to us by William and Ralph. First, there is the framing narrative—the discovery of the children, their appearance and behaviour, and their ultimate fate (this chapter). To all of this, if we believe our sources, there were a number of witnesses—the harvesters in the fields, the villagers of Woolpit, Sir Richard de Calne and his household, and any number of 'persistent questioners'. We can treat these reported 'witness statements' with the same respect, but healthy distrust, as any other similar representations of 'fact'—the *res gestae* ('things that were done') of medieval historians.

Secondly, we have the story told by both children (according to William of Newburgh) or by the surviving child, the girl (according to Ralph of Coggeshall)—the description of their homeland and of the circumstances surrounding their arrival in our land (Chapter 7). Here we have what is at best the unsupported story told by a distraught child or children in response to searching adult questions. Our attitude to this must be very different— and William of Newburgh as well seems to have been rather dubious of the children's story, since he treats it much more cursorily than the surrounding narrative.[1]

The two elements of the story are analysed separately in this chapter and Chapter 7—first the external narrative (Table 1) and then 'the children's story' (Chapter 7, Table 2). The versions by Ralph of Coggeshall and William of Newburgh are summarized in parallel columns in these tables. Incidents and themes are numbered in sequence and are referred to by these numbers in the text. Episodes common to both authors are highlighted in the table, and are referred to in the text by a number in angle brackets thus: <9> (for both agree the children were coloured green). Where Ralph and William disagree, or one includes an episode not found in the other, the number is accompanied by an initial—for example, <R14> (the information, found only in Ralph's account, that the girl had thought the food they were offered was 'inedible') or <W2> (William's dating of events to the time of King Stephen). The full texts in both Latin and English, however, are included in an Appendix.

Table 1.   A comparison of the two accounts

	William of Newburgh	**Ralph of Coggeshall**
	'Concerning the green children'	'Concerning a certain boy and girl who emerged from the ground'
1	(Many people reported it, and William was convinced by the testimony of so many good witnesses.)	see <R26>
2	In the time of King Stephen	
3	at a village 4 or 5 miles from Bury St Edmunds	At St Mary Woolpit in Suffolk
4	two children, a boy and a girl,	a boy and his sister
5	appeared to harvesters	were found by the inhabitants
6	emerging from certain ancient ditches called 'wolf-pits' (which give their name to the village).	At the mouth of a pit.
7	They wandered in amazement through the fields,	
8	until they were caught by the harvesters.	
9	Their bodies were green	Their skin was coloured green.
10	and their clothing was of an unusual colour and made of an unknown material.	
11	see <W22>	No one could understand their speech.
12	They were taken to the village.	They were taken weeping to the house of Sir Richard de Calne at Wykes.
13	For some days they would not touch the food they were offered, in spite of their hunger.	They would not touch the food they were offered, in spite of their hunger,
14		because (as the girl later said) they did not think it was edible.
15	However, seeing fresh-cut bean plants they seized them,	However, seeing fresh-cut bean plants they made signs to be given them,
16	but looked for the beans inside the stalks, and wept when they found nothing.	But opened the stalks instead of the pods, and wept when they found no beans.
17	A bystander tore the beans out of the pods for them, and they ate them.	Bystanders opened the pods for them, and they ate the beans avidly.

(cont.)

Table 1 (cont.)

	William of Newburgh	Ralph of Coggeshall
18	For some months they ate only beans,	For a long time they ate no other food.
19	see <W24>	The boy languished and died,
20	until they got used to bread.	But the girl got used to other kinds of food,
21	As the nature of our food affected them their colour changed and they became like us,	and lost her leek-green colour and gradually regained her ruddy complexion
22	and they learnt our language.	see <R11>
23	They were baptized	She was baptized
24	but the boy, who seemed the younger, died soon after.	see <R19>
25	His sister flourished.	And she lived for many years
26		in the service of Sir Richard de Calne; but she remained very wanton and impudent, as Ralph heard many times from Sir Richard and his household.
27	She was no different from women of our own kind, and was said to have married a man in Lynn and to have still been alive a few years before William wrote.	
28	(Some marvels, says William, are illusions caused by 'evil angels', but he confesses he is unable to explain the case of the children who are said to have emerged from the ground.)	

A shared source?

The accounts by Ralph and William run in parallel, though with some inconsistencies, from <3> to <25>. They contain, as Howlett wrote of a similar case, 'the same substance though in different though equivalent words' (Howlett 1884: xxx). The similarities in narrative content are worrying if we wish to use one version to test the 'truth' of the other. Two reporters (and neither was an eyewitness) whose stories are so consistent can rarely be truly independent. Given William's reputation for recasting his sources in different words rather than simply quoting them (ibid.: x–xi), we should not perhaps place much reliance on the differences in vocabulary!

The similarities suggest that Ralph and William must have derived parts at least of their accounts from a single source. This is a disappointing conclusion if we had hoped for independent testimony from the two authors. It confirms, however, that a story was circulating. Yet it raises the question of what the common source was and how the two authors may have treated it.

William of Newburgh's *Historia Rerum Anglicarum* ends abruptly in 1198 and he probably died in that year (Gransden 1974: 263). The earliest surviving manuscript of Ralph's *Chronicon*, which looks like a draft copy, with changes of handwriting, additions and corrections, covers the period from 1066 to 1224—six years after Ralph had resigned as abbot of Coggeshall because of ill-health (ibid.: 322–24). Gransden notes that 'from Richard I's last years [before 1199] the chronicle has passages which were written up with the help of more or less contemporary information' and that the annal for 1223 must have been written in about 1226 (ibid.: 324). However, as we have noted, Ralph's account of the Green Children occurs as part of an interruption in his narrative of the beginning of the Fourth Crusade in 1199—itself an element within the section of the *Chronicon*, from 1187 to 1205, that can with some confidence be attributed to the sole authorship of Ralph himself (Freeman 2002: 180). David Carpenter (1998: 1216) has concluded that the account of the years from 1195 to 1200 'was written up soon afterwards, perhaps in 1201'.

Ralph claims to have 'heard' stories of the girl's later life and behaviour from Richard de Calne and his family and household—that is, before Sir Richard's own death in about 1187 (below)—and it is a natural assumption that the story of the children's discovery and the girl's account of their origin came to him in the same way. No one seems to have queried the truth of his claim to have spoken with Richard de Calne and his family; it would certainly match what is known of his methods, for he seems to have depended largely on oral evidence for his knowledge of recent events—indeed, he rarely made use of contemporary documents (Gransden 1974: 324–25). The changes seen in style and in hands in the *Chronicon* after the year 1205, and the apparent interpolation of a set of brief annals covering the years 1206 to 1212 (Freeman 2002: 180), may perhaps reflect Ralph's appointment as abbot in 1207—a post that one might think would allow little time for historical endeavours thereafter. This was perhaps twenty years after the death of Ralph's informant Richard de Calne and ten years after the death of William of Newburgh. The *Chronicon* was not to be 'completed' with the additions up to 1224 for another twenty years, and Ralph, with his duties as abbot and his later ill-health, perhaps had less direct involvement in its compilation during this period.

This chronology at first sight would allow that *Ralph* might have had access to a complete copy of *William*'s work—but not the reverse. Yet, although we can suggest when the extant manuscripts were written, it is not evident which of our authors wrote the earlier account of the Green Children. We know that Ralph lived close to the events he describes and preferred to use (and credit) oral sources, while William was far away in Yorkshire and is well known for paraphrasing uncredited written accounts. Richard Howlett (who edited William's *Historia* in the Rolls Series) discusses another case where William and Ralph both tell us of the same events—Richard I's misadventures on his return from the Third Crusade (Howlett 1884: xxix–xxxvi). Though the vocabulary largely differs, the accounts are so similar in narrative content and in the sequence of events ('the same substance though in different though equivalent words') that Howlett considers the two historians' sources must ultimately have been one and the same. Now Ralph claims to have *heard* this story direct from Anselm, Richard I's chaplain; but Anselm is known to have *written* a life of the king—although no copy survives (Gransden 1974: 239). Howlett's conclusion was that while Ralph had indeed heard the story from Anselm, William must have had access to Anselm's lost work and must have drawn on it without crediting his source.

In the case of the Green Children, the similarities suggest that William and Ralph drew at least part of the story from a common source—and Ralph himself may have been William's intermediary. It is surely likely that Ralph, if not already writing his *Chronicon* sequentially in the 1190s, was at least collecting material—he might have written down a version of the de Calne story at that time. William says that he had received accounts of the Green Children from a number of people <W1>; could an early draft by Ralph of Coggeshall have been one of these accounts? Augustinian Newburgh Priory lay only a mile and a half from Cistercian Byland Abbey, with which it had strong connections (Gransden 1974: 290 and n.165)—William must have known Byland's own historian, Abbot Philip. And it was, as we have seen, Abbot Ernald of Cistercian Rievaulx, not many miles further away, who had encouraged William to begin his *Historia*. The monks of Byland and Rievaulx would have been in regular communication with Cistercian houses in south-east England—such as Coggeshall. If William had sight of a text written by Ralph, he would certainly have recast it in his own words when incorporating it into his *Historia*, as was his normal practice. Indeed William's use of the obscure words *legumen* and *thyrsus* where Ralph has the more common *faba* ('bean') and *stipes* ('stalk') looks suspiciously as if he is deliberately avoiding identical words in order to distance a paraphrase from the original.

Michael Staunton (2017: 121) notes the existence of other cases where William 'appears to provide a more developed version of a passage found in Ralph's *Chronicon*'. He also (ibid.: 119) points out that an early version of

Ralph of Coggeshall's history that extended only up to 1195 was apparently in circulation at one time, being drawn on by Roger of Wendover, chronicler of St Albans, in the 1220s (Powicke 1906).[2] If that supposed lost version of the text were written in the same sequence as the surviving manuscripts it would not, of course, have included an account of the Green Children, which Ralph inserted, as we have seen, only *after* his description of events that took place in 1199. David Carpenter (1998: 1216) concluded that the account of the years from 1195 to 1200 formed 'a separate and unified part of [Ralph's] chronicle'. As we have noted, he considered that 'There are a variety of reasons for thinking that it was written up soon afterwards, perhaps in 1201.' And it is incorporated into this part of the chronicle that we now find the story of the Green Children and Ralph's other tales of wonders. But the possibility that a manuscript containing an earlier version of Ralph's account of the Green Children might have been in circulation in time to come to the notice of William of Newburgh when he was writing his own *History* between 1196 and his death in 1198 must remain conjecture.

There is no direct evidence of contact between William of Newburgh and Ralph of Coggeshall. However, if Ralph correctly credits his source, the similarity of the accounts is such that the origin of the basic story as told by William must also lie, like that of Ralph, in the de Calne household. And it has been suggested that the presence of canons of William's own order at Ixworth, 2 miles from the de Calne home, may have provided another route by which the story might have travelled (Harris 1998: 83).

The de Calne version, then, is common to both authors. However, William claims to have heard or read a number of other reports about the Green Children. If so, it is only to be expected that they differed in details. The story, as he relates it, probably represents his attempt to combine a number of inconsistent versions into a coherent whole. He comments at the end that the children said many other things in response to persistent questioners ('*curiose percunctantibus*')—and we have no basis on which to judge how he decided what to include and what to omit, or what changes he might have made in the interests of credibility. Ralph of Coggeshall's account, on the other hand, is claimed to come from a single source—or at least a single household. It is likely to be 'truer' (at least in so far as it represents truly the story as it was told by Sir Richard de Calne and his family). However, it might well have developed accretions during Sir Richard's long life, and even in Ralph of Coggeshall's own mind, if he wrote down the final version long after Sir Richard's death.

The date

William dates the event to the reign of Stephen (1135–1154) (Fig. 8, left)
<W2>; indeed, by including it in the first book of his history, which closes
with the death of Stephen (William of Newburgh 1988: 132–33), he confirms
his belief in that dating. As we have seen, his chapters 27 and 28, on the Green
Children and other 'marvels and prodigies', are closely framed by chapters
dealing with events in 1153–1154. Ralph, on the other hand, gives no date in
his text. But he includes the story of the Green Children between his accounts
of a wild man discovered at Orford in Suffolk 'in the time of king Henry the
second' (1154–1189) (Fig. 8, right) and of 'giant's teeth' found in Essex 'in
the time of king Richard' (1189–1199) (Ralph of Coggeshall 1875: 117–20),
apparently implying that the event fell in one of those reigns.

However, Ralph does supply other, circumstantial, evidence that may help
us date the children's appearance. For it was to the house of Richard de Calne
at 'Wikes' that the children were taken <R12>.[3] We have no reason to doubt
Ralph's circumstantial account, although William does not mention Sir Richard
or his manor.[4] The later history of the manor at Wykes or Wicken was reconstructed by Copinger (1905–1911: 1:266–70), although Copinger seems to
have conflated its history with that of the separate place called Wyken Hall
(ibid.: 270), which survives today as a house.

Fig. 8.   King Stephen (1135–1154) and King Henry II (1154–1189),
as depicted by Matthew Paris in his *Historia Anglorum* (c.1255). Courtesy of
the British Library Board, Royal MS 14 C VII, ff 8v and 9r (details).

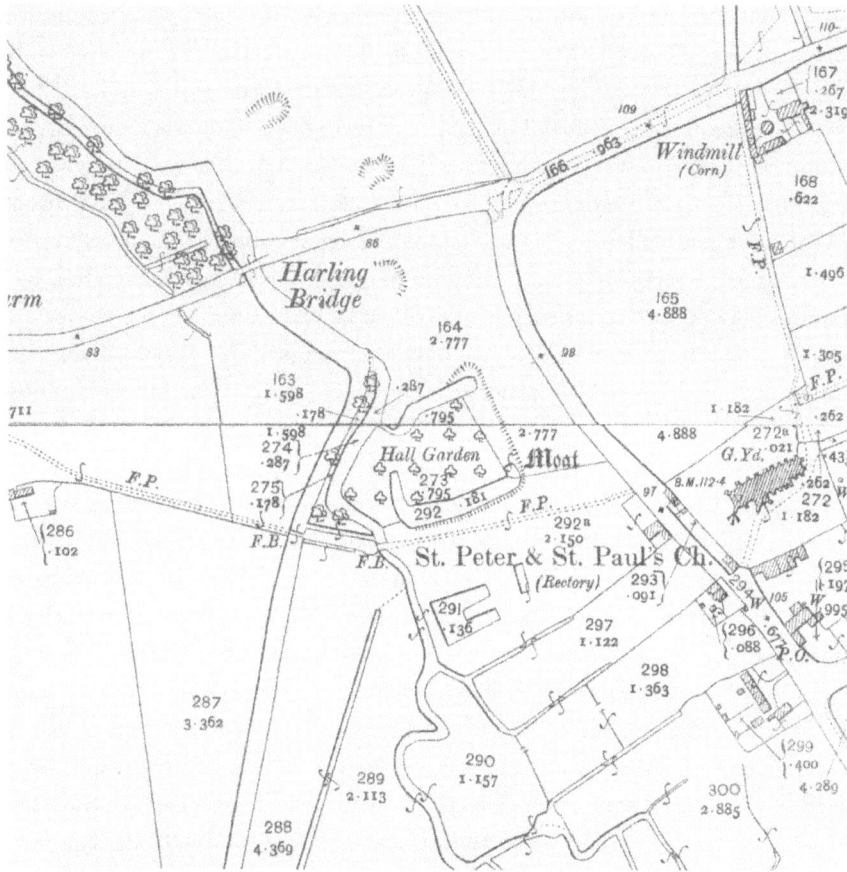

Fig. 9.   Map of Bardwell village at the beginning of the twentieth century,
showing the now lost moated site west of the church, possibly the site of
Richard de Calne's manor house of Wykes. Detail from Ordnance Survey
County Series maps, Suffolk (25 inch) XXIII, 14; XXXIV, 2 (1904).
Reproduced with the permission of the National Library of Scotland.

Wykes lay in the large parish of Bardwell 8 miles (13 km) north of Woolpit
and carried with it the advowson of Bardwell church (Map 2; Fig. 9). Although
often identified as 'Wyken Hall' (Suffolk Historic Environment Record 2023:
BAR 069), the site of the original manor house of Wykes is debatable. From
eighteenth-century maps, Duncan Lunan identified a site on the northern edge
of the parish, at Bowbeck (Lunan 2012, 52–55). An alternative is the moated
site that was bulldozed in 1959 but was previously visible in a field just to the
west of Bardwell church, at National Grid Reference TL93937363 (Fig. 9)
(Suffolk Historic Environment Record 2023: BAR 005—listed as 'Site of a
former Medieval moated manor house and fishpond').

The manor was certainly the property of the de Calne family—presumably originally from Calne in Wiltshire—at the turn of the twelfth and thirteenth centuries (Rye 1900: 42; Davis 1954: 40). Richard de Calne himself has proved more elusive, although the name seems to occur more than once in the family. Unfortunately, the authoritative prosopography of *Domesday Descendants* has little to say of Richard de Calne (Keats-Rohan 2002: 371). As a result of intensive and wide-ranging study of documentary sources, Duncan Lunan (2012: *passim*) reconstructed a detailed biography of Richard de Calne, his family connections and his role in what might be termed the 'secret history' of the twelfth century, for which I can only refer readers to his book. I have not attempted to pursue or to question his references, and feel that his conclusions can only be regarded as, in the terms of the subtitle of his book, 'a subjective treatment'.[5]

Ralph of Coggeshall gives no reason why the children were taken to Wykes rather than, for example, to Bury St Edmunds. Bury was hardly any further away—and Woolpit, after all, belonged to the abbot. Few commentators have considered *why* the villagers would in the midst of the harvest abandon work— or at least send a deputation—to walk 8 miles or so with the children 'weeping inconsolably' to the home of Richard de Calne. Retellers of the story, at least those who have prioritized Ralph's account and realized that Wykes was a separate place and that Sir Richard was not 'lord of the manor' of Woolpit, have seen the incongruity and felt it necessary to elaborate: 'Sir Richard's a traveller [...] He's travelled far and wide, almost to the ends of the earth. Perhaps he's heard of green children' (Crossley-Holland 1966: n.p.); 'He was the constable of the Hundred, and would know what to do' (Hartsiotis 2013: 15).

It may be significant that Wykes was one of the very few places in the vicinity where the chief or sole landowner was *not* St Edmund's Abbey (Page 1911: 556–57 and 573; map facing 357), and where as a result the villagers from Woolpit might expect to find a 'lord'—someone of evident authority—in residence.

Duncan Lunan (1996: 47–48; 2012: 75–78 and *passim*) suggests a historical context when the villagers might have been reluctant to take a problem to the Abbey—a period between 1161 and 1182 when Henry II 'annexed' Woolpit. This is a tempting circumstance, but I believe it is a misreading of the historical evidence. As we shall see, during this period (and indeed, according to Abbot Samson, considerably earlier) the advowson and revenues of its church were alienated (Arnold 1890: 252–54; Jocelin of Brakelond 1989: 43–45). However, the manor of Woolpit still belonged to the abbot, and lay within the juris-diction of the Abbey—the Liberty of St Edmund, comprising the whole of

West Suffolk (Scarfe 1987: 39–40, fig. 2; Jocelin of Brakelond 1989: xv–xvi; Map 2). Within this area, the abbot was effectively the king's viceroy (Cam 1944). Richard de Calne would seem to have had no authority over the village.

Lunan (1996: 46; 2012: 50) concludes that Richard de Calne held the manors of Wykes and Knettishall (a few miles to the north) by 1135. If this is so, it would certainly be possible for the Green Children to have been taken to him some time in the reign of Stephen—though Lunan himself dates their discovery much later, to 1173 (1996: 46–47; 2012: 99–103). And it may well be true, as we shall see, that Richard de Calne already held Wykes before the death of Henry I in 1135.

The earliest *contemporary* record of Richard de Calne seems to be in 1148, when he witnessed the confirmation of a grant of property at Lambourne in Essex by Peter de Valognes, lord of Benington, Hertfordshire, and a great landowner in East Anglia (Gervers 1982: 137–38). Later it becomes clear that Richard was a tenant of the Valognes fiefdom (Keats-Rohan 2002: 371). He is listed among the 'knights' of Peter de Valognes in 1158 (Pipe Roll Society 1884a, 4) and of Peter's successor, his brother Robert de Valognes, in 1166 (Hall 1896: 360). However, the latter list of Robert's knights, in the Red Book of the Exchequer, indicates that Richard was *already* a Valognes dependant in the time of Henry I ('in the time of King Henry, the grandfather of our lord the King'), that is, before 1135. It gives no clue as to the location of any land(s) he held at that time or later.

The Peter de Valognes of 1148 and 1158 was the second of that name. His grandfather, also Peter, the first lord of Benington (Sanders 1960: 12), was prominent in the Domesday Book, with large landholdings in many counties (Keats-Rohan 1999: 322–23). Among them was a manor at Wykes ('*Wicam*') in Suffolk (Page 1911: 556–57). Richard de Calne could well have held the manor from the de Valognes—and could well have done so even before 1135.

The de Calnes appear three times in the long consecutive series of Pipe Rolls (records of the Exchequer) for Suffolk and Norfolk—the two counties being assessed together—compiled in the reign of Henry II; unfortunately only one isolated Pipe Roll survives from before Henry II's time. Although the property to which the records relate is not named, it seems likely that it is the manor of Wykes. In 1158/59 Richard de Calne paid money to the Exchequer (Pipe Roll Society 1884a, 12); payment of a sum outstanding was made in the following year 1159/60 (Pipe Roll Society 1884b, 4). The most likely circumstances in which this money would be due to the Crown would be as payment of feudal relief on the death of Richard's lord Peter (II) de Valognes in 1158 (Gervers 1982: 138). Richard was also recorded in the roll for Essex at this time (Pipe

Roll Society 1884a, 4)—the Essex record makes it clear that it is the same man, and that he was one of the Valognes knights. The manor of 'Canes' or 'Cawnes' in North Weald Bassett, near Epping (Map 1), where a Richard de Calne (clearly a later generation) and his brother Walter are recorded in 1204–1205, seems to have taken its name from this same family (Powell 1956: 288). The earlier Richard's involvement in the transaction concerning nearby Lambourne in 1148 (above) may suggest that he was already present here at that date.

Thus the beginning of Richard de Calne's tenure of Wykes cannot be dated securely. It might well have been before 1135, when he was already a knight of the Valognes fiefdom; it was almost certainly before 1158, when he was assessed for feudal relief in Suffolk.[6] Thus William of Newburgh's dating of the appearance of the Green Children to the reign of Stephen (before 1154) is feasible, in spite of the implications of its placing by Ralph of Coggeshall *after* an episode in the reign of Henry II. And Ralph introduces his version of the Green Children story with the words: 'Another wonder also, not unlike the previous one, happened in Suffolk at St Mary Woolpit.' This might suggest that he incorporates it at this point in his text because of its similarity in content to the Orford episode (both entailed the mysterious appearance of strange humans or human-like beings), not necessarily because it was contemporary or subsequent (Clark 1999: 272). We should remember that Ralph's wonder tales are grouped out of any strict chronological sequence, interrupting his historical narrative at the beginning of the Fourth Crusade in 1199 (Freeman 2002: 193–95).

The date of Richard's death is, of course, another limiting factor in our assessment of when the Green Children appeared. It also, as we suggest above, affects our understanding of how long Ralph of Coggeshall may have had to ponder and improve the story before he wrote his final version of it, since he claims to have heard about the green girl from Richard de Calne himself as well as from members of his household <R1>.

In 1187/88 we find a *Walter* de Calne recorded in the Norfolk/Suffolk Pipe Rolls (Pipe Roll Society 1925: 66). This date seems to provide a *terminus ante quem* for the death of Richard de Calne, Walter presumably being his heir.[7] And that Richard did indeed die at about this time seems to be confirmed by an entry in the *Kalendar* of Abbot Samson of Bury St Edmunds, the first section of which was apparently compiled between 1186 and 1188 (Davis 1954: xii). Here an entry under the heading 'Berdewelle' (Bardwell, the parish in which Wykes lay) refers to *'Heres Ricardi de Caune'*—the (unnamed) *heir* of Richard de Calne (ibid.: 40). Thus Richard was already dead by 1186/88—though perhaps so recently that the name of his heir was not yet known in Bury.

Ralph tells us that the girl was a servant in the de Calne household 'for many years' <R25–26>—certainly possible if she and her brother had arrived in the reign of Stephen, before 1154. A caveat should be noted. William of Newburgh had heard that the girl was still alive (although no longer in Wykes) a few years before he wrote in 1198 <W27>. If she had been a child in the days of Stephen (and apparently a sick and malnourished one), this would make her unusually long-lived for a lower-class woman of that period (Clark 1999: 272, quoting, on the basis of statistics derived from the study of medieval skeletons, a 90 per cent chance of death before the age of forty-five and an *average* lifespan of closer to thirty years). Yet William clearly did not find her age surprising; he was, of course, over sixty years of age himself when he wrote his *Historia*—and if our reconstruction is correct, Richard de Calne must have been in his seventies when he died.[8]

Lunan (1996; 2012) and Harris (1998) favour dates in the 1170s for the discovery of the Green Children, on the basis of which each constructs a distinctive historical context and a very different interpretation of the event. This is to ignore William's categorical statement *'quod sub rege Stephano in Anglia noscitur evenisse'*—'it is known to have happened in England in the time of King Stephen'. Apart from the position the episode occupies in the sequence of Ralph's narrative, there is no substantial evidence to contradict William's dating of the coming of the Green Children to the reign of Stephen—and it may even have occurred where he places it in the chronological sequence of his chapters, in 1153 or 1154. And such a late date, at the very end of Stephen's reign, would not be entirely inconsistent with the implications of Ralph of Coggeshall's text, that he believed that the event occurred in the reign of Stephen's successor Henry II. Thus our tentative conclusion is a compromise: that the Green Children appeared in Woolpit—or rather that the story of their appearance there first became current—at a time at the end of Stephen's reign or the beginning of that of Henry II, in about 1153 or 1154.

Beans in season

> … the green-hued wanderers among the sheaves. (Walsh 2000: 247)

William <W5, W42> tells us that the children were found at harvest time. Medieval calendars portraying the 'labours of the months' consistently illustrate haymaking in July and the corn harvest in August (Henisch 1999: 111–16). In the late fourteenth century an English poet wrote of August 'quen corne is corven with crokez kene' ('when corn is cut with keen sickles') (ibid.: 112), and a fifteenth-century poem on the activities of the months includes the lines:

Julij   With my sythe my mede I mowe [with my scythe my mead I mow]

Auguste   And here I shere my corne full lowe [and here I shear my corn full low]. (Ibid.: 3)

Similarly, in the sixteenth century, Thomas Tusser (1524?–1580) assigns hay harvest to July, wheat and barley harvest to August (Tusser 1984: 114–15 and 122–23).

The presence of fresh-cut beans <15> confirms the summer date. The beans would have been faba (or fava) beans (*Vicia faba*), commonly known as 'broad beans' (Fig. 10)—other types such as runner beans and French or haricot beans are later introductions from the Americas (Huxley et al. 1992: 1:313–15). Faba beans were among the earliest of plants to be domesticated and are now grown and consumed widely (Salunkhe and Kadam 1989: 1:224; Belsey 1973: 1). Broad beans are best plucked for eating when young, and can be cropped throughout the summer (Huxley et al. 1992: 1:313); in sixteenth-century East Anglia Thomas Tusser was advising housewives to pick their garden beans in

Fig. 10.   Bean plant (*Vicia faba*), showing the bean stalk and the pods that contain the beans. Photo © Biopix.dk: J.C. Schou.

July (Tusser 1984: 116). Tusser's garden beans were a large-seeded variety intended for human consumption; smaller-seeded 'field beans' were grown for animal fodder (Bond 1995: 312–13).[9] In Britain broad beans only made the transition from a 'garden' crop to one farmed on a large scale, particularly for freezing and canning, in the 1960s (Gane et al. 1975: section 1:3). Grown largely in the eastern counties, they are now harvested over a period of ten to fourteen days in early August (ibid.: section 3:35).

The events take place, then, in high summer. In spite of Martin Walsh's arguments in his paper on the celebration and significance of Martinmas (Walsh 2000: 247), to which we shall return, the discovery of these children from 'St Martin's Land' cannot easily be associated with that November festival.

The geographical setting

> There is a village in East Anglia four or five miles distant, it is said, from the noble monastery of the blessed king and martyr Edmund. Near that village can be seen certain very ancient ditches which are called *Wolf-pits* in English—that is, 'wolves' ditches'—and these give their name to the nearby village. (William of Newburgh)

The discovery of the Green Children is quite closely defined in time. The same is true of its geographical context. It has been noted of twelfth-century historians that 'topography, or the special setting, seems to be an unusually prominent concern in English history and hagiography' (Otter 1996: 2). This concern with locality seems to be an aspect of an unwritten contract between the medieval historian and his readers that what he presented was *historia* (history—*res gestae*—things that had happened), not *fabula* (fiction) (ibid.: 9). A firm basis in the real landscape, copious reference to named places—these, like the identification of individuals concerned and witnesses to the events, were seen as guarantees of the 'truth' of the story. The contract was one that could easily be broken by an unscrupulous writer. It may perhaps be recognition of the fragility of the contract that led one of our historians, William of Newburgh, to devote his prologue to a scathing attack on Geoffrey of Monmouth. William claimed that Geoffrey had in his *Historia Regum Britanniae* taken *fabulae* about King Arthur and 'cloaked them with the honourable title of *historia*' (William of Newburgh 1988: 28–37). William seems to be particularly incensed at the way in which Geoffrey made his fictitious king conquer real nations of the known world, and assigned fictitious archbishops to real places (ibid.: 33–35).

Yet even in accounts of the discovery of the relics of saints, which often contain much that today would be dismissed as fiction and which in their adherence to a standard narrative pattern show signs of deliberate 'story-telling', the precise definition of place is clearly regarded as essential if the story is to carry conviction. Thus Goscelin of St Bertin, writing in about 1080 of the chance discovery of bones later revealed by a dream to be those of St Yvo, sets the scene 'in the village of Slepe, eight English miles from Ramsey and three from the town of Huntingdon, right on the River Ouse'—the place now known as St Ives (Otter 1996: 42).

It is with this in mind that we can note the precision with which both Ralph and William specify the locality where the discovery of the Green Children took place. It was in the fields near 'a certain pit' or 'certain very ancient ditches called "wolf-pits"' on the edge of the Suffolk village of Woolpit <3–6>, a few miles from Bury St Edmunds (although William <W3> underestimates the distance). Ralph (as we have already seen) introduces also the nearby manor of Wykes and names its lord <R12>, and William ends his tale with the girl living in Lynn <W27>.

Woolpit (Fig. 11; Map 2) lies in East Anglia (Map 1), which in the early Middle Ages was the most agriculturally productive and most densely populated part of rural England (Darby 1936: 209 and 232). The village had belonged to the Abbey of Bury St Edmunds since before the Domesday Book survey of 1086, having been given to the abbot by Earl Ulfketel (Copinger 1905–1911: 6:354; Page 1911: 498–99). Jocelin of Brakelond, the Abbey's chronicler, lists Woolpit among the manors and churches that belonged to the abbot himself, rather than those belonging to the monks (Jocelin of Brakelond 1989: 57). However, in the early twelfth century the Abbey seems to have lost its right to appoint the priest to Woolpit church and its revenue from the church. In 1183, the newly appointed Abbot Samson said that this had been the case for more than sixty years past (Arnold 1890: 252–54; Jocelin of Brakelond 1989: 43–45). Two high-ranking royal servants in succession were granted the benefice: Geoffrey Ridel (later Bishop of Ely) in about 1161 and William de Coutances (later Bishop of Lincoln) in about 1174. Only after William's preferment to Lincoln in 1182 and Samson's appointment as abbot of Bury—and as a belated consequence of a mission that Samson himself had undertaken twenty years earlier to see Pope Alexander III in Rome—did the Abbey regain its rights in Woolpit church.

The Abbey's records also provide us with lists of the tenants in Woolpit in the times of Abbot Baldwin (1065–1098) (Douglas 1932: 32–3) and Abbot Samson (1182–1211) (Davis 1954: 15–16)—the latter list of about thirty names, which can be dated to about 1186–1188 (ibid.: xii), presumably includes

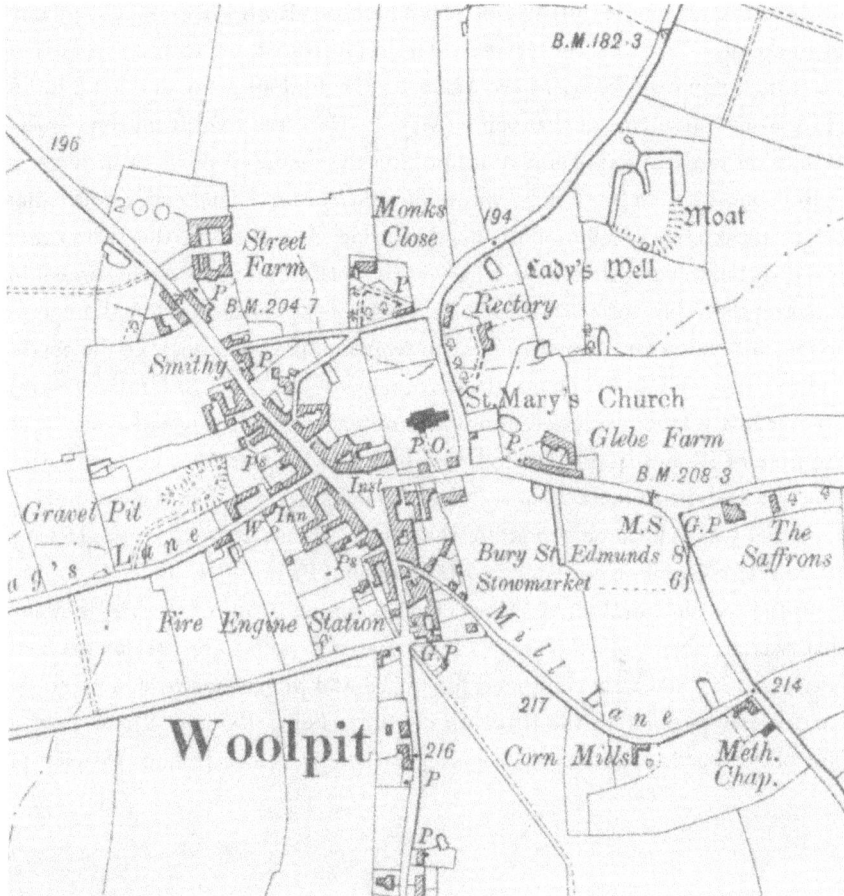

Fig. 11. Woolpit village in 1905, showing the site of Our Lady's Well to the north-east of the church. Detail from Ordnance Survey County Series map, Suffolk (6 inch) XLV.SE (1905). Reproduced with the permission of the National Library of Scotland.

men who, or whose parents, had met the Green Children.[10] Later there was to be a long-running dispute between the incumbents of Woolpit church and the Abbey about church revenues that the Abbey's hosteller claimed (Arnold 1896: 78–114). Although these surviving records give us no information on the discovery of the Green Children, they provide a useful background, and throw light on the relationship between the Abbey and its manors like Woolpit, and how, perhaps, the tenants regarded it.

Outside the gates of St Edmund's Abbey lay a flourishing market town—a town whose population in the twelfth century included a well-established Jewish community, until anti-Jewish feeling led to a massacre in 1190 and the expulsion of the survivors on the initiative of Abbot Samson (Roth 1964: 24–25; Jocelin of Brakelond 1989: 10 and 41–42). The road from Bury to the east was at one time known as 'Wolpetweye' (Lobel 1932: foldout map), and led 8 miles (13 km) to the village of that name (Map 2). Here the road from Bury made a junction with an important route linking the medieval ports of Ipswich in Suffolk and Lynn in Norfolk by way of Stowmarket and Thetford, a route that originally skirted Woolpit on the northern side. At some time this main route was diverted to run through the village itself, perhaps after the establishment of a market there (Taylor 1979: 136–37). A map of the eastern part of Woolpit in about 1568 shows both the 'ancient highway from Bury to Ipswich' to the north, and the 'cart-way to Woolpit village' (Scarfe 1987: 195). Just 6 miles (9 km) further east was Stowmarket, an important place that already had a market at the time of Domesday Book (Hollingsworth 1844: 36 and 68; Letters 2013). Woolpit itself had a market later, and an annual fair perhaps first mentioned in 1286 that was to become famous for the sale of horses (Kirby 1735: 62; Hervey 1925: 2:151; Dymond and Martin 1989: 60–63; Paine 1993: 8).[11]

In the parish church of St Mary (Fig. 12) was an image of the Virgin Mary that was an object of pilgrimage. Pilgrims to Woolpit are first mentioned between 1211 and 1214, although the image and pilgrimage to it were to be particularly popular in the fifteenth century (Paine 1993: 8–9). In 1430 a Norfolk Lollard, John Skylan, on trial for heresy before Bishop Alnwick of

Fig. 12.   St Mary's church, Woolpit. Photo: John Clark.

Norwich, recanted. Among the heresies he abjured was his condemnation of pilgrimage to three specific shrines, punning on Woolpit as 'Foulpette' ('foul-pit') together with the more famous Walsingham ('Falsyngham') and Canterbury ('Cankerbury') as sites of superstition and idol-worship:

> Also that no pilgrimage shuld be do to the Lefdy [Lady] of Falsyngham, the Lefdy of Foulpette and to Thomme [Thomas] of Cankerbury, ne to noon other seyntes ne ymages. (Tanner 1977: 148)

To the north of the church, on the south edge of an enigmatic moated enclosure, lies Our Lady's Well or the Lady Well (Figs 11 and 13), a natural spring now encased in brickwork with an iron grille. It was first mentioned by that name in 1573–1576—although the presence in Woolpit in 1286 of a woman called Petronella de Fonte ('of the well') may confirm its existence, though not its dedication, much earlier (Paine 1993: 10; Hervey 1925: 2:151).[12] Paine (1993: 10–11) concluded that the tradition that it was a holy well dedicated to the Virgin Mary, noted for its healing powers (particularly for diseases of the eyes) and attracting visitors from as far away as Ireland, could be traced no earlier than 1827. However, more recently, Francis Young has noted that the Roman Catholic Catharine Burton (1668–1714), from Beyton (just west of Woolpit) recorded in her autobiography that she made several pilgrimages to the nearby holy well dedicated to the Virgin Mary—certainly that at Woolpit (Young 2006: 215).[13] Young suggests that Jesuits encouraged Catharine and others in their devotion to the well—'unless some residual devotion to the holy well had survived among the local people' (ibid.: 217). Jeremy Harte (2008: 83) notes that many wells named after the Virgin Mary or Our Lady seem to be late—'not gaining any real popularity until the fifteenth century'. He allows the possibility that popularity of wells dedicated to the Virgin may have succeeded an earlier shrine or chapel slighted at the Reformation (ibid.: 84–85).

The area did not escape the impact of national events during the twelfth century. In October 1173 Robert, Earl of Leicester, in rebellion against Henry II, led his army (including 3,000 Flemish mercenaries) to a catastrophic defeat north of Bury St Edmunds, near Fornham St Genevieve—only 8 miles (13 km) from Woolpit (Poole 1955: 335–36; Bartlett 2000: 55–56, 257–58).

This was not, then, an isolated district in which nothing ever happened. The villagers of Woolpit would have been used to travellers of all sorts. Nor would it be surprising if the story of certain local events in the mid-twelfth century spread rapidly and widely.

Fig. 13.   Our Lady's Well Woolpit. Photo: John Clark.

'Certain ditches called "wolf-pits"'

At first sight, writers on place-names seem to support William's contention that the village of Woolpit took its name from certain ancient ditches known as 'wolf-pits' <W6> (Ekwall 1960: 533; Briggs and Kilpatrick 2016: 157).[14] However, the name of the village, which appears as *'Wlfpeta'* in Domesday Book, is usually *singular*—although it does appear as *'Wulpettas'* in 1045×1065 and *'Wulpetes'* in 1203 (ibid.), and we may note that both William of Newburgh (*'Wlfpittes'*) and Ralph of Coggeshall (*'Sancta Maria de Wulpetes'*) use plural forms. Thus the name has generally been derived from the Old English singular form *wulf-pytt* (Toller 1921: 751)—usually assumed to be a pit baited with carrion for catching wolves (Pluskowski 2006: 99–100), although perhaps an abandoned wolf-den.[15]

Oliver Rackham (1986: 35) was sceptical about the implications of this name: '[Woolpit] is not evidence for wolves in Anglo-Saxon Suffolk, any more than "Giant's Grave" is evidence for giants.' However, Aybes and Yalden (1995: 204–05), take it—together with some forty other instances of similarly derived place- or field-names (ibid.: 206–10)—to indicate the presence (at one time) of a pit to trap wolves. Pluskowski (2006: 19–20) supports this view, although recognizing that the term 'wolf' may be used metaphorically.[16]

Ralph of Coggeshall mentions a single pit where the children were found (*'iuxta oram cuiusdam foveae'*—'near the mouth of a certain pit') <R6>. He does not associate this pit with wolves or suggest any connection between the pit and the name of the village. He does, however, as we have noted, name the village in the plural (*'apud Sanctam Mariam de Wulpetes'*—'at St Mary of (the) Wolfpits')—as in the independent references from 1045×1065 and 1203. William of Newburgh uses the plural form 'wolf-pits' in both English and Latin: *'quaedam antiquissimae fossae* [...], *quae sermone Anglico Wlfpittes, id est, luporum fossae, dicuntur, et vico cui adiacent suum nomen indulgent'*—'certain very ancient ditches which are called *Wolf-pits* in English—that is, wolves' ditches— and these give their name to the nearby village' <W6>.

There is a significant difference in the terminology used by our two authors. Ralph's *fovea* is a good equivalent for Old English *pytt*—in classical Latin it even has a particular meaning 'a pit with a concealed mouth used to trap game' (Souter et al. 1968–1982: 729). Although in medieval Latin it is sometimes applied more widely to 'quarry' and even 'moat', the original significance of 'pit' is generally preserved (Niermeyer 1976: 450; *Dictionary of Medieval Latin from British Sources* 2018: s.v.).[17] Thus the reader of an English translation of

Ralph's text, seeing the word 'pit', may make a subliminal connection with the name of the village and with wolves, and picture the children emerging from a wolf-trap—indeed the majority of recent writers retelling the story seem to have done just that!

William, however, uses the word *fossa*—in classical Latin 'a long narrow excavation' (Souter et al. 1968–1982: 728)—and insists that there were more than one *fossa*. In later Latin (although it gains a special meaning of 'grave') *fossa* generally refers to a ditch, dyke, watercourse or similar linear trench, or even an embankment (Niermeyer 1976: 449; *Dictionary of Medieval Latin from British Sources* 2018: s.v.). It may be that William, or more likely a local informant, understood (rightly or wrongly) the name of the village to be plural, as in Ralph of Coggeshall and the two references cited by Briggs and Kilpatrick (2016: 157), and to refer to features of the landscape much more noticeable than a (singular) wolf-trap. In 1735 John Kirby, describing the road from Stowmarket to Bury, noted the existence at Woolpit of 'large and deep Ditches, that are conjectured to be Roman Works' (Kirby 1735: 62). The idea that these ditches were Roman in origin seems to have been first put forward by the antiquary Dr Thomas Gale (1635?–1702), High Master of St Paul's School and later Dean of York, who considered that Woolpit stood on the site of Roman *Sitomagus* (Camden 1722: 443).[18] Are these the same as the 'very ancient ditches' mentioned by William of Newburgh? Neither William's 'very ancient ditches' nor Kirby's 'Roman Works' are convincing evidence of the actual date or function of these features. However, it may be possible to identify their location, on a map if not on the ground.

Suffolk historian Norman Scarfe (1923–2014) discussed a manuscript map of part of Woolpit, drawn in about 1568, in the library of Lord Stafford at Swynnerton Park, Staffordshire (Scarfe 1987: 194–96, fig. 17; Skelton and Harvey 1986: 349–50). This shows 'the alde ditch called the Fraunchise bancke' crossed by the Bury–Stowmarket road on the eastern edge of the parish. Parallel to it on the east lies another 'ancient ditch dividing Grass-field from Woolpit Heath'. These may have been the ditches that Kirby thought were 'Roman Works', but Scarfe noted that in the Middle Ages the 'Franchise Bank' (whatever its original date and original purpose) was prominent enough to serve as the eastern boundary of the jurisdiction of the Abbey of Bury St Edmunds (the 'Liberty of St Edmund' of 1044) and thus later of the county of West Suffolk (Scarfe 1987: 194). With the aid of the map of *c.*1568, the sites of these ditches can be located on a nineteenth-century Ordnance Survey map (Fig. 14—and see Map 2).

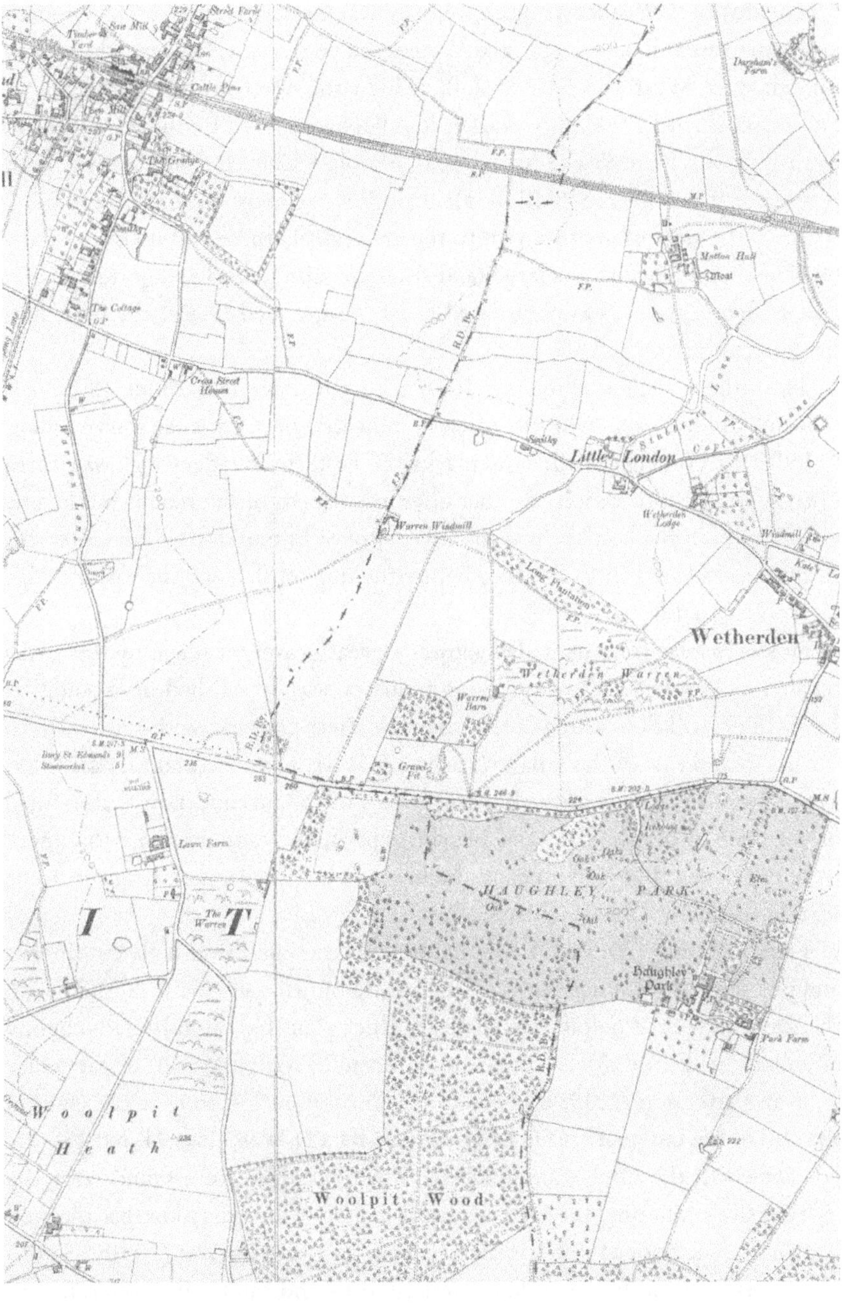

Fig. 14. Map of the eastern edge of Woolpit at the beginning of the
twentieth century, showing the possible alignment of the 'Franchise Bank'
and the boundary of the Liberty of St Edmund. Detail from Ordnance
Survey County Series map, Suffolk (6 inch) XLV.SE; XLVI.SW (1905).
Reproduced with the permission of the National Library of Scotland.

The line of the Franchise Bank is apparently marked by the parish boundary between Elmswell on the west and Wetherden on the east, formerly the county boundary of West and East Suffolk. This runs north from the old Bury–Stowmarket road ('Old Stowmarket Road'), superseded by the A14 Woolpit bypass, about 1¼ miles (2 km) east of Woolpit Church—at National Grid Reference TL99336238 (Suffolk Historic Environment Record 2023: EWL 016). At the time of my first visit to the area (2001) there was no trace of any bank or ditch. Since then a large (and still expanding) sand and gravel quarry, Lawn Farm Quarry, has obliterated Scarfe's suggested line of the Franchise Bank in this area.

The other 'ancient ditch' of 1568 seems to have lain about 180 yards (160 m) further east, where a track is indicated on Ordnance Survey maps (TL99506235) (Fig. 14). It now marks the eastern boundary of Lawn Farm Quarry. Any continuation of either alignment south of the road is masked by woodland, but the boundary of the Liberty of St Edmund itself ran eastwards along the road for a short distance before turning south along the eastern edge of Woolpit parish.

However, the 1568 map also shows 'a great gravel pit made by the lord's tenants of Woolpit'. A brick-making industry was established in Woolpit by 1573/1577, still flourishing in the early twentieth century, with brickyards to the north and east of the village (Kirby 1735: 62; Dymond and Martin 1989: 118–19 and 152). Among such disturbances of the ground, now water-filled or occupied by new housing and a business park, one cannot be sure that there were not once other 'very ancient ditches' or even an original 'wolf-pit' to be seen in the vicinity of the village.

Francis Young (2019: 39) comments that 'the confusion between ditches and pits suggests that neither William nor Ralph was personally familiar with the geography of Woolpit'. He suggests other plausible candidates, including boundary banks and ditches in Great Wood and Woolpit Wood. In particular he draws attention (2019: 39–40) to the moated enclosure near the church, the site of the enigmatic Our Lady's Well or Lady Well (Figs 11 and 13). He concludes: 'If the ditches in which the green children were found were the moated site containing the well, then this could be an indication that the well had fairy associations in the twelfth century'—citing Purkiss (2000: 65–66) for the association between holy wells, fairies and saints. In a reference to the Green Children in his 2023 study of British fairies, Young returns to this conjecture, and the possible identification of female fairies encountered at wells with female saints and their holy wells, and surmises: 'The green girl of Woolpit, on this interpretation [...] perhaps re-emerges as the Virgin

Mary' (F. Young 2023: 87). This, however, seems to be a circular argument, depending upon the prior identification of the children as 'fairies'. Moreover, at least according to William, the children emerged from the ditches and were found by harvesters 'in the fields'—could this be said of a site so close to the centre of the village?

All these candidates are tempting. However, perhaps we should admit that we shall never know exactly where the Green Children first appeared to Woolpit's villagers.

'A boy with his sister'

Our two sources agree that the children were brother and sister (<R4>, <W25> and the reference to their father in <W35>)—information that could only have come from the children themselves, although it would have been a natural assumption. Although William records the impression that the boy was younger <W24>, and modern tellers of the story such as Crossley-Holland and Mitchell have portrayed an older sister looking after her younger brother, there is no proof of their relative ages. Yet the weakness and premature death of the boy ('*semper quasi languore depressus*' <R19>; '*immatura morte decessit*' <W24>) fits well with the suggestion that he was the younger. Sickness, starvation or exposure—whatever experiences the children had been through together would have borne hardest on a younger child.

It is fruitless to speculate as to the actual age of either child. The *puer* and *puella* of our authors give no clue. In Latin a *puer* could be any age up to seventeen, even when the term was applied strictly in law, while *puella* might refer even to a young married woman (Lewis and Short 1879: s.v.). Our only other real clue is that the children, at least according to their own account, had been old enough to look after their father's herd of cattle (see <35> in Table 2).

Harris (1998: 89) suggests that William of Newburgh's description of the girl (after she lost her green colouring) as '*nec in modico a nostri generis feminis discrepante*' ('not in the least different from the women of our kind' <W27>) implies that she reached puberty soon after she was found. This, he argues, supports his view that the girl was suffering from chlorosis—a condition that was thought at one time, as we shall see below, to be prevalent among adolescent females. This is an interesting point, but not I think convincing. We shall turn instead to those particulars in which the children palpably *did* differ from the perceived human norm.

What colour were the Green Children?

> [T]he tone of green of the children's skin must have been something
> unprecedented and unusual, exceeding the imagination of the
> inhabitants of Woolpit. (Madej 2020: 125)

Both our authors agree that the children were green in colour <9>. However,
Thomas Keightley (1850: 281) translated Ralph of Coggeshall's phrase '*tota
superficies cutis eorum viridi colore tingebatur*' as 'the whole surface of their skin
was tinged of a green colour'. This translation, in what became the 'standard'
version of the text, may mislead the reader.[19] In both classical and later Latin
the verb *tingo/tingere* is used chiefly of the process of *dyeing*; it implies nothing
about the *density* of the colour, and unlike the modern English word 'tinge' it
does not carry the connotation of a mere tint or slight coloration.

Although both William and Ralph employ the normal Latin adjective for
green, *viridis*, Ralph later uses the words *prassinus color* of the girl when he
describes how she lost her green colour and 'regained' a ruddy complexion
<R21>—literally her 'leek-green colour', since *prassinus/prasinus* is a loan-word
in Latin from Greek πρασινος, itself derived from πρασον, a leek (Niermeyer
1976: 822; André 1949: 192; *Dictionary of Medieval Latin from British Sources*
2018: s.v.).

Jacques André (ibid.) cites the treatise *De coloribus* attributed to Aristotle
for the description of the shoots of plants that start out light green 'like grass'
(ποωδης) and then 'darken' as they grow to become 'leek-looking' (πρασοειδης).
Thus the colour term in Greek refers to the dark bottle-green of the leaves of
a leek, rather than the pallid root of the plant (Fig. 15).

The two teams that dominated chariot-racing in the eastern Roman Empire,
and the popular 'circus factions' that supported them, were the Blues and the
Greens—and the latter colour is consistently represented by Latin *prassinus/
prasinus* or Greek πρασινος (André 1949: 192; Cameron 1976: 45–73). André
provides no direct evidence from Roman usage, where the term was often
applied to textiles, to confirm this identification, but has no doubt that '*prassinus
color*' was a true dark green ('vert foncé'). Michel Pastoureau (2014: 30)
identifies it as 'a loud, garish green'—'vert épinard' or 'spinach green'. In
later usage, the once authoritative dictionary of medieval and later Latin, 'Du
Cange', identifies the colour '*prasinum*' as '*viride acutissimum, herbaceum*'—an
'intense, vegetable, green' (Du Cange et al. 1886: 477).

Du Cange, Niermeyer (1976: 822) and the *Dictionary of Medieval Latin from
British Sources* (2018: s.v.) all note its use of *emeralds*—in particular '*smaragdus*

Fig. 15.   Leeks (*Allium porrum*). Photo © Biopix.dk: J.C. Schou.

viridissimus qui Prasinus dicitur'—a 'very green emerald that is called "Prasinus"'. Thus, in modern scientific usage a rare monitor lizard (the Emerald Tree Monitor of New Guinea), a bird (the Emerald Toucanet of Central/South America), and a couple of frogs (Bokerman's Lime Tree Frog from Brazil and the Rio Calima Glass Frog from Columbia) are respectively *Varanus prasinus*, *Aulacorhynchus prasinus*, *Sphaenorhynchus prasinus* and *Nymphargus prasinus*. All are striking if not garish green!

We may assume that when Ralph of Coggeshall (who claimed to have spoken to eyewitnesses who had met the Green Children) applied the term to the green girl's complexion he was thinking of a truly deep green coloration, not a tint of pale green on a pallid skin. As Madej (2020: 125) comments: 'In this particular case, were we to believe the story at face value, the tone of green of the children's skin must have been something unprecedented and unusual, exceeding the imagination of the inhabitants of Woolpit.'

This colour can hardly be 'the slightest imaginable tint of olive green in the shadow beneath the chin' which assisted nineteenth- and early twentieth-century medical men in their diagnosis of chlorosis in young patients (Humphreys 1997: 160). Nor is it the extreme ashen pallor of sixteenth- or seventeenth-century sufferers from 'green sickness' or '*morbus virgineus*' (Dixon 1995: 238–41; Humphreys 1997: 160–61).

Yet colour terms are notoriously uncertain (and unstable) in meaning—and particularly problematic when one is dealing with usage in different languages, in different cultures or in different periods (Gage 1999 *passim*). There is little doubt about the meaning of Latin *viridis* and *prassinus*—yet neither Ralph nor William saw the Green Children, and we do not know in what language the story was first recounted.[20]

When considering the word 'green' it is difficult to avoid reference to the Celtic adjective *glas*, a word common to Irish and Scots Gaelic, Welsh and Breton. This can signify a range of colour including blue, grey and the green of vegetation (Dineen 1927: 543; Bevan et al. 1967–2002: 1401).[21] The word can, when used to describe a person's appearance, simply mean 'pallid' or 'grey'—as with fear or cold. It belongs to a group of colour terms found in a number of languages for which an equivalent English word *grue* (green/blue) has been coined (Biggam 1997: 18). If the Green Children had been simply *glas* we could interpret it as 'pallid' and would have little difficulty in finding a rational explanation for their colour.

An Old English word *hæwen* had some of the connotations of *glas*—blue, pale grey, perhaps sometimes grey-green (Biggam 1997: 115–218). But in her meticulous study of Old English terms for blue, Carole Biggam suggested that *hæwen* 'came gradually to specialize in pale blue, in the face of the establishment of *grene* as the green BCT [basic colour term]' (ibid.: 213). The existence of the compound *hæwengrene* 'blue-green' (ibid.: 245) confirms that the two words were seen as having distinct meanings.

Thus, in its recognition of 'green' as a colour distinct from blue-grey, Old English seems to have been closer to Modern English than to the Celtic languages. In Modern English 'green' is relatively unambiguous. Yet phrases such as 'green about the gills' show that it too can, when used of skin colour, have an unexpected meaning. It is in this context perhaps not unlike the 'leaden *or green*' colour that was a symptom of *furor uterinus* (a medical term for a condition apparently similar to that later identified as chlorosis), according to a medieval English translation of a standard gynaecological text (Dixon 1995: 72). And thirteenth-century English supplies other examples, such as 'þat weren for hunger grene and bleike'—'who were from hunger green and pale' (*Middle English Dictionary* 1952–2001: s.v.).

A similar correlation seems to hold true of the word *vert* in early French writing, where, although commonly applied to grass (indeed 'l'erbe verte' is something of a cliché in twelfth-century French romances), '*vert* may sometimes be used to express paleness and the approach of death' (Curta 2004: 46; see Tobler and Lommatzsch 1989–2002: 325–8). Thus the children's colour, although 'green', might still be regarded by those who saw them as symbolically presaging 'the approach of death'.

Certainly 'green' and 'pallid' races were not unknown to the medieval world, at least in travellers' tales. To his history of Hamburg and its archbishops written between 1072 and 1076, Adam of Bremen added a geographical and ethnographical account of Scandinavia and the northern seas, and the people of those areas, which formed part of the vast archdiocese of Hamburg-Bremen. Among the strange races to be found around the Baltic Sea, he tells us, were '*homines pallidi, virides et macrobii, quos appellant Husos*'—'pale, green and long-lived people that they call "Husi"' (Adam of Bremen 1846: 375–76; 1959: 200–01). Given that the neighbours of these 'Husi' are Amazons, Cynocephali ('dog-heads') and Anthropophagi ('cannibals'), there seems little point in trying to identify them among the medieval peoples of Finland and northern Russia. They are simply people 'on the edge'—a concept to which we shall return.

However, one can only conclude from our authors' use of '*viridis*' and '*prassinus color*' that whatever word, in whatever language, was first applied to the Green Children, they were certainly remembered as of a striking 'green' colour, not simply 'pallid' or 'greenish-grey'.

Were the children fairies?

Central to the interpretation of the story of the Green Children as a 'folktale' is, presumably, the identification of the children as fairy-folk, strays from some imagined hidden, perhaps subterranean, Otherworld. And we have noted that Katharine Briggs included the children in her *Dictionary of Fairies, Hobgoblins, Brownies, Bogies and Other Supernatural Creatures* (1976: 200–01). The question, perhaps, should rather be, in the twelfth century, would those who met the Green Children or heard about their strange appearance and behaviour identify them as 'fairies'—or perhaps rather, to use the earlier English term, 'elves'?[22] We shall continue, as most folklorists do, to use the term 'fairy'—without implying similarity to any modern or early modern concept of such creatures.

Ronald Hutton (2014: 1135) regretted that 'There seems at present to be no history of British fairies'. He emphasized that understanding of and attitudes to those entities that were called 'fairies' (or equivalent terms) changed and developed over time.

What seems to be missing so far, from all this admirable body of work, is a sustained sense of how British concepts of fairies developed and mutated from the opening of recorded history to the early modern period, at which time they arguably attracted the most attention and generated the most debate; and which bequeathed most of the key images of them to modernity. This would be a study of the making of a 'tradition', defined as a body of ideas and beliefs handed down between generations. (Ibid.)

Francis Young has made a major contribution to this lacking 'history of British fairies' with his comprehensive study *Twilight of the Godlings* (F. Young 2023).[23] He suggests that there was a persistent belief in popular culture in what Terry Pratchett called 'small gods', intermediary between humans and the higher deities of the contemporary 'official' religion, and fulfilling small and local tasks—and that medieval 'fairies' were such 'godlings'. He notes the difficulty that medieval authors, writing in Latin and with a knowledge of classical sources, would face in interpreting the names used in vernacular languages for these beings (ibid.: 45–46, 263–73). By applying vocabulary derived from classical authors such as 'faun' and 'nymph', they might lead themselves and their readers to conclude that these beings shared the character, powers and behaviour of their Greek or Roman predecessors.

Of course neither of our authors identifies the Green Children as 'fairies'— or any vernacular or Latinate equivalent word. Fortunately, therefore, we do not have to discuss in detail the nature of Gervase of Tilbury's *portuni* or the *nymphae* and *fauni* of other contemporary authors (Hutton 2022: 16, 78; F. Young 2023: 264–65, 284–89), or what the equivalents in popular belief were.

William of Newburgh admitted his puzzlement <W28>—clearly the children did not appear to him to be like either the *mali angeli* who misled people 'with conjuring and fantasy' or the mischievous *daemones* seen by second-sighted Yorkshire peasant Ketellus (to which we shall return). To Ralph of Coggeshall, Malekin of Dagworth was 'a fantastical spirit' (*fantasticus spiritus*). Their contemporary and Ralph's friend Gervase of Tilbury introduces us to *portuni*—small household fairies in England who can be both helpful and mischievous (Gervase of Tilbury 2002: 674–77; F. Young 2023: 284–89).[24] Walter Map provides tales of beautiful fairy brides and a red-faced pygmy king (Map 1983: 26–27; 154–55). Elidurus, in Gerald of Wales's account of his Welsh underworld adventure, met diminutive people 'no bigger than pygmies', but beautiful and with long fair hair (Gerald of Wales 1868: 75–78).

In setting out his approach to the study of *Elves in Anglo-Saxon England* (2007: 17) Alaric Hall came to

> the optimistic conclusion that although Anglo-Saxons encountered more, and more varied, resources for constructing their *ælf*-lore than now remain to us, the processes of construction were fundamentally similar: Anglo-Saxons encountered the word *ælf* and surmised its significance, primarily, from the linguistic and discursive contexts in which it appeared.

Ronald Hutton (2014: 1138–39) drew on Hall's work and on other sources to provide an overview of medieval understandings of the 'fairy' world under six headings, tabulated here:

1. 'a parallel world to the human one, with human-like inhabitants who occasionally have their own sovereign, and are longer-lived than, and in some ways superior to, people'.
2. 'the ability of such beings to enter our own world, and sometimes to steal human children away from it,[25] while humans could blunder into their realm'.
3. 'beautiful supernatural women, who dance in secluded areas at night, and who can be wooed or abducted by mortal men'.[26]
4. 'such non-human beings are often associated with the colour green, either in their clothing or even their flesh'.[27]
5. 'they can give blessings to people who entertain them or otherwise treat them graciously, but also afflict them, notably by leading them astray at night into pits or bogs'.
6. 'human-like creatures which live in or enter homes, where they can make themselves useful to the human occupants by helping them with tasks, or play mischievous tricks on them'.

This is perhaps the context within which those who met or heard about the Green Children would interpret them. Hutton traces subsequent developments in fairy beliefs, and greater cohesion, culminating in the period 1560 to 1640, when fairies appear on stage and at the trials of witches, and there is intense debate about their nature. But perhaps we should not expect our early medieval Green Children to resemble closely the fairies of William Shakespeare, Ben Jonson and their contemporaries.

Once the children had learnt our language and spoken about their strange twilight home and their subterranean wanderings, their status as visitors from an Otherworld would no doubt be obvious. But before that, when they first appeared, would the circumstances—their colour, their choice of diet, their behaviour, language and clothing—be sufficient to convince those who met them that they were elves, *mali angeli*, *daemones* or fairies?[28]

And were fairies green?

The application by Briggs (1971: 1:263) of Stith Thompson's Motif F233.1 ('Fairy is green') to the story of the Green Children begs the question: if the children were indeed green would the villagers of Woolpit have regarded this as proof of their fairy nature? Alternatively, should we assume that the children's colour, however strange, was interpreted and described as 'green' because they were considered to be fairy-folk? In other words: were fairies green in twelfth-century Suffolk? Indeed, have fairies characteristically ever been green?

In his discussion of medieval fairy beliefs and the reactions of the medieval Church, Richard Firth Green refers to the Green Children only once, in a paragraph on the various colours of fairy that were described in his sources (Green 2016: 4). He notes John Walsh, a Devonshire (*sic*, properly of Netherbury, Dorset) cunning-man, who in 1566 categorized fairies as white, green or black ('the black Fairies be the worst') (see Anon. 1566; Gibson 2000: 29); grey fairies in *The Merry Wives of Windsor*; a mysterious 'little red man' recorded by the St Albans chronicler Thomas Walsingham; and a 'polychrome' fairy dog given to Tristram.

To the white, green and black fairies of John Walsh one can add *red* fairies, according to an anonymous text 'Of Fairies' contained in a manuscript in the Bodleian Library, Oxford, datable to the second half of the seventeenth century (Harms 2018).[29] The anonymous author of this text (who credits information from a friend who 'in his youth was much conversant with [fairies], & beloved of them') describes white fairies (who are 'aery' and do little harm), black fairies (who are 'tarrestiall' and malignant), red fairies ('not so evill, yet they have power to hurt & kill') and finally green fairies ('which some call Elves or nymphs'). Of these last our seventeenth-century author tells us rather more:

> The green faires doe commonly frequent houses, gardens, green
> meddows & such places having power to doe good & evill to men
> or women as to enrich or to imperish, to hurt thoes offending them
> [...] finally these fairies which some call Elves or nymphs are clean
> spirits desiring to be in houses, or else w[h]ere, that are kept with
> cleanly people, to such they give Gifts of rewards which in respect

of them brush, sweep, & garnish their roomes, setting faire & fresh water in place with faire fyer light, many times, they leave them mony which they find on the harth of the chimney, or in their shoes or other places, as it hath been reported, they are very familiar with whom they shew themselves to, & very desirous of their company, filling their ear with rare musick, they are to shew themselves with sweet & mild behaviour, with Dances, much myrth, their statue like little children most beautified & faire, using many illusions. (Harms 2018: 196)

Thus of all four types of seventeenth-century fairy, it is the green fairies who have most dealings with humankind, and whose behaviour reflects many familiar fairy traits (at least, familiar in early modern times), such as delight in music and dancing, and giving rewards for good housekeeping. However, we are left uncertain whether these colour terms describe the fairies' actual skin colour or their clothing, or simply reflect and define their *nature*—as may be implied by John Walsh and the anonymous author of the Bodleian text; both of them, for example, regard black fairies as malignant.

But this categorization of fairies by colour was probably itself a post-medieval development, along with their identification as elementals or spirits.[30] Hutton (2014: 1154) identifies a great concern with fairies in the late sixteenth and early seventeenth centuries with 'an interest in the nature of spirits in general, and the attitudes that should be adopted to them, consequent on the complete re-evaluation of religious doctrine produced by the Reformation'. It represented a new, scientific approach to the study of fairies. The 'green' fairies described in the Bodleian manuscript would seem to have little in common with the Green Children—or with any other early medieval Otherworldly folk.

Of medieval fairies Green (2016: 4) says 'green is sometimes mentioned— as with the green children of Woolpit—but is by no means universal'; but he cites no other specific medieval examples of greenness, and they seem hard to identify.

Green clothing presents no such problem. The three Otherworldly riders who in the fourteenth century reportedly (according to an account of a miracle at the shrine of St Cuthbert on Farne Island) abducted the peasant Richard of Sunderland were riding green horses, like the more familiar Green Knight, but were themselves merely clad in green (Craster 1951: 101; Wade 2008: 18).[31] And in perhaps the most well-known later medieval Otherworldly adventure, the lady encountered on Huntley Bank by Thomas (the Rhymer) of Erceldoune was wearing a skirt of 'grass-green' silk (John Murray 1875: lii, l. 5).[32]

In a study of the 'unlucky' colour green, John Hutchings drew attention to its reputation even in recent times as a fairy colour—but generally as the colour of fairy clothing, not of fairies themselves (Hutchings 1997: 58–59). Indeed, in spite of some evidence for green fairies in Irish literature (Cross 1952: 245), reports of actual green-skinned fairies seem to be quite uncommon, except as we have noted above. Baughman (1966: 204) cites only two instances from Scotland and from the Yorkshire moors.[33]

Similarly, although in her book *Fairies: Real Encounters with the Little People* Janet Bord makes much of green as the fairy colour, and the colour of plant life, and compares the Green Children to twentieth-century reports of 'little green men' (1997: 112), the number of such accounts she can muster (for example, ibid.: 71–72 and 76–78), whether they are of fairies from fairy hills or extraterrestrials from UFOs, is surprisingly limited.

But we can now draw upon two sources of information on recent encounters with fairies, both made available by the enterprise of Simon Young. Marjorie Johnson's book *Seeing Fairies*, begun in 1955 but not published until 2014, contains reports of many people's sightings of fairies that date mostly from the 1920s to the 1960s. Encounters with green-skinned fairies are occasionally described: Johnson herself, in a letter to the magazine *John O'London's Weekly* in 1936, recalled her own encounter, at the age of six, with 'a quaint little creature from four to six inches in height. Its body was like shiny green jelly surrounded by an aura of green light, and on its head a red, pointed cap of the same protoplasmic substance' (Johnson 2014: 240). Her description emphasizes the differences between such modern diminutive 'protoplasmic' fairies and fairy sightings and the solid, essentially human stature and appearance of Woolpit's Green Children. Although other twentieth-century green fairies are recorded, particularly in Johnson's chapter 'The Case of the Green Wood Elves' (ibid.: 115–22), a search in the text for the word 'green' shows that observers most often applied the term to fairy clothing rather than to the fairies themselves.[34]

Young's own report of the first results of the Fairy Census, 'an ongoing internet questionnaire about who sees fairies, when and why' (Young 2018b: 11), includes some 500 reports, many of recent encounters, others of childhood experiences. Of these, nearly thirty describe the fairy as 'green' or 'greenish'—in rather more cases the fairies are dressed in green. In a couple of cases, the figure is described specifically as 'the Green Man' or 'a classic green man'—presumably the leafy spirit of vegetation that we shall identify below as a relatively modern concept.

In one instance (ibid.: 59–60, case 68) the respondent recalls an encounter that took place in the 1950s when, as a young girl, she was walking with her father and her sister along a quiet lane in Lancashire, adjacent to a stream: they came across two children, a girl and a boy, both with 'pale greenish skin, pure white short hair, longish clothes', who seemed 'to float in the reeds'.[35] The contributor thought that the girl was about six or seven, the boy about four or five. 'I became alarmed, when my Dad spoke to them. They didn't answer. [...] They didn't speak, smile, or acknowledge us in any way [...] We walked on, and then looked back, no sign of them at all.' Although this episode presents more interaction between the viewers and the putative fairies than other cases reported by Young (most of them merely brief sightings of enigmatic entities)—even if it was failed interaction, since the children did not respond when addressed—it still lacks the circumstance and the long-term relationship and communication that developed between the Green Children of Woolpit and their hosts.

Green-skinned fairies, then, are acceptable as a class but not particularly commonly reported, and the colour has certainly never uniquely identified a fairy. Thompson (1955–1958), indeed, allows for other colours (red, silver, brown, black) as further subdivisions within his Motif F233 'Color of fairy'.

However, discussion of 'green' fairies—particularly Celtic ones—is bedevilled by the dangers of equating colour terms in a variety of languages. For example, the name of the Irish Eochu Glas, an adversary of Cúchulainn (MacKillop 1998: 187), can be translated 'Eochu the green' or 'the green rider' and 'may be a sign that he belongs to the Land of Death' (Brown 1947: 58–59). Yet, as we have seen, the meaning of *glas* is such that 'the pale (or blue-green-grey) rider' seems an equally likely translation.

Ireland's Eochu Glas, then, seems not to be related to that English 'green rider' better known as the 'Green Knight'—even if one accepts a 'Celtic' origin for the latter. In an important study of the fourteenth-century poem *Sir Gawain and the Green Knight* and its parallels, George Kittredge (1916: 195–99), while tempted to identify the Green Knight as 'the demon of vegetation', noted the existence of 'The Green Knight of Knowledge' ('Curadh Glas an Eolaig') in Connaught tradition; but he pointed out that owing to the ambiguity of *glas* the latter name could mean 'grey knight' (ibid.: 197).

This is not the place to ponder the folkloric significance (if there is any) of the story of Gawain and his dealings with the Green Knight. The subject has been dealt with extensively elsewhere, and Michelle Miller has discussed some of the 'innumerable speculations about its mythic nature' (in Lindahl et al. 2000: 925–29). Though Martin Walsh identified the Green Knight as an 'older cousin' of the Green Children (Walsh 2000: 247),[36] this being, not only green of face but with bushy green hair and beard, green clothing and gear, and a green horse, holding a holly branch in one hand and an axe in the other, is a very different figure from our children (Tolkien and Gordon 1949: 5–7, ll. 136–220). Brewer (1997: 183) comments on the Green Children: 'There are no other characters in medieval European literature that I am aware of, apart from these unfortunate children, who have green complexions. If there were it would mean that they were ill. All the more striking is the vivid green complexion of our Green Gome [the Green Knight] who is clearly in the best of rude health.'

At first sight the Knight seems to have more in common with the 'Green Men' of English pageantry discussed by Centerwall (1997: 26–27) and the 'Wild Men' of Christmas mummings (Lindahl et al. 2000: 929). Yet even here the similarities are not close. It is worth noting how unique the figure of the Green Knight is in medieval literature—as the quotation above from Brewer (1997: 183) indicates. Larry Benson (1965: 62–72) compares him with—or rather distinguishes him *from*—both 'literary green men' who, like the allegorical figure of Youth in a contemporary poem *Parlement of the Thre Ages*, are merely green clad, and 'literary wild men' who come in two guises, 'leaf-clad' and 'hairy' (ibid.: 72–83). 'Green skin', he writes (ibid.: 90), 'is not a conventional feature.' Nor do Centerwall's Green Men of pageantry have green skin and green hair—they are leaf-clad, but they have bare faces and black bushy beards and hair (Centerwall 1997: 26–27).

In her paper 'How Green is the Green Knight?' Bella Millett (1994) takes to task those who, like John Speirs (1949) and many popular writers since, have identified the Green Knight as a vegetation spirit—the so-called Green Man. She finds no evidence in the poem to support Speirs's reading, and reminds us (ibid.: 148) that the very name of the Green Man was the creation of Lady Raglan in 1939, and that his perceived mythic nature depends upon the work of those late nineteenth-century scholars whom Andrew Lang once dubbed 'the vegetable school, the Covent Garden school of mythologists' (Lang 1901: 206; quoted by Millett 1994: 139). She concludes that the present popularity of the concept of the 'Green Man' may be read as 'a temporary [...] embodiment of human desire, the product of twentieth-century fears of industrialisation and nostalgia for [...] "our oneness with the earth"'—and that the Green Knight 'has more than once been caught up with this embodiment' (Millett 1994: 150–51).[37] This popular embodiment tells us nothing about the Green Knight's significance in his original context.

We must accept that in this instance at least we are faced with an Otherworldly entity whose skin is indeed green (*enker grene*—'very/bright green'). But as an apparently unique literary creation whose possible basis in medieval belief and whose significance in the context of the poem are both debatable, he provides no hint of how we should interpret the Green Children's skin colour.

What do we mean by 'colour' anyway?

> [S]ome appeared of an azure, some of a deep purple, some of a grass-green, some of a scarlet, some of an orange-colour, etc. (Cavendish 1992: 133)

Today, we are perhaps more familiar with the concept of strangely coloured 'non-humans', whether it is the 'little green men' of early journalistic accounts of flying saucers (Trudel 2005: 10), the more recent extraterrestrial 'Greys' who carry out abductions, or aliens in popular science fiction, such as the blue-skinned Andorians of *Star Trek* (who refer to people from Earth as 'pink-skins'), or (for an older generation) the green-skinned Treens encountered by Dan Dare on Venus—and that colour is overt, the colour of the aliens' skin.

Yet this seems not to have always been the case. Even as Europeans became aware of human races with different skin tones, the terms adopted to describe them do not reflect their 'real' hue, but are simply relative to the 'norm' of European complexions ('white'). North American 'redskins' were not scarlet; writers who warned against the 'Yellow Peril' did not believe the Chinese were the colour of lemons. The complexities of normal human skin coloration, and the difficulties of categorization, were obvious to Daniel Defoe, who described Robinson Crusoe's companion Friday at some length:

> The Colour of his Skin was not quite black, but very tawny; and yet not of an ugly yellow nauseous tawny, as the *Brasilians*, and *Virginians*, and other Natives of *America* are; but of a bright kind of dun olive Colour, that had in it something very agreeable; tho' not very easy to describe. (Defoe 1927: 1:238; quoted in Anderson 2003: 144)

By default, then, human beings are human-coloured. And colour terms applied to people did not necessarily refer to the colour of their skin. It is generally assumed that, for example, Norse explorer Erik the Red had red hair. The 'black Irish' (a term first recorded in the nineteenth century) were not negroes—they had dark complexions, dark eyes and black hair. And when

Samuel Pepys described an Italian waiting woman as 'black' he was presumably using the word in similar sense (Iyengar 2005: 221).

Early author of science fiction Margaret Cavendish, Duchess of Newcastle, writing in 1666, obviously felt that the concept of a skin colour outside the normal human range would be novel to her readers, and would require fuller exposition. She uses it explicitly to distinguish the people of her 'Blazing World' from earthly humans (who are 'white, black, tawny, olive or ash-coloured'):

> [A]s for the ordinary sort of men in that part of the world where the Emperor resided, they were of several complexions; not white, black, tawny, olive or ash-coloured; but some appeared of an azure, some of a deep purple, some of a grass-green, some of a scarlet, some of an orange-colour, etc. (Cavendish 1992: 133; Iyengar 2005: 220)

She chooses very specific colour terms—'azure', 'scarlet', '*grass*-green', '*deep* purple', '*orange*-colour'—lest her readers interpret 'red' as 'of reddish complexion, ruddy', 'green' as 'greenish, pale' and so on. Was it for the same reason that Ralph of Coggeshall tells us that the Green Children's complexion was *prassinus*—leek-green?

When Domingo Gonsales, the supposed narrator of Francis Godwin's *The Man in the Moone*, first meets the Lunar inhabitants, he is astounded both by their great size and by the colour of their skin. Godwin/Gonsales expands on this unusual colour: 'a colour never seen in our earthly world' ([Godwin] 1638: 71). It would be as fruitless to attempt to describe it, he tells us, as to explain to a blind man the difference between blue and green.[38] Their 'otherness' is emphasized by—indeed is inherent in—their colour.

The attention given by these later writers to the skin coloration of strange races suggests that if fairies had ever been thought of as set apart from humans by the colour of their skin it would have been noted as a particular matter of interest—instead, they were presumably by default 'people-coloured'.

Fairies in Suffolk and elsewhere

It seems that in Suffolk itself more recently one may look in vain for green fairies—perhaps in part because of the prevalence of reports of 'sandy-coloured' fairies in the area around Stowmarket.[39] Our knowledge of this type of fairy is largely thanks to the enterprise of the Rev. Arthur Hollingsworth of Stowmarket in including in his history of that town an appendix on witches and local fairylore dating back to the eighteenth century (Hollingsworth 1844: 247–48; drawn on by Gurdon 1893: 36–39, Porter 1974: 77–78, Westwood 1985: 159–61, Westwood and Simpson 2005: 704–05, and Young 2019: 82–86). For example, his informants told of encounters with fairy-folk 'quite small and sandy-coloured' with 'sandy hair and complexions' in the hamlet of Onehouse, only 3 miles (5 km) from Woolpit (Map 2; Fig. 16). Certainly, in the eighteenth century, Woolpit must have lain well within the range of these sandy-coloured 'ferriers'.

Yet one must question whether the small distance that separates Onehouse and Stowmarket from Woolpit can be as significant as the 600 years that separate the Rev Arthur Hollingsworth's reports from those of Ralph of Coggeshall and William of Newburgh. We should not expect a long-lived and consistent vision of 'fairy-folk'.

But there are comparable instances of Otherworld inhabitants or beings that today we might call 'fairies' in the works of Ralph and William and their contemporaries. An examination of these may indicate whether green coloration entered into twelfth-century concepts of such beings.

First, Ralph of Coggeshall himself tells us of Malekin—'Malkin' being a diminutive of Matilda/Maud, though presumably without the pejorative sense

Fig. 16. St John the Baptist church, Onehouse. Its twelfth-century
round flint tower was shortened when it became unsafe in 1990.
Woolpit church may have had a similar tower in the time of the Green
Children, before its rebuilding in the fifteenth century. Photo: John Clark.

of 'slut' it later acquired (Breeze 1995). Malekin was a 'fantastical spirit' who in the time of King Richard I (1189–1199) haunted the house of Sir Osbern de Bradwell (Ralph of Coggeshall 1875: 120–01; Westwood 1985: 149; Westwood and Simpson 2005: 690–91; Young 2019: 48–51; F. Young 2023: 291–92). Again the report comes from the vicinity of Stowmarket, for the de Bradwell house was at Dagworth, only 2 miles (3 km) north of Stowmarket and 4 miles (6 km) from Woolpit (Map 2). Malekin, by her own account, had been stolen away as a baby when her mother left her at the edge of a field while working on the harvest at *Lanaham*—assumed to be Lavenham, about 10 miles (16 km) distant to the south-west.[40] She had spent seven years with a mysterious 'other woman'—it would be a further seven before she could return to human company.[41] Malekin spoke English with a local accent ('*secundum idioma regionis illius*'—'according to the idiom of that region'), but was equally at home discussing the Scriptures in Latin with Sir Osbern's chaplain. She begged for food, which was set out for her to take.[42] However, she normally appeared only as a disembodied voice; she could not be seen since, she said, she wore a special cap that made her invisible. A housemaid, who once persuaded her to show herself, described her as looking like a very small child in a white dress. Malekin is puzzling: not quite a fairy, not quite a house-spirit, not quite a poltergeist, not quite a changeling. When she allowed herself to be observed, she looked perfectly human, if diminutive.

William of Newburgh as well introduces us to human-seeming 'fairy-folk'. He provides a version of a widespread tale of a theft from a fairy hill (William of Newburgh 1988: 118–21; Westwood 1985: 350–51; Westwood and Simpson 2005: 846–47).[43] He tells how a villager who lived near the stream known as the Gypsey Race (Humberside/East Riding of Yorkshire), close to where William himself was born, was returning to his home drunk late at night and heard singing coming from a nearby mound (*tumulus*). This mound has been identified as the large round barrow (possibly Neolithic) called Willy (or Willie) Howe, near Wold Newton (Heritage Gateway 2012). Other stories of fairies and hidden treasure there were recorded much later (Wright 1861: 1:32–35; Grinsell 1976: 168–71; Briggs 1971: 2:396–97; Westwood 1985: 352).[44] According to William, the villager found an open door in the mound, and inside it a large well-lit hall with people seated at a feast. William himself attributes this appearance to the machinations of demons or 'evil angels' (*mali angeli*)—they misled the villager 'with conjuring and fantasy' (*praestigialiter et fantastice*). Yet, though the cup that the villager stole from the feast was 'of unknown material, unusual colour and extraordinary form', there is nothing to suggest that, in the story as it reached William, the feasters themselves were of unusual appearance.

But William was also aware of beings that were of other than 'human' coloration. These were the *daemones* (perhaps the same as the entities he elsewhere calls 'evil angels'?) seen by a peasant called Ketellus (perhaps in English Ketil) from the village of Farnham (near Knaresborough, North Yorkshire, and 15 miles (25 km) from Newburgh). Ketellus apparently developed this 'second sight' quite suddenly.[45] Returning from the fields one day, he was thrown from his workhorse (a *iumentum*—a draught animal, probably a mare) when it 'fell to the ground as though it had struck a low obstacle'. He saw 'two little men who looked like Ethiopians, sitting in the road and laughing' (William of Newburgh 2007: 86–87). The two little men were equally surprised that he could see them. Thereafter,

> [h]e received from God this gift of keeping demons in view from that day onward; they could not lurk hidden from him, however much they sought to do so.

The first two demons were presumably *black* 'like Ethiopians'—sadly Ketellus made no comment on the colour of others he later saw:

> He used to say that some demons were big, strong, cunning, and extremely harmful if given scope by a higher power, whereas others were small, contemptible, feeble physically, and dull mentally, but that all according to their modest measure were hostile to men, and they took great pleasure in causing people even a modicum of inconvenience. (William of Newburgh 2007: 90–91)

Occasionally he saw them, invisible to all others, sitting 'like apes' on the shoulders of men in a tavern, and spitting in their ale (ibid.). These 'black' demons that are 'hostile to men' seem to have a lot in common with the much later sixteenth- and seventeenth-century fairies described by John Walsh: 'the black Fairies be the worst' (Anon. 1566; Gibson 2000: 29), and the anonymous author of the text 'Of Fairies' to which we have referred—whose black fairies are 'tarrestiall and very malignant and deadly' (Harms 2018: 195).

Other twelfth-century accounts of brushes with Otherworldly beings are well known. In Gervase of Tilbury's story of the swineherd who followed a lost pig through Peak Cavern, Derbyshire, and emerged in the land of the Antipodes (Gervase of Tilbury 2002: 642–45; Westwood 1985: 204–06; Westwood and Simpson 2005: 172), there is no reason to believe that the harvesters he saw in the fields there or the local ruler he spoke to were of anything but human appearance (and they presumably spoke English since he was able to communicate with them).

Gerald of Wales relates the story of the Welsh monk Elidurus who claimed that, as a boy, he had had dealings with the inhabitants of a land reached through an underground tunnel (Gerald of Wales 1868: 75–78; 1978: 133–36; Westwood 1985: 295–96)—a story to which we must return later for some similarities to that of the Green Children. The people of that land were small ('no bigger than pygmies') and beautiful, with long fair hair. Unearthly beauty was also the characteristic of Eadric the Wild's fairy wife and her sisters as described by Walter Map (Map 1983: 154–55; Westwood 1985: 246–49), but combined with greater stature ('greater and taller than our women'). The 'little red man' ('*homunculum rubeum*') of an encounter that, according to Thomas Walsingham of St Albans, occurred 'in northern parts' in 1343 seems, in spite of his own strange appearance, to have been the servant or attendant of 'a most beautiful lady [sitting] with many girls like her'. She, as her subsequent actions show, was an Otherworldly figure with strange powers (Wade 2008: 11–12). And the Otherworldly riders who tried to tempt the peasant Richard of Sunderland to his damnation 'were beautiful of stature and of countenance' (Craster 1951: 101).

On the other hand Walter Map also tells us of the Otherworld ruler who invited the British king Herla to his wedding feast: a pygmy, no bigger than an ape, 'his visage was fiery [*ardenti facie*], his head huge; he had a long red beard [*barba rubente*] reaching to his chest [...]: his belly was hairy and his legs declined into goats' hoofs' (Map 1983: 26–27; Westwood 1985: 251–53; Westwood and Simpson 2005: 331; F. Young 2023, 240–41). One hesitates to second-guess the great scholar M.R. James, who translated '*ardenti facie*' as 'his visage was fiery red', but the *colour* red is implied rather than explicit. Yet we should recognize that this pygmy king with his 'fiery' face and red beard might well have been described, in medieval terms, as a 'little red man'. Wade (2008: 15–16) makes a similar comparison between the king and the '*homunculus rubeus*' of Thomas Walsingham's story. Later, having mysteriously grown to more normal size, Walsingham's 'little red man' is described as '*ille rubeus et rufus*'—which Wade (ibid.: 11–12) translates as 'that ruddy red-haired man'. But Walter's portrayal of the pygmy king is clearly influenced by classical descriptions of Pan, to whom he likens him ('*vir qualis describi posset Pan*'), and of fauns, and by his book-knowledge of both pygmies and apes, rather than necessarily by local concepts of Otherworld inhabitants or fairy-folk (F. Young 2023, 240–41).

Otherworld people might thus be of unusual appearance, or differ in stature and in beauty from humans. It would surely have warranted comment if they differed in *colour*—there is no comment, and we are left to assume that their colour was unexceptional within normal human limits.

There is nothing to suggest that greenness was considered a general attribute of medieval fairies. But our sources are inconsistent as to their actual appearance. Perhaps various types of fairy were envisaged—possibly in different regions—with different characteristics, or perhaps fairies should be considered to be polymorphous and able to change their appearance at will. Certainly, as we have seen, one of our informants, William of Newburgh (1988: 120–21), concluded that 'evil angels' could confuse people 'with conjuring and fantasy'.

Yet even if green skin was not an 'unmistakable mark' that would identify a fairy in twelfth-century Suffolk, there was already enough strangeness about the Green Children's appearance and their behaviour that would have led people to wonder if their origin lay beyond this normal, human, world. The Green Children may have been—probably were—identified as Otherworld visitors even before they spoke of their journey from sunless St Martin's Land. But if someone wished to concoct a story of such visitors, there would have been no reason in local belief or preconception for them to describe the children as green. It is not a characteristic that would have been imposed on them by their status as 'folktale'. Hence, we have every right to suppose that the story is true in at least this regard: if the Green Children existed at all, they *were* green. This places the onus upon 'rationalizers' to identify a real life basis for green-skinned children. They do not seem to have met the challenge very successfully.

'[T]heir skin was all dyed'?

Both our authors agree that the children's green coloration was temporary. Both seem to have believed that their colour was caused by, or at least was contingent upon, their diet <21>. William of Newburgh says: 'At last, as the nature of our food prevailed, they gradually changed their colour and became like us'; Ralph of Coggeshall says of the green girl (the boy having already died): 'Becoming used to all sorts of food she totally lost her leek-green colour, and gradually recovered the ruddy appearance of her whole body.'

Ralph may have suspected, however, that their coloration was not only temporary but *artificial*—a colour applied to the skin. As he puts it:

> [I]n colore cutis ab omnibus mortalibus nostrae habitabilis discre-
> pabant. Nam tota superficies cutis eorum viridi colore *tingebatur*.

> [T]hey differed in the colour of their skin from all the mortal inhab-
> itants of our world; for the whole surface of their skin was *imbued/
> stained/dyed* with a green colour.

He uses the same term when recounting the green girl's description of her homeland <R32>:

> [O]mnes habitatores et omnia quae in regione illa habebantur viridi
> *tingerentur* colore.

> [A]ll the inhabitants and all things that existed in that country were
> *imbued/stained/dyed* with a green colour.

The significance of Ralph's words, emphasized by the repetition 'tingebatur' and 'tingerentur', is obscured by Keightley's misleading translation of the first as 'tinged' and omission of the second (he simply says that the inhabitants and everything in the green girl's world were 'of a green colour').

In classical Latin the verb *tingo/tingere* means 'to immerse something in liquid' and in particular 'to immerse something in colour, to dye' (Lewis and Short, 1879: s.v.), and this seems to have been its usual connotation in medieval writing (*Dictionary of Medieval Latin from British Sources* 2018: s.v.).[46] The related noun *tinctor* was the regular term for a dyer. Although the verb did sometimes have a more generalized meaning, 'to impart colour to something' (ibid.), it is tempting to conclude that Ralph, or one of his informants, believed that the children's skin had been dyed or artificially stained green—and by extension that the same procedure had been applied to the inhabitants and everything else in the children's homeland, if the girl's account was to be believed.

Lunan (2012: 8) correctly translates the verb as 'dyed' in both instances, and discusses its significance within the context of his hypothesis of an extrater-restrial colony of humans, perhaps conditioned to eat only genetically modified green foodstuffs (Lunan 1996: 44; 2012: 375–81),[47] and themselves coloured green similarly, or perhaps as a result of their diet. Although Harris (1998: 82) quotes Keightley's translation 'tinged', his hypothesis that the children came from an immigrant Flemish family, perhaps with connections with the clothworking industry, leads him to suggest that the family, in hiding from anti-Flemish violence, might have 'dyed themselves green as camouflage' (ibid.: 91)—though he goes on to prefer chlorosis as the cause of the children's green colouring.

Yet the concept of dyeing the skin green, either deliberately 'as camouflage' or accidentally, perhaps while working in a cloth dye-works, raises a problem in a medieval context. There are natural vegetable sources of green dye—for example, ferns, nettles or foxgloves—but these do not provide a rich or stable green colour, and do not seem to have been used in practical cloth dyeing in the medieval period. Dominique Cardon, in her authoritative study of *Natural Dyes*, says: 'It is a strange paradox of the vegetable kingdom that there are almost no plants that will give a true green directly. The greens produced by dyers in all parts of the world have traditionally been obtained on a ground or base of indigo before a second bath of yellow dye' (Cardon 2007: 360–61). Writing in the 1890s, William Morris contrasted traditional dyeing techniques with modern industrial processes, and commented that in traditional practice 'Green is obtained by dyeing a blue of the required shade in the indigo-vat, and then greening it with a good yellow dye, adding what else may be necessary (as, *e.g.*, madder) to modify the colour to taste' (Morris 1893: 203).[48] The process of a first dyeing with blue, then a second dyeing with yellow, is apparently recorded on a Babylonian clay tablet of the seventh century BCE (Cardon 2007: 359–60).

In the medieval period, green was produced by this two-stage process, first dyeing the cloth blue with indigo dye extracted from the leaves of the woad plant (*Isatis tinctoria*), then dyeing it a second time with a yellow dye such as that derived from weld (the plant *Reseda luteola*) or from 'dyer's broom' (*Genista tinctoria*), the final colour depending very much upon the depth of the blue imparted by the original dyeing with woad (Hurry 1930: 47; Munro 2003: 211–12; Cardon 2007: 173, 361; Pastoureau 2014: 116).[49] Writing in praise of wool and its uses in 1068–1070, Winric of Trier described woollen cloth made in Flanders 'in green or blue-green or deep blue colours'—the sorts of colours that could be readily produced by woad alone or with a second dyeing with weld (Uytven 1983: 154). This same technique was presumably used to produce the 'green cloth of Ghent' that was admired in the thirteenth century (ibid.: 156).

A medieval dye-house would not contain a vat of green dye, nor apparently would it provide any ready way to colour the skin green. The hypothesis that the children's skin was coloured by a natural dye that faded in time is a tempting one, and it may well be that this is what Ralph of Coggeshall suspected. In practice, its adoption in a medieval context is problematic. If the Green Children were stained green, it was not with any readily available green dye used on cloth.

Arsenic, chlorosis or favism?

> Just as sufferers from the Black Death did not turn black, so girls
> suffering from green sickness did not need to be, literally, green.
> (H. King 2004: 25–35)

Ralph of Coggeshall's use of the word '*tingebatur*'—which could, as we have seen,
mean 'was dyed'—of the children's green skin <R9>, and his statement that
the girl 'regained' her ruddy complexion ('*sanguineam habitudinem totius corporis
paulatim recuperavit*') <R21>, may suggest that he, or perhaps his informants,
thought that the children's colour was *artificial*. But it was at most a temporary
condition, perhaps (both our authors seem to imply) brought on by their diet
<20–21>. For only when the children became accustomed to more normal food
than their original diet of raw beans did their green colour begin to fade.

We have already noted a suggestion, possibly local to Woolpit, that the
children's coloration was due to *arsenic* administered by a wicked uncle (Maxwell
1926: 108; Roberts 1978: 84–85). Unfortunately for this theory green skin is
not apparently a symptom of arsenic poisoning—though yellowness, through
jaundice, might be (Macpherson 1999: s.v. Arsenic). Chronic poisoning with
low levels of arsenic can indeed lead to changes in skin pigmentation, notably
to a 'raindrop' pattern of pale hypopigmented spots on a background of brown
hyperpigmented skin, or even to a patchy, piebald appearance (Subcommittee
on Arsenic in Drinking Water 1999: 101–03). But clearly this does not explain
the greenness of the children's skin. Perhaps those who have suggested arsenic
as the cause had in mind the notorious 'Paris green' pigment containing arsenic
that was used in wallpaper and paint in the nineteenth century, and were
unconsciously misled by its name.

More widely, to those seeking a 'natural' explanation of the Green Children's
colour, chlorosis (or 'green sickness'—the earlier English designation that
continued in use alongside the medical term chlorosis) has long been a popular
suggestion (Brewer 1997: 182; Harris 1998: 89; Warren 2001),[50] although
the term is one no longer familiar to the medical profession (Humphreys
1997; H. King 2004). It was prevalent as a medical diagnosis in the nineteenth
century, when the condition was particularly identified among adolescent girls
and young women and 'overwhelmingly frequent in females between fifteen
and twenty-five' (Taylor et al. 1896: 720). Helen King (2004: 1) defined it as
'a historical condition involving lack of menstruation, dietary disturbances,
altered skin colour and general weakness once thought to affect, almost exclu-
sively, young girls at puberty'.

A *greenish* pallor, although sometimes mentioned, does not seem to have been the defining symptom of this condition. Most of the symptoms reported appear to be attributable to iron-deficiency anaemia (hypochromic anaemia).[51] But other descriptions have led some modern writers to identify, in at least some of the sufferers, a form of what today would be called anorexia nervosa (Loudon 1984; Humphreys 1997: 163–64; H. King 2004: 2). Others have seen psychological significance in the fact that the malady was common in a period when young women were bound as much by the constraints of Victorian society as they were physically by tight corsets (Dixon 1995: 240–41).[52] Nancy M. Theriot has discussed its social and psychological implications within nineteenth-century American families (Theriot 1996: 101–13).

In any case, contemporary accounts do not describe the sort of greenness implied by Ralph of Coggeshall's description of the children's skin as of '*prassinus color*' ('leek-green colour'), as we have already discussed. The eminent physician Marshall Hall (1790–1857), author of a volume on *Some of the More Important of the Diseases of Females* in which he devoted a chapter to chlorosis, described its effects on the patient's complexion as follows:

> The incipient state of this morbid affection is more particularly characterized by paleness of the complexion, an exanguious [bloodless] state of the prolabia [lips], slight tumidity [swelling] of the countenance, and puffiness of the eyelids, especially the upper one. There is sometimes with this marked state of the counte-nance a slight tinge of green, of yellow, or of slate-colour. In the confirmed stage of chlorosis, the state of pallor of the complexion is still more marked. (Hall 1827: 53)

Hall refers us to his Plate IV: 'This plate pourtrays the state of the complexion, of the eyelids, and of the prolabia, in confirmed chlorosis.' The (hand-coloured) plate shows the face of a girl or young woman that is indeed pale, but shows no trace of greenness (Fig. 17).

By the end of the nineteenth century the nature and the symptoms of chlorosis were being questioned. Dr Frederick Taylor (1847–1920) of Guy's Hospital, opening a discussion on anaemia reported in the *British Medical Journal* in 1896, described 'a peculiar tint suggesting green—I scarcely dare go further' (Taylor et al. 1896: 720). He concluded:

> The green tint of the face or of the skin from which the name is derived is a somewhat uncertain feature. Some authors deny its

existence; others believe it is only recognisable in those of dark complexion.

Similarly, an American medical man wrote in 1915:

> If one exercises a great deal of imagination, one may possibly see the slightest imaginable tint of olive green in the shadow beneath the chin, but that is all. To the ordinary eye, the color is a yellowish pallor in brunettes and a whitish, although extreme, pallor in blondes. (quoted in Humphreys 1997: 160)

Irvine Loudon (1984: 27) concluded that 'there are good reasons for believing that the green colour was certainly not a constant feature and may have been a myth'. One wonders how many Victorian doctors and their predecessors were misled by the name of the condition to identify a green complexion when none was present.

Fig. 17.   Marshall Hall, *Commentaries on Some of the More Important of the Diseases of Females* (1827), plate IV: 'This plate pourtrays the state of the complexion, of the eyelids, and of the prolabia, in confirmed chlorosis.' Courtesy of Wellcome Collection (public domain).

The term 'chlorosis' (from Greek χλορος 'pale green, bleached') seems first to have been coined by French physician Jean Varandal of Montpellier (1563–1617) in his *De morbis et affectibus mulierum*, printed posthumously in 1619 (H. King 2004: 19, 43–45).[53] He defines it as 'the disease of virgins', a term used earlier by German physician Johannes Lange, in an account of its multifarious symptoms and its best cure—marriage (ibid.: 43–49, 142–3; Lange 1554: 74–77). Lange says that the disease does not have a proper name, but 'it may be designated "the disease of virgins" [*morbus virgineus*]; which is what the women of Brabant usually call "white fever" [*febrem albam*], on account of the pale face, as well as "love fever" [[*febrem*] *amatoriam*]' (H. King 2004: 47, 142; Lange 1554: 75). This latter designation perhaps explains the condition of the pale and languid young women depicted in seventeenth-century Dutch paintings with titles such as *The Lovesick Maiden* or *The Doctor's Visit*. The artists depict little more than pallor—nothing that would immediately strike an onlooker as 'green' (Dixon 1995: 59–91, 109–12, plates 1 to 8).

The contemporary, and indeed earlier, term used in England was 'green sickness'. The earliest medical use of the term found by Helen King was in the notes of Dr Barker of Shrewsbury in 1596, who equated it with '*morbus virgineus*' (H. King 2004: 19–20), but it seems to have been in popular use earlier. For example, Margaret Countess of Cumberland wrote that she had suffered from green sickness until her marriage at the age of seventeen, in 1577 (ibid.: 21). Ursula Potter has discussed the several references to supposed cases of green sickness in stage-plays in the sixteenth and seventeenth centuries, including Shakespeare's *Romeo and Juliet* (Potter 2002; 2013), and later the condition was defined succinctly in the second edition of Francis Grose's *Classical Dictionary of the Vulgar Tongue* as 'the disease of maids occasioned by celibacy' (Grose 1788: s.v. 'Green sickness').

Like their successors in the nineteenth century, earlier physicians treating the green sickness did not expect as a matter of course that their patient's complexion would appear green. Daniel Turner, writing in 1714 'Of the Green-Sickness, so called', described it as 'The Green (or rather give me leave to call it, the Pale or White) Sickness (since in its worst State the Complexion is rarely if ever true Green, tho' bordering on that Hue)' (Turner 1714: 90, quoted by H. King 2004: 33).

Discussing 'How green was green sickness?', Helen King (2004: 25–35) concluded: 'Just as sufferers from the Black Death did not turn black, so girls suffering from green sickness did not need to be, literally, green.' Those who have attributed the Green Children's colour to chlorosis have perhaps simply been misled by the name once given to this condition, rather than considering medical accounts of the symptoms of the disease.[54]

However, not all modern medical authorities deny the possibility of a green complexion in rare medical circumstances. Dr William H. Crosby, writing in the *Journal of the American Medical Association* in 1987 (quoted in H. King 2004: 5), reported: 'Based on my own experience, I am convinced that chlorosis did exist, for I have seen a chlorotic woman. It was in about 1955 [...] her face was green, its color accentuated by flaming red hair. The word was passed and doctors came from all over the hospital to gaze at her' (Crosby 1987, 2799). The patient was thirty-five years old, and was diagnosed as suffering from severe iron-deficiency anaemia due to uterine bleeding. 'With thera-peutic iron and a good diet' she quickly regained her health and lost her green colour. Crosby suggests (ibid.: 2800) that a combination of anaemia and a lack of sufficient protein in a person's diet might produce such 'chlorotic' symptoms—a reduced level of melanin in the skin, leading to a yellow tone, combining with a bluish tone resulting from low haemoglobin to give the appearance of green. He compares this to the colour of a maturing bruise—blue, with a fringe of yellow, shading to green between the two areas. Thus, though he does not describe the shade of green displayed by this unfortunate patient, we can perhaps assume it to have been a yellowish green.

Crosby, 'considered by many to be one of the founding fathers of modern hematology' (according to Wikipedia), could cite no other similar cases from his own long experience, but 'my series of one case was convincing and memorable' (ibid.: 2800). He continues: 'It's been 30 years since my last case of chlorosis. Another is due any day.' It may in fact have taken nearly a further twenty years for another case to be recognized, and Crosby died in 2005, his expectation apparently unfulfilled. But in 2006 Dr Perdahl-Wallace and Dr Schwartz of the Inova Fairfax Hospital for Children, Falls Church, Virginia, USA, reported the case of a nine-year-old girl with 'a remarkable and unmistakable green complexion of the forehead, nasal bridge, and the medial aspects of both cheeks and chin' (Perdahl-Wallace and Schwartz 2006: 187). The same coloration was visible on the backs of her hands and fingers. The authors reproduce a colour photograph of the girl's face (ibid.: 188, figure 1). Although at first sight her complexion appears mostly *yellow*, it certainly shades to a greenish tinge on her temples and cheeks. This coloration had persisted for two months. The girl complained of mild fatigue, and her mother had noticed a loss of appetite. Extensive medical examination revealed no predis-posing condition that might account for this 'bizarre' (the doctors' own word) complexion—except for 'iron deficiency with mild hypochromasia'. Treated with doses of iron (iron salt therapy), the girl regained her normal colour, her energy and her appetite within a few days.

Perdahl-Wallace and Schwartz (ibid.: 189) expressed their belief that this was 'the first medically witnessed, well-documented, and photographed case of classical chlorosis in a young girl in the past 70 years'. If one is permitted to question their diagnosis, this was surely far from a 'classical' case of chlorosis. The prepubescent nine-year-old Virginian child was not a typical sufferer from chlorosis or green sickness, reported, as we have seen, as 'overwhelmingly frequent in females between fifteen and twenty-five' (Taylor et al. 1896: 720). A green complexion was never the defining symptom of the condition, and the girl seems to have shown little sign of the other distressing symptoms reported by Victorian and earlier writers.

Perhaps we should conclude instead that in rare circumstances iron-deficiency anaemia—whether or not itself contributing to the condition formerly known as chlorosis—can cause a strange yellow tending to greenish coloration of the skin of the sufferer.[55] The rarity of this effect would account for the confusion of medical writers as to whether 'green sickness' entailed actual greenness. As we have seen, Loudon (1984: 27) concluded that 'there are good reasons for believing that the green colour was certainly not a constant feature and may have been a myth'. It was not a constant feature—but nor was it a myth; simply a very rare symptom.

What then of the Green Children? Leaving aside the fact that chlorosis, the 'disease of virgins', as defined and studied by the medical profession, would probably have affected only the girl, not the boy, the pallor described by Victorian doctors and by earlier writers, or depicted by early Dutch painters, would surely have aroused no particular excitement in medieval Suffolk.

The Green Children did not suffer from 'chlorosis' as the term was used by early physicians, with all its associated symptoms. However, they may well have suffered from iron deficiency and anaemia—many medieval children did. Examination of medieval skeletons has identified traces in the bones left by chronic childhood anaemia, probably the result of poor diet (White 1988: 41–42; Roberts and Cox 2003: 185–87, 234–35; Lewis 2007: 111–13).[56] Suffolk villagers would surely have recognized the normal symptoms of anaemia, if not the cause—many of their own children probably suffered from the condition. The green skin of the children found at Woolpit was apparently something far outside local experience.

Yet the case of the young girl treated by Drs Perdahl-Wallace and Schwartz in Virginia suggests that a very rare result of iron-deficiency anaemia may be a temporary but distinctive yellow/yellowish-green pigmentation. This rare condition would be something that neither the villagers of Woolpit nor Sir Richard de Calne would be familiar with—it would certainly add to the 'foreignness' or 'otherness' of these strangely dressed children with their unknown language. And even without the treatment with iron recommended both for chlorosis and for anaemia, an improved diet would presumably eventually restore the iron levels in their blood—but perhaps too late for the boy, who, according to Ralph of Coggeshall, 'always suffered a sort of weakness and died in a short time' <R19>.

Of course, there remain problems with this interpretation. William of Newburgh says that the children were green over their whole bodies ('*toto corpore virides*') <W9>; Ralph of Coggeshall that 'the whole surface of their skin was imbued with a green colour' ('*tota superficies cutis eorum viridi colore tingebatur*') <R9>. In the one modern case of which we have a proper record, the nine-year-old girl from Virginia, both the doctors' report and the published photograph indicate a patchy appearance—yellow shading to green in some areas. Yet the Green Children's appearance might of course have been exaggerated in descriptions, as the story passed around and as people unconsciously elaborated it in their own memories.

We are left with the problem of Ralph's use of the term '*prassinus color*' and its reference to an intense, dark green colour—far from the pale yellowish-green of the patient treated by Drs Perdahl-Wallace and Schwartz. Ralph claimed to have spoken to people who had met the Green Children—but he was writing more than ten years after the death of his chief informant, Richard de Calne, and perhaps nearly fifty years since the Green Children arrived in Woolpit. By the time he wrote his account, Ralph had no doubt that the children had been dark green in colour when the villagers of Woolpit first found them and when Richard de Calne gave them shelter. Had an original description of them as 'yellowish-greenish' been elaborated as the story circulated, and then in Ralph's own mind, to a much more distinctive 'vivid/dark green'?

The case must remain open. The greenness of the Green Children of Woolpit, and the extent to which their green skin could be attributed to a medical condition, is still undecided. We may conclude that the Green Children did *not* suffer from chlorosis, green sickness or the disease of virgins. They may have had iron-deficiency anaemia—one of the factors thought to have contributed to the condition once known as chlorosis. Whether even the rarest symptoms of anaemia and its effects on skin colour would have been sufficient for the children to be called 'green', more particularly 'leek-green', remains debatable.

If the children's recognition of beans as foodstuff indicates that they had been foraging among the bean plants for food for some time, an alternative diagnosis of their condition might be *favism*.[57] Favism is an inherited allergy to some of the chemicals in faba (broad) beans, causing acute haemolytic anaemia, which can triggered by eating beans or even by breathing the pollen of bean plants (Belsey 1973; Salunkhe and Kadam 1989: 1:233–35; Macpherson 1999: s.v. Favism). It particularly affects young children, and especially boys. The symptoms include weakness, dizziness, pallor and jaundice, culminating in some cases in kidney failure and death. The condition could explain both the death of the younger child (according to Belsey (1973: 7) mortality is greatest in the youngest children) and the girl's return to health once she assumed a more usual diet. And a tendency to favism is genetic. It is found today chiefly in the populations of Sicily and Sardinia and of the Middle East (Belsey 1973: 4; Simoons 1998: 216–49; Macpherson 1999: s.v. Favism). If we accept the diagnosis of favism, we have a real clue to the geographical origin of the Green Children—and a reason why the nature of their illness was not recognized in England.

Yet no amount of special pleading can explain why children with anaemia and jaundice should have been described as 'leek-green'. We may also leave aside (as perhaps her own fantastic elaboration) the girl's contention (reported by Ralph of Coggeshall) that everybody and everything in her homeland was green <R32>.

Both William and Ralph seem to have regarded the children's green colour as a temporary condition, perhaps brought on by their strange diet. It was after getting used to ordinary food that the girl '*recovered* the sanguine/ruddy appearance of her whole body' <R21> and 'as the nature of our food prevailed' that the children 'gradually changed their colour and became like us' <W21>. Ralph's choice of *prassinus color* ('leek colour') to describe the girl may also hint at a supposed link between the children's fondness for a vegetable diet and their leaf-like colour. However, his use of the phrase *sanguineam habitudinem* to describe the girl's new healthy appearance may of course also be significant. He may imply that it was an imbalance of the humours that had led to her strange coloration; in any event, the boy who died *languore depressus* was clearly *melancholic*, unlike his once more *sanguine* sister.

'Clothing of an unusual colour'

A description of the children's clothing is found only in William's account <W10>: '*coloris insoliti, ex incognita materia veste operti*' (they were 'dressed in clothing of an unusual colour, made of unknown material'). In the context of their strange appearance, this is perhaps only to be expected. Yet the variety and bright colours of fairies' clothing are also recognized in a series of folktale motifs—Thompson's F236 as an example.

There is a disturbing similarity in William's phraseology to that which he uses a few pages later to describe another 'wonder'—a cup stolen from a fairy hill: *'vesculum materiae incognitae, coloris insolitis, et formae inusitatae'* ('a vessel of unknown material, unusual colour and extraordinary form'), which was given to King Henry I and by him to King David I of Scotland, and later returned to Henry II (William of Newburgh 1988: 118–21). However, this may simply be a verbal reminiscence on the part of William—it need not reflect on the reality or otherwise of either clothing or cup. In any case, the survival, now in the Victoria and Albert Museum, of the Islamic glass beaker known as 'The Luck of Edenhall' proves that vessels 'of unknown material, unusual colour and extraordinary form' *and* reputed to have come from fairy hills are not unknown to reality (C[harleston] 1959; Westwood 1985: 303–05; Tyson 2000: 96; Westwood and Simpson 2005: 131–32; Davies 2010). This vessel, a beaker of fine, transparent and almost colourless glass, decorated with intricate patterns in coloured enamels and gilding, was probably made in Egypt or Syria in the thirteenth century. It was an inheritance of the Musgrave family of Edenhall, Cumbria, and was said, at least by the eighteenth century, to have been acquired from local fairies by a Musgrave ancestor. Although made rather later than William of Newburgh's time, it or its like would certainly have looked exotic enough to any English viewer to inspire William's description of a *'vesculum materiae incognitae, coloris insolitis, et formae inusitatae'*.

It is perhaps pointless to ask what colour of clothing the villagers of Woolpit and Sir Richard de Calne's household would have regarded as 'unusual' or what material would have been 'unknown' to them. In support of his case that the Green Children were of Flemish origin, Harris (1998: 90) writes of the weaving skills of immigrant Flemings and their use of dye colours not seen in England before, as we shall discuss below. Yet much of the medieval trade passing through England's east coast ports, such as Ipswich and Lynn, was with Flanders and the Low Countries (Darby 1936: 327–29). The children's clothing sounds considerably more exotic than the fashions to be found just over the North Sea.

'No one could understand their speech'

The children's inability to speak English and the strangeness of their language is a common feature of both Ralph's and William's stories <R11; W22>. To those seeking a 'down-to-earth' explanation this is simply a foreign language—or even an English dialect from a distant village (Shuker 1996: 29). As with the clothing, it seems fruitless to debate what languages the villagers of Woolpit (living beside a route used by travellers from two major ports and perhaps already with a shrine of the Virgin Mary that attracted pilgrims, and close to a town with annual international trading fairs) or Richard de Calne (one of the French-speaking Anglo-Norman ruling class) would fail at least to recognize the sound of.

England's annual trade fairs attracted foreign merchants both to sell their own goods and to buy local products such as wool. These fairs were at their peak in the late twelfth century (Oksanen 2012: 161), and the greatest of them—at Bury St Edmunds, Boston, Stamford, Northampton, St Ives and Lynn—lay in the East Midlands and East Anglia (Moore 1985: 8 map; Oksanen 2012: 173).

By the fourteenth century, Bury St Edmunds hosted four fairs each year, on and around the saints' days of St Edmund (20 November), St Peter (29 June), St James (25 July) and St Matthew (21 September) (Lobel 1935: 188–89, quoting the Abbey's 'Pinchbeck Register'—see Hervey 1925). Of these, the greatest was the winter fair around the feast of the town's own saint, King Edmund the Martyr, which lasted from the eve of the saint's day (19 November) until Christmas Eve. It was a major event in the town's economic calendar. Already by the end of the twelfth century tenants of the Abbey with shops and workshops in the marketplace were required to relinquish them for the accommodation of visiting traders for the duration of the fair (Lobel 1935: 101). However, the St James's fair in July was the first to be recorded. Only two days in duration by the time of the fourteenth-century Pinchbeck Register, it originally lasted six or seven days. In the early twelfth century Abbot Anselm (1121–1148) obtained a grant from King Henry I, dated between 1124 and 1129, which allowed him to hold an annual fair for 'seven days', comprising the Feast of St James the Apostle (25 July), three days before it and two days after it (sic—the original arithmetic seems suspect, unless the eve of the feast is counted!) (Douglas 1932: 73–74, no 43; Letters 2013). Whether it lasted six days or seven, this fair in late July would have brought many foreign merchants to the town. Some must have used the road passing through or just north of Woolpit village, which, as we have seen, led to the port of Ipswich. Is it coincidence that the Green Children must have appeared in Woolpit at just about this time—at harvest time and, as we have seen, when fresh beans were available? Could they have been strays from a party of foreign merchants en route to or from St James's Fair at Bury St Edmunds?

The children's exotic language fits at least as well into a 'lost foreign children' scenario as it does into one of 'fairy-folk'. Indeed, there is little evidence in the twelfth century for a belief that Otherworld inhabitants spoke an incomprehensible language—most communication (for example, Eadric and his fairy wife, King Herla and the pygmy king) seems to have been assumed to be in mortal language. William Peverel's swineherd apparently had no difficulty explaining himself to the ruler of the antipodean land he reached by way of Peak Cavern. Malekin of Dagworth was a linguist, conversing in both Latin and English (above)—but she was of course a stolen human child. An exception must be made for the underworld people who entertained the young Elidurus in Wales. Although Elidurus had no difficulty in communicating with them, presumably in Welsh, they, it seemed, spoke a strange language of their own that, on the basis of a few words that Elidurus claimed to remember in old age, Bishop David of St David's identified as a form of Greek (Gerald of Wales 1868: 77; 1978: 135–36). Yet stories of human interaction with fairies, at any date, usually involve easy communication between the two. We may well take their incomprehensible language as an indication that the Green Children were *not* fairies.

'By chance some beans were brought in'

Both Ralph and William recount, in very similar words <13–18>, the children's refusal to eat ordinary food, their joyful recognition of bean-plants (though unaccountable expectation that the beans were to be found in the stalks) and their survival on a diet of beans 'for a long time' or 'for some months'.

This episode is clearly thought to be significant, yet neither folklorists nor 'rationalizers' seem to have asked why the children, though they recognized the bean-plants, should have expected the edible beans to be found within the stalks rather than in the bean-pods <16>; nor indeed why the fresh-cut beans were brought into the house still on their stalks <15> (for Ralph says '*fabae noviter cum stipitibus abscissae in domo asportarentur*'—'some beans, newly cut with their stalks on, were carried into the house'). As we have seen, garden beans are best plucked in their pods from the plants when young (Huxley et al. 1992: 1:313). Indeed, Thomas Tusser advised sixteenth-century housewives to pluck the lower pods and leave the plant growing to provide a second crop:

> So gather the lowest, and leaving the top
> Shall teach thee a trick, for to double the crop. (Tusser 1984: 116)

Similar advice is given to gardeners today, and the ripening pods are plucked by hand over a period of weeks, the stalks afterwards being forked in (Biggs

1999: 100–01). This seems to be the traditional and widespread practice. In recent times broad beans grown on a large scale for canning or freezing are machine cut, the cut plants being left in windrows for twelve or twenty-four hours until a second machine (the 'viner') collects them, threshes them and automatically shells the beans (Gane et al. 1975: section 7:16–26; Biddle 2017: 145). The smaller-seeded 'field beans' cultivated for cattle food are left to mature until the pods are black and dry, and are harvested with combine harvesters—the dry stalks either being used as fodder or litter, or chopped and ploughed in (Knott et al. 1994: 146–51). So the gathering of fresh beanstalks complete with bean-pods does not seem to feature in modern agricultural or horticultural practice. But study of medieval or traditional agriculture may yet indicate a purpose. As we have seen, it seems to be uncertain when the distinction between large-seeded broad beans and the smaller-seeded 'field beans' and their categorization respectively as human or animal food would have first been recognized in England. Certainly if by the twelfth century English villagers were aware of the variation and considered the larger variety of bean better suited for human consumption, the suspicion that the children were other than human would have been strengthened if it was field beans that they instead chose to eat.[58]

Both William and Ralph lay stress on the fact that the children expected to find beans in the *stalks* of the bean-plants <16>:

> They seized them and looked for the beans inside the stems. (William of Newburgh)

> [T]hey opened the stalks, not the bean pods, thinking that the beans were contained in the hollow of the stalks. (Ralph of Coggeshall)

It is difficult to think of circumstances in which children would be able to identify bean-plants as food-bearing plants without also knowing where to look for the edible beans (Fig. 10). According to Belsey (1973: 10), many cases of favism, the dramatic allergic reaction to beans found among children in some populations, occur in the Middle East at harvest time, when children assist their parents in the bean fields and eat raw beans straight from the pods. In any other part of the world where beans are grown as a food crop one would expect children in rural communities to help with the harvest from an early age and to be quite familiar with bean-plants, pods and beans. This episode, although no one seems to have commented on it, remains one of the more puzzling aspects in the story of the Green Children.[59]

In those parts of the world where the genetic tendency to favism exists, the connection with beans has long been understood—although Simoons points out (1998: 223) that the condition and its cause were not recognized by ancient Greek medical authors. Folk wisdom in Iran, for example, dictates that beans should not be fed to children—particularly uncooked beans or beans with their skins on (Belsey 1973: 10). This advice would have been unknown to the villagers of Woolpit, who might have thought it unusual for children to eat raw beans, but would have seen no harm in it.

Yet even in Europe beans seem to have had a reputation as unwholesome food. In the seventeenth century, dieticians warned of the dangers of eating beans—especially when raw, as Robert Burton wrote in 1621:

> They fill the Braine (saith *Isaack*) with grosse fumes, breed blacke
> thicke blood, and cause troublesome dreames. And therefore that
> which *Pythagoras* said to his Schollers of old, may be for ever applied
> to Melancholy men, *a fabis abstinete*, Eat no Pease, nor Beanes.
> (Burton 1989: 216–17)

Indeed, it has been suggested that Pythagoras's instruction to his followers to abstain from beans was based upon a fear of favism, an illness certainly found in Greece today (Brumbaugh and Schwartz 1980). Simoons, however, disputes this, and argues that the Pythagorean ban was based on culture or religious belief (Simoons 1998: 218–49).[60]

Folklorists have seen significance in the children's fondness for beans. Stith Thompson (1955–1958) provides a perhaps relevant Motif C224.1 'Eating beans forbidden'; but it is disappointing to note that his only citations are of Frazer's *The Golden Bough* and Pausanias, second-century Greek geographer. Katharine Briggs comments (1967: 8): 'It is perhaps a coincidence, but beans are traditionally the food of the dead.' It is not clear to what specific tradition Briggs is referring. However, beans are in many cultures strongly associated with the dead (Vries 1974: 37–38; Binde 1998: 214–15; Simoons 1998: 250–66) or 'regarded as intermediaries between the dead and the living' (Holden 2000: 6–8).[61] It seems unlikely that this was the rationale for the taboo on eating beans that was common to Pythagoreans, Orphics, Eleusinian initiates and the Egyptian priesthood (Holden 2000: 6).

Simoons notes that early varieties of broad beans had black skins (1998: 196).[62] He suggests that 'people came to associate beans considered black [...] with death, the underworld and underworld forces, impurity, and unhappiness' (ibid.: 214). The association with death certainly seems to be widespread.

Simoons (ibid.: 251–52) refers to a tradition of eating dishes of beans at funeral meals in parts of France and Italy, while elsewhere on All Souls Day cooked beans, lentils and peas were given to the poor.[63] He devotes four chapters of his book to the broad bean and an Indian equivalent, the urd bean (*vigna mungo*) (ibid.: 158–266), concluding that there was an association of beans not only with death, but with sex and the spirit of life (ibid.: 262).

In a regional study of the folklore and folk practices of southern Italy, Per Binde (1998: 214–17) reviews both Pythagorean and pagan Roman belief as well as more recent Italian customs. Of the eating of beans and other seeds on ceremonial occasions, as on saints' feast days and at funerals, he suggests that 'by eating seeds, human beings could symbolically incorporate the seed's natural fertility and regenerative capacity' (Binde 1998: 216), while of offerings of beans to the dead he concludes:

> The offerings may thus be seen as a sophisticated exorcism. The threat posed by the discontent and dangerous dead, jealous of the living, is counteracted by the living offering them a prospect of a new life, not by coming back to the world of the living but by moving further away from them and returning to the mundane in a renewed form. (Ibid.: 217)

Moreover, when beans were ceremonially given to the poor and to beggars on All Souls Day, it was as to 'earthly representatives' of the dead (ibid.: 204; 217).[64] Binde quotes Piero Camporesi (1993: 15) on the importance of the bean in Italian tradition:

> Broad beans [...] represent the link with the underworld of the dead, in the duplex, multi-faceted and ambiguous valency of old and new, fear and hope. The broad bean holds uneasy, fearful connotations but also a potential ferment of unexpressed energies and hidden lives [...] Fathers and children, grandparents and grandchildren are joined in an infinite genealogical sequence: the eternal, repeated but ever new alternation of generation and extinction, presence and disappearance.

Can we associate such thinking with the people of Suffolk in the middle of the twelfth century? If we do, how would they then regard the children's appetite for beans?

In different traditions, witches rode on beanstalks and the King of the Bean was chosen as master of merrymaking on Twelfth Night (Vries 1974: 37–38; Simoons 1998: 257–58). In later folklore beanfields themselves seem sometimes to have been regarded as perilous. Simoons (1968: 255) cites an English folk belief that if you slept in a beanfield overnight, you would have awful dreams and go mad. One wonders if this might be associated with the belief recorded by Roy Vickery that the scent of broad bean flowers was an aphrodisiac (Vickery 2019: 235): 'There ent no lustier scent than a beanfield in bloom' (Oxfordshire, c.1920), or

> Peas and beans inflame lust [...] best of all traditional aphrodisiacs was the scent of the bean flower, for this not only stimulates passion in the man, but extreme willingness in the girl. (Suffolk, between the two World Wars)

However, none of these associations seems appropriate in twelfth-century Suffolk or to the situation of the Green Children.

More significant may be the simple fact that the children's choice of food— uncooked beans—was not a normal human diet, and the girl's later explanation that when faced with ordinary food 'they believed all foodstuffs of this sort were inedible' ('omnia huiusmodi cibaria incomestibilia esse credebant') <R14>.

Lunan (1996: 44; 2012: 380–81), as might be expected, puts forward a characteristically startling hypothesis. He takes note of the girl's reported claim that everything in the children's homeland was green <R32 below>. He translates the text as 'all plants that were held in that land/world were dyed (tingerentur) with the color green'—although one should note that the Latin original refers not to 'all plants' but to 'all the inhabitants and all things' (see Appendix). Lunan's view, as we have noted, is that the children came from a colony of human 'abductees' on an alien planet. He suggests that terrestrial food plants growing there had been dyed or genetically modified to be green, to distinguish them from inedible native plants. It is impossible to comment meaningfully on this suggestion—yet I suppose there may indeed be a hint in the original story that it was the greenness of the bean plants 'newly cut with their stalks on' that persuaded the children they were edible.

But why should they think ordinary foodstuffs ('bread and other food'— 'panis ac caetera cibaria' according to Ralph) were incomestibilia? Did the bread the villagers offered appear so unlike anything they had ever eaten that they could not identify it as food? Or did they recognize it as in some way 'unlawful'? There exist in the everyday world of reality many cultural and religious reasons why people abstain from particular types of foodstuff, or insist that food must be processed or cooked in certain ways (Holden 2000: 94–105). Was this the sort of objection the children had to the food they were given?

Holden (2000: 100–01) reports Anna Meigs's conclusion, after research in Papua New Guinea, 'that food taboos are a means of recognising and defining both social and religious categories and of stressing opposition and difference'. And similar dietary differences and preferences serve to differentiate not only between two human categories but also between the human world and the Otherworld. Concepts of special Otherworld or fairy food are widespread (Thompson's Motifs F183 and F243, etc.). A contemporary description of such food is that by Elidurus, the Welsh monk whose boyhood adventures, recounted by Gerald of Wales, have a number of similarities to the Green Children's story. Elidurus reported on the diet of the diminutive people he met in the Otherworld: 'They never ate meat or fish. They lived on various milk dishes, made up into junkets and flavoured with saffron' (Gerald of Wales 1868: 75; 1978: 134). This milk diet is very different from the Green Children's choice of beans—though similar in its exclusion of meat.

And avoidance of the Other's diet is mutual. The traditional view that Otherworld food is dangerous for mortals—its consumption usually condemning them to dwell forever in that Otherworld—has as a corollary an understanding that human food is dangerous for fairies. The familiar Motif C211 'Tabu on eating in other world' has its equivalent and complementary Motif C211.3.2 (or C212.1 according to Cross 1952) 'Tabu on fairies eating mortal food'. Consequent upon this is Motif C661 'Girl from elfland must eat earthly food in order to remain [among mortals]'. The demands that the stolen human child Malekin of Dagworth made for food and drink from her mortal friends perhaps reflect a similar concept—only by eating human food could she ensure her eventual return to the human world (Ralph of Coggeshall 1875: 121; Westwood 1985: 149; Westwood and Simpson 2005: 691).

In this context, the green girl's later explanation that the children had thought that the bread and other foodstuffs they were offered were 'inedible' and William's claim that 'as the nature of our food prevailed, [the Green Children] gradually changed their colour and became like us' <W21>, mirrored by Ralph's 'becoming used to all sorts of food she totally lost her leek-green colour' <R20–21>, both take on an added, and at first sight folkloric, significance. Thus Katharine Briggs (1970: 95) commented that the Green Children 'lost their green colour and became mortal people *after they had eaten mortal food*' (my italics).

Yet the idea that 'wild' or 'marginal' people would not eat, and perhaps would not even recognize, the food familiar to us was well enough known in the Middle Ages. It certainly cannot be used to argue that the Green Children were *ipso facto* identifiable by their contemporaries as fairy folk. Thus the distant race called the 'Homodubii' in a tenth-century Anglo-Saxon account of *The Wonders of the East* ate nothing but raw fish (Bildhauer and Mills 2001b: 11). And in what has been termed 'The Wonders of the West', Gerald of Wales's description of Ireland in his *Topographia Hibernica*, Gerald reports the tale he had heard from some sailors whose ship had been driven off course in a storm off the north-west coast of Ireland (Gerald of Wales 1867: 170–71; Mittman 2001: 107–08). When the storm had subsided they saw two men in a skin-covered boat—presumably a *currach*—and took them on board. The men spoke the Irish language, but expressed amazement at the ship and everything they saw on it, and had never heard of Christ. They asked for food, but had not seen bread or cheese before and at first, like the Green Children, refused to eat them. They said they fed only on meat, fish and milk. Eventually, the men set off home in their boat and 'took with them a loaf of bread and a cheese, in order to show to their own people for their amazement the sort of food that foreigners ate'.

Gerald's account is entirely matter-of-fact. He had earlier commented that the primitive Irish had never developed beyond a pastoral way of life (1867: 151; Bartlett 1982: 158–66, 176), and this seems no more than an extreme example of that way of life. Although they were not Christian, there was nothing Otherworldly about these visitors. They were simply dwellers on the fringes of the known world. The Green Children's choice of food would have aroused no surprise if reported as a traveller's tale from the far East or the far West. It is the *location* of the story, in a village in the heart of England, that makes the children's diet so exceptional.

Baptism and after

Although William and Ralph agree that it was thought appropriate to baptize the children <23>, presumably in Bardwell parish church, they differ as to whether the boy died soon after baptism <W24> or before it could take place <R19>. This difference in the sequence of events is likely to be less significant than the decision to baptize them and the fact of the boy's death. Baptizing the children, says William, seemed prudent ('And it seemed good to prudent people that they should receive the sacrament of holy baptism'). This was a precaution lest the Green Children should die unbaptized—both an act of kindness and an act of self-protection for the villagers: 'children who die before baptism remain in a liminal situation, condemned to return to earth as ghosts and bad spirits' (Lindahl et al. 2000: 832). But it certainly suggests that they were considered so 'alien' ('foreign' in modern English) that they could not be presumed to be already baptized Christians. Perhaps then they were already considered to have come from an Otherworld, rather than simply from a foreign country, even before the girl told her story of St Martin's Land. And there would have been a doubt in people's minds whether such an Otherworld could be Christian. For example, Elidurus's little people had no overt form of worship ('*cultus eis religionis palam nullus*'—Gerald of Wales 1868: 76; 1978: 134). It comes as something of a surprise to us, as it surely did to her questioners, when the girl eventually reveals that their land was after all a Christian one with churches <W30>.

The fate of the souls of children who died without baptism was much debated by theologians in the twelfth and thirteenth centuries—in reaction, it seems, against the harsh views of St Augustine, who had consigned them to all the torments of the damned in hell (Herbermann et al. 1907–1918, 9:256–59). The concept of a *limbo* (*limbus infantium*—the limbo of children), literally a 'border' place, to which such children went in the afterlife, developed only slowly, and it seems unlikely that the 'prudent' people of Woolpit would have been aware of it. But the urgency of the baptism of infants was certainly recognized (Fisher 1965: 110–13). Fisher cites Bernard of Clairvaux (d. 1153) who wrote that 'while the grace of baptism is denied to them, the life of Christ is unattainable to the children of Christians, and the way to salvation is closed to them' (ibid.: 112), and Pope Innocent III in 1201 regretted the great numbers of children who died each day who 'but for the grace of baptism would have perished eternally' (ibid.: 113). In spite of the prescription of Canon Law that baptisms should take place only on the eves of Easter and Whitsun, there were frequent statements exempting infants—whether or not in immediate danger of death—from this ruling: 'the baptism of infants was not to be delayed, because for all sorts of slight causes they might die'. Thus Bernard of Saintes (1141–1166) ordered that newly born infants be brought for baptism with all haste, and in 1279 John of Peckham, archbishop of Canterbury, decreed that only the baptisms of those children born in the week before Easter or Whitsun should be delayed till the feast days—and then only if there was no danger to the child (ibid.: 111).

So vital was baptism that, if death threatened the child, it could be carried out by anyone who knew the proper procedure and form of words—either in Latin or the vernacular. In 1199 Gerald of Wales, by now presumptive bishop of St David's, wrote a volume of advice addressed to the priests of the diocese, the *Gemma Ecclesiastica*. In chapter 12 of the first part, he tells priests that they should instruct their parishioners in the form of baptism, so that they can carry out the ritual correctly 'if they should perhaps be far from a church and priest and should see a child in peril of death'. For any lay person ('even a woman') can do so, 'lest the soul of the child perish' (Gerald of Wales 1979: 35–36).[65]

Whether those who decided it was necessary for the Green Children to be baptized did so because they saw their emergence from the ground as a symbolic birth, or were simply unsure of their status as Christians, they were in any case doubly prudent. In addition to the concerns expressed by churchmen, there may have been a popular belief that, before baptism, the newborn child was vulnerable to demons or witches. Furthermore, if the Green Children died unbaptized there was a very real danger that their unhappy ghosts might haunt those who had taken them in (Lindahl et al. 2000: 832–33; Simpson and Roud 2000: 16). Simon Mays (2016) has concluded that whereas, in medieval belief, sinful or vengeful adults might return as revenant corpses, unbaptized children would normally return as ghostly apparitions or in dreams. Thus, for example, the mother of the French monk Guibert of Nogent (*c.*1064–*c.*1125) was haunted by a vision of the crying ghost of her husband's illegitimate child, a baby who had died unbaptized (Joynes 2001: 23–25).

William and Ralph agree about the early death of the boy:

> But the boy, who seemed the younger of the two, lived only a short time after baptism and died a premature death. <W24>
>
> Now the boy always suffered a sort of weakness and died in a short time. <R19>

There is nothing unexpected in the death of the younger, weaker child—though it, perhaps coincidentally, embodies a folktale motif (F329.4.2 'Lost fairy child found by mortals but it pines away'). Indeed, in the context of the narrative it seems inevitable, and in Kevin Crossley-Holland's retellings of the story the death of the boy is a central and moving episode (LeFanu and Crossley-Holland 1990; Crossley-Holland and Marks 1994).

Ralph tells us that the girl remained 'in the service' (*in ministerio*) of Richard de Calne for many years <R25–6>. The word *ministerium* can be applied to the role of anyone from a household servant to a trusted bailiff or reeve, or a high royal or public official (Niermeyer 1976: 687; *Dictionary of Medieval Latin from British Sources* 2018: s.v.). In the absence of any hint to the contrary, it seems likely that Ralph intends the term in its most general, basic meaning—though Lunan takes it to imply a much more responsible position in the de Calne household, leading, in effect, to the girl's adoption into the family and marriage to a royal official (Lunan 1996: 49–50; 2012: 141–43).

On the other hand, according to William of Newburgh, the girl was reported to have married a man in *Lenna* <W27>. There need be no contradiction in this—it would be possible for the girl both to have worked for the de Calnes and later to have married. William's *Lenna* is modern King's Lynn, in Norfolk (Map 1).[66] In the twelfth century Lynn was a cluster of three settlements growing up on the fringes of an estuarine lake at the mouth of the River Little Ouse: a town belonging to the monks of Norwich in the centre, the independent South Lynn to the south of it and the new planned town of Bishop's Lynn to the north (Parker 1971: 19–22). Indeed, at this time the new plantation town, the initiative of Bishop William Turbe of Norwich (1146–1174), would have been an inviting place for settlers from other parts of East Anglia. The green girl would not have been the only person to move there. Lynn was rapidly becoming a major trading town and by the reign of King John was one of the four wealthiest ports in England (ibid.: 3–4). William of Newburgh himself calls it elsewhere 'urbem commeatu et commerciis nobilem' ('a town outstanding for its trade and commerce' (Howlett 1884: 309)). William may have had a source of information in Lynn, for he writes in some detail of the massacre of Jews that took place there in January 1190 (ibid.: 309–10).

'[S]he remained very wanton and impudent'

He never saw anyone so pert. (Sands 1986: 212)

The same Calne family informants, including Richard de Calne himself, who told Ralph of Coggeshall of the girl's long service in the household had (according to Ralph) added that the girl 'remained very wanton and impudent' ('*nimium lasciva et petulans exstitit*') <R26>.[67] In the context of this girl who was clearly an 'outsider', probably already suspected to be a visitor from an Otherworld even before she spoke of her origins in the twilight land of St Martin, it may well be that Ralph's informants had in mind reports of 'fairy' temptresses and their lascivious ways—and that Ralph included this information because it supported his own interpretation of the children's origin.[68]

The Motif index gives us Motifs F300 'Marriage or liaison with fairy' and F302 'Fairy mistress. Mortal man marries or lives with fairy woman'. Tales of human men and their fairy mistresses or wives seem to have been particular favourites of Ralph and William's contemporary Walter Map: 'Not only Eadric the Wild but also Gwestin Gwestiniog, Henno *cum dentibus*, and Gerbert/ Silvester II all conform to this pattern' (Green 2016: 99). And Gervase of Tilbury claimed to have heard several accounts of the ill fortune that befell men who had taken fairy mistresses and then abandoned them:

> But here is something we do know, confirmed daily as it is by men who are above all reproach: we have heard that some men have become the lovers of *larvae* of this kind, which they call fays [*fadae*], and when they have transferred their affections with a view to marrying other women, they have died before they could enjoy carnal union with their new partners. And we have seen many men who had attained the summit of worldly happiness, but then, as soon as they renounced the embraces of fays of this kind, or spoke about them in public, they lost not only their worldly prosperity, but even the solace of a wretched life. (Gervase of Tilbury 2002: 730–31)

For more on fairies as mistresses and temptresses, and the dangers that might face their human lovers, see the chapters in Corinne Saunders' *Magic and the Supernatural in Medieval English Romance* (2010: 185–93) and James Wade's *Fairies in Medieval Romance* (2011: 109–45). Richard Firth Green (2016: 76–109) also devotes a chapter to the perceived relationship between medieval 'fairies', male and female, and the entities otherwise known as *incubi* and *succubi*. Green (ibid.: 80) quotes an early fifteenth-century tract, *Dives et Pauper*:

> The fiends that tempt folk to lechery be most busy for to appear in man's likeness and woman's to do lechery with folk and bring them to lechery, and in the speech of the people they are called 'elves'. But in Latin when they appear in the likeness of man they are called '*incubi*', and when they appear in the likeness of woman they are called '*succubi*'. (my modernization)

Thus, sexual relationships with Otherworldly females were accepted as a possibility, if a perilous one, for human men. Whether they were identified as 'fiends', fairies or elves, they were widely perceived as temptresses. Thus Green (2016: 102) quotes from the late fourteenth-century *lai* of *Sir Launfal*, by Thomas Chestre. Launfal, invited by two maidens he meets in a wood to come and speak to their mistress, finds the lady Triamour (the daughter of the 'kyng of Fayrye') in a pavilion, lying half-naked on 'a bed of prys':

> For here her cloþes down sche dede
> Almost to her gerdylstede [her girdle/waist-band].
> ...
> He seygh neuer non so pert. (Sands 1986: 212, ll. 289–90; 294)

'He never saw anyone so *pert*.' While the *Middle English Dictionary* (1952–2001) cites this same passage for 'pert' meaning 'attractive, comely', Green (2016: 102) comments that it is surely here punning upon the base meaning 'exposed'. To this we might add those occurrences where according to the same *Middle English Dictionary* entry it means 'saucy, forward'—which reminds us of Ralph of Coggeshall's comments on Woolpit's green girl.

So it would not be surprising, as the green girl grew to adulthood, if those who knew her and suspected her Otherworld origin would look for evidence in her behaviour—and find it. Perhaps she even played up to their expectations.

Ralph of Coggeshall reports their suspicions. It becomes increasingly clear as we read his account that Ralph himself had concluded that the children were indeed from an Otherworld, and (as we shall see) he may even have improved upon the story to conform with his preconceptions of how one might journey from one world to another.

William of Newburgh, however, seems to have remained unconvinced of the children's Otherworldly origins. Instead he comments of the girl that 'she was not in the least different from the women of our kind' ('*nec in modico a nostri generis feminis discrepante*') <W27>. Once she had lost her green coloration and grown to adulthood, there was nothing to make her stand out among the ordinary human inhabitants of 'our world'. Perhaps William had in mind a contrast with the 'unearthly beauty' that distinguished so many fairy mistresses. Such unearthly beauty was the characteristic of Eadric the Wild's fairy wife and her sisters as described by Walter Map; they were also 'greater and taller than our women' (Map 1983: 154–55). Green quotes a description of one of these Otherworldly beauties from an anonymous French *lai*:

> Have you ever seen so beautiful a face, such beautiful hands, such beautiful arms, so fair a body in a robe adorned with laces, more beautiful hair, finer or better arranged and coiffed? Never was born so beautiful a creature. (Green 2016: 103)

Or there was Dame Triamour, her skin 'whit as lilie in May | Or snow that sneweth in winteris day', and 'The here upon her hed | As gold wire that shinith bright' (ibid, 102; Sands 1986: 212, ll. 292–93; 229, ll. 938–39).

William's description of the Woolpit girl in later life as 'not in the least different from the women of our kind' hints at no such unearthly beauty—and her liaison was not with a knightly hero of romance like Sir Launfal but with 'a man at Lynn'!

The Flemish connection

> This province [Flanders] makes this excellent cloth in green or blue-green or deep blue colours. (Winric of Trier, quoted in Uytven 1983: 154)

The Otherworld explanation will not satisfy most modern commentators, of course. The most detailed and fully argued attempt to provide a 'down-to-earth' explanation of the Green Children is that by Paul Harris, published in the short-lived series *Fortean Studies* (Harris 1998 and 1999). Although he preferred to identify the children's coloration as due to chlorosis—a conclusion we have seen reason to question (above)—his interpretation of the children as foreign strays and his identification of their national origin and background in the circumstances of the twelfth century deserves fuller and careful consideration. As we have noted, Brian Haughton has identified Harris's hypothesis as 'the most widely accepted explanation at present', one that 'certainly suggests plausible answers to many of the riddles of the Woolpit mystery'. He concludes, however, that 'the theory of displaced Flemish orphans [...] does not stand up in many respects' (Haughton 2007: 237–38).

Harris's hypothesis was that the children were strays from a family of immigrant Flemish clothworkers, domiciled in England—possibly in Fornham St Martin (to be, he considered, identified with 'St Martin's Land' in William of Newburgh's account, <W30>), a few miles from Woolpit—who had suffered violent attack either as a result of Henry II's measures in 1154 to banish Flemings from England, or in 1173, when Flemish mercenary troops in the army of the Earl of Leicester, fighting in support of the rebellion of 'Young King Henry' against his father, were slaughtered after their defeat at the Battle of Fornham.

Since Harris wrote, the publication of Eljas Oksanen's *Flanders and the Anglo-Norman World, 1066–1216* (2012) has provided a new basis on which to revise our assessment of these events, and the place of Flemings in England. Oksanen discusses evidence for a 'gradual trickle' of immigrants from Flanders to England in the late eleventh and the twelfth centuries, to the extent that they eventually formed a small but quite significant proportion of the population (Oksanen 2012: 178–218). By the mid-twelfth century there was a permanent community of Flemish merchants based in London; there were Flemish households in Canterbury, Bristol and Gloucester, and no doubt in other towns (ibid.: 208, 212).

> These immigrants did not comprise just soldiers and knights but, hailing from the most industrialized region in western Europe, included craftspeople, burghers, traders and merchants, and their families, all of whom had skills and resources that could benefit growing local economies. (Ibid.: 208)

Harris quoted William of Newburgh's description of the children's clothing 'of an unusual colour, made of unknown material' <W10> in support of his identification of them as Flemings, recalling the famously fine and beautifully dyed cloths produced by weavers in Flanders (Harris 1998: 90). Harris quoted from J. Arnold Fleming's *Flemish Influence in Britain* (a popular account of Flemish immigrants and their descendants in Britain, mostly in Scotland, that may not be entirely reliable): 'webs woven with shuttles filled with threads of purple and many other colours flying from side to side' (Fleming 1930: 1:176). Sadly, the quotation comes from a work by the Anglo-Saxon bishop Aldhelm of Sherborne, writing in about 680 CE, and has nothing to do with twelfth-century Flemish weavers.

However, Raymond van Uytven (1983: 154) quotes a more nearly contemporary opinion, from Winric of Trier, who wrote a treatise in praise of wool in 1068–70, and mentioned Flemish woollen textiles in particular: 'This province [Flanders] makes this excellent cloth in green (*viret*) or blue-green (*glaucus*) or deep blue (*ceruleus*) colours. Those cloths [...] you are exporting, Flanders.' Uytven (ibid.: 156) goes on to cite other early medieval writers 'impressed by the technical know-how of Flemish cloth-makers and by the variety and splendour of their dyeing', and later (ibid.: 180–81) states that 'all were obviously fascinated by the rich variety of brilliant colours of Netherlandish cloths'. Oksanen (2012: 154–55) confirms that Flemish cloth was exported widely, as far as Italy and Russia. It was favoured in England since it was better quality than locally made woollen cloth, while silk was also among items imported into England by merchants from Flanders.

Yet the children's unusual clothing presumably merely marked them as 'foreigners'—not necessarily as wearing the products of Flemish looms, still less as Flemish themselves.

There were indeed Flemings in England—those that Henry II ordered to leave England in 1154 were mercenary troops serving in the private armies of English noblemen that the new king was attempting to bring under control (Oksanen 2012: 138, 242–44). However, there seems to have been a flourishing Flemish colony in south Wales, in Pembrokeshire, established by Henry I in about 1108 (ibid.: 213–17). Oksanen quotes William of Malmesbury's disapproving account of this event:

> Many Flemings who had trooped over in his [King Henry's]' father's [William I's] time, relying on their kinship of his mother [Matilda of Flanders, wife of William I], were lying low in England, in such numbers as actually to seem a burden on the realm itself; and so he collected them all together, as though into some great midden, in the Welsh province of Rhos [in Pembrokeshire] with all their belongings and relatives. (Ibid.: 213)

Yet there seems to be nothing in Oksanen's work to suggest that Flemish clothworkers, in particular, settled in England and set up workshops in competition with English craftspeople.

The Flemish mercenaries who accompanied the Earl of Leicester's army in 1173 were certainly dismissed by a contemporary chronicler, Jordan Fantosme, as 'weavers' who 'did not know how to bear arms like knights' (Fantosme 1981: 72–73). The characterization of them as weavers, simple workmen untrained in warfare, was no more than a slur on their nationality—like Napoleon's reputed dismissal of the English as 'shopkeepers' or the (perhaps more friendly) term 'diggers' applied to Australian soldiers in the First World War. Fantosme goes on to claim the Flemings shouted 'We have not come to this country to stay but to destroy the king, Henry, the old warrior, and to get for ourselves the wool that we so much desire.' Says Oksanen: 'Fantosme's conceit is simple: these Flemings are not even a proper army but only a mass of foreign thieves who seek to rob the riches of England' (Oksanen 2012: 240).

Flemish weavers did indeed desire English wool, but were willing to pay for it. The reputation of Flemish cloth was equalled by the reputation of the English wool from which it was made. The export trade in English wool was already significant by 1100 and grew during the following century—and it was the supply to the weavers of Flanders that constituted the bulk of that trade (Oksanen 2012: 153; Lloyd 1977: 1–24). Indeed the first chapter of T.H. Lloyd's authoritative volume on the English wool trade is titled 'The growth of the Flemish connection'. And the trade was largely in the hands of foreign merchants, including traders from the Low Countries and Flanders (Oksanen 2012: 157).

Uytven (1983: 180) and Oksanen (2012: 163) both tell the story of a group of Flemish merchants who in 1113 sailed from Wissant to England, with 300 marks (£200) in silver to buy English wool. They rented a large warehouse in Dover, and travelled around England buying up wool until their warehouse was full. Unfortunately—supposedly because they had failed to fulfil a religious vow made when they survived an attack by pirates on the voyage from Wissant—the warehouse burned down.

Presumably it was at England's great trade fairs such as that at Bury St Edmunds that these Flemish merchants bought their wool. It is possible to imagine that a foreign merchant travelling from an east coast port—such as Ipswich—to one of these fairs (most of them, as we have noted, situated in the East Midlands), or vice versa, might have his family with him. Foreign merchants travelling in England did so under the king's protection, and indeed when in the 1160s a Flemish merchant travelling through Blackheath Hundred in Kent (just south-east of London) was killed by an unknown assailant, a murder fine was levied on the whole local community (Oksanen 2012: 172). Perhaps if the villagers of Woolpit suspected the children were strays from a group of foreign merchants who might have suffered some such misfortune they were wise to pass the responsibility, and the problem, on to someone else, Sir Richard de Calne, as soon as possible.

That the Green Children were the children of a Flemish clothworker resident in Suffolk, as suggested by Paul Harris, seems unlikely. That they were the children of a foreign merchant passing through the area (possibly even a Fleming, selling Flemish cloth or buying English wool at one of the great fairs) is certainly feasible—if one could only explain their green coloration!

Who was Agnes Barre?

Neither of our two authors, William of Newburgh and Ralph of Coggeshall, gives names to the Green Children or to the husband that (according to William) the girl married in King's Lynn. Yet many recent accounts, particularly those found online, claim that she took the name 'Agnes' and married a royal official called Richard Barre.[69] Where does this additional information come from? It depends entirely upon the research of one author, Duncan Lunan. And yet so accepted has this identification of the girl as 'Agnes' become that in two of the most recent retellings of the story, by J. Anderson Coats (2019) and Edward Carey (2019), and in Don Nigro's playlet *The Recollection of Green Rain* (2021), the girl is given or adopts the name 'Agnes'.

In 2012 Scottish astronomer Duncan Lunan published his in-depth study of the Green Children of Woolpit, *Children from the Sky*, subtitled 'A Speculative Treatment of a Medieval Mystery—the Green Children of Woolpit' (Lunan 2012), to which we have already referred. Setting aside his adoption of what might be termed the 'extraterrestrial option' in explanation of the appearance (in both senses) of the children, we must admire his enthusiastic and exhaustive research over many years into contemporary documents to reconstruct the historical context for the events in Woolpit.[70]

Not the least startling of his conclusions is that the green girl (far from being a servant in the household of Richard de Calne for many years and/or marrying 'a man at Lynn') had been baptized with the name 'Agnes', was adopted as Richard de Calne's ward, perhaps bore an illegitimate child, married Richard Barre, ecclesiastic, justice and royal ambassador,[71] was still alive, as lady of the manor of Aston, Birmingham, until about 1238 or 1239, and has descendants today, including, at the time Lunan was writing, one sitting in the House of Lords (Lunan 2012: *passim*).[72]

Lunan (ibid.: 144) records that the breakthrough in his search for the name and identity of the green girl as Agnes, wife of Richard Barre, came with his discovery of a record from 1197, when at a session of the royal justices held in Bedford 'Richard and his wife Agnes and John and his wife Sibylla' petitioned for the return of land in 'Eiton' that was the joint inheritance of Agnes and Sibylla (Hunter 1835: 9–10; Pipe Roll Society 1898: 3).

No family names are given (Lunan does not suggest that they are). Nor does the document specify the source of the inheritance that Agnes and Sibylla claimed—but Lunan had apparently no hesitation in identifying it as from Walter de Calne, son and heir of Richard de Calne, the landowner who had taken the Green Children in, and simply calls it 'their joint inheritance from Richard de Calne's son, Walter' as if he were paraphrasing the published document (Lunan 2012: 144). This is disingenuous.

'Sibylla' was indeed the name of Walter de Calne's daughter, Richard de Calne's granddaughter, but there is not the slightest evidence to connect her with the Sibylla involved in this legal case about the land at 'Eiton'. Further, Sibylla de Calne was indeed married to a 'John'—his name was John fitz Bernard. The coincidence of this pairing of names is surely just that—there is no reason to identify the fitz Bernard couple with the otherwise unidentified

'John and Sibylla' of the 'Eiton' record. To go further and identify 'Agnes', otherwise unknown in the de Calne family, as a putative ward or adoptee in the family, sharing in Sibylla's inheritance, goes far beyond any historical probability. It is simply misleading, as are Duncan's assumptions that the Richard of this record was Richard Barre, royal official and archdeacon of Ely, and that John was John fitz Bernard.

These misapprehensions seem to have arisen from Lunan's interpretation of items in the indexes of the two printed editions of the medieval documents known as the 'Feet of Fines' that he consulted. He comments:

> The 1835 edition Index reads as if Richard was a clerk in Stafford and John a chaplain in Buckinghamshire, but this is misleading. The Pipe Roll Society edition identifies them correctly.[73] (Lunan 2012: 145)

In fact the indexes in both editions contain (not surprisingly) entries for a number of different Richards and Johns (hardly uncommon names at this time, in the reigns of King Richard I and King John). In Joseph Hunter's edition of 1835, comprising documents dating to the period 1195–1214, the name in the first index entry is set out in full, in those that follow the repeating name 'Ricardus' or 'Johannes' is replaced by a 'ditto' mark in the form of a long dash. Thus the first index entry under the name 'Ricardus' is 'Ricardus clericus' (Richard the clerk) referring us to cases on pages 195 and 216, followed by the entry '——— et Agnes uxor eius' ('ditto and his wife Agnes') that refers us to the involvement of a married couple named Richard and Agnes in the 1197 case about 'Eiton' printed on page 10. The printer is indicating by a long dash the repetition of the name 'Ricardus' without intending us to assume that all the Richards in the index (some thirty-seven of them, all but two, the first in each of two columns of text, being represented only by long dashes followed by their surname, patronymic or other designation) are the same man! Similarly, under 'Iohannes' we find the entry 'Iohannes capellanus' (John the chaplain) referring us to a case on page 237 (concerning land at Leckhampstead in Buckinghamshire), followed immediately below by the entry '——— et Sibilla uxor eius'—the (different) John and his wife Sibylla of the 'Eiton' case on page 10. We are not intended to infer that John the chaplain of Leckhampstead had a wife called Sibylla.

In the index of the Pipe Roll Society edition (Pipe Roll Society 1898), which includes only the records for a single year, 1197 to 1198, most people are listed under their surnames or their patronymics or other description.

Only those who are referred to in the text simply by their first name without other designation are indexed under the first name. And the first entry in the index for the name Richard is indeed '*Ricardus et Agnes uxor sua*'—the second entry is a 'see also' reference ('*vide*' in the original) to two other Richards, '*Elyensis archidiaconus*; *Molendarius*' who appear under those head words in the index—Richard the archdeacon of Ely (that is, Richard Barre, who occurs many times in these records, *not* as litigant but as one of the presiding justices) and a certain Richard *molendarius* (the miller), who was involved in a suit about land in Bergholt, Essex.

It seems to be this unfortunate conjunction, in the index, of references to three distinct personages that led Lunan to the mistaken conclusion that the Richard of the first entry, who had a wife called Agnes, was identical with one (or both) of those in the second entry, and thus that Agnes was the wife of Richard Barre. And contrary to Lunan's claim, the index of the Pipe Roll Society edition does *not* identify the John of the Eiton record as John fitz Bernard. There is no entry for any fitz Bernard in the index, since none of that name was involved in any legal proceedings in the single year covered by that printed edition.

When discussing the claim made by Agnes and Sibylla and their husbands, Lunan adds: 'Nevertheless, in 1202 Richard and Agnes had to bring another case in Nottingham about it' (Lunan 2012: 144). In June 1202 a couple called Richard and Agnes were indeed claimants in such a case (jointly with another couple, Gilbert of Lindsey and his wife Emma), which was heard before the justices in Nottingham (Hunter 1844a: 18–19).[74] Our puzzlement that the case should be heard in *Nottingham*, so far from the assumed site of the 'Eiton' of the Bedfordshire records, is allayed when it becomes clear that it appears among records of cases relating to properties in the neighbouring county *Derbyshire*— at a place called 'Eston'. This was presumably one of the several places in Derbyshire now called 'Aston'. There is nothing to suggest that the Richard and Agnes of this record are to be identified as the same couple who were involved in the Bedford case—and Derbyshire's 'Eston' is certainly not the 'Eiton' of Bedfordshire.

And where was the 'Eiton' of the earlier record? Lunan says it was 'Eyton, also spelled Eiton or Eston' and on the following page claims that '[t]here are a number of Estons, etc., and this one is Aston Clinton, Buckinghamshire, but it's connected with Aston (Estone) in Warwickshire, now part of Handsworth in Birmingham' (Lunan 2012: 144–45). He offers no explanation for the trans-mutation of 'Eiton' to 'Eston' (both editions of this text in the Feet of Fines give '*Eitoñ*' abbreviating the Latin form '*Eitona*') and the place is clearly *not* in

Buckinghamshire but in Bedfordshire (Hunter 1835: 9–10; Pipe Roll Society 1898: 3).[75] There are several other references to this Bedfordshire place in the Feet of Fines (Hunter 1835: 45, 51, 78–79) and it is probably Eaton Bray, near Dunstable (Page 1912: 369–75).

Is this catalogue of misunderstandings and wildly optimistic reworkings of history typical of Lunan's research? Sadly, it seems to be. In the immediately previous paragraph to that on his page 144 with which we are concerned, he draws on the 'Red Book of the Exchequer' (Hall 1896), a legal compilation from the reign of King John, for the following information:

> By 1195 [Sibylla de Calne's] son, Walter Fitz-Bernard, had land in Reed [Hertfordshire], 'with the daughter [...] of Walter de Calna'. Sibylla was only fifteen in 1195, so it must be very soon after his birth. Like other clues in the story, it's been added to the record later, in a different hand, and it's an odd way to indicate Walter's mother. (Lunan 2012: 144)

It seems to be true that Sibylla de Calne was fifteen years old in 1195. A document from ten years earlier, 1185, the *Rotuli de dominabus et pueris et puellis* ('Rolls of ladies and boys and girls'—that is, widows and orphans holding property at the disposal of the king) confirms that the (unnamed) daughter of Walter de Calne, already an orphan and a royal ward, was five years old when she was given in marriage by the king to an (unnamed) son of Thomas fitz Bernard (Round 1913: 77; Walmsley 2006: 114–15). Although the late Thomas fitz Bernard had left three sons, the oldest being ten years old (Walmsley 2006: 128–29), it seems evident from other sources (I agree with Lunan on this) that the son in question was John, and that Walter de Calne's daughter was Sibylla, Richard de Calne's granddaughter.

Lunan is puzzled by the record in the Red Book of the Exchequer that apparently suggests that in 1195 fifteen-year-old Sibylla had a son of legal age. Yet the answer is surely simple—Lunan has misdated the record. A marginal note in the printed edition (Hall 1896: 581) dates it to 1211–1212, when Sibylla would have been in her thirties. Nor, indeed, does the document refer to a son of Sibylla called Walter holding the property jointly with his mother. From the Red Book, the editor Hall prints the line concerning the holding of the property—'*Walterus filius Bernardi tenet*'—'Walter fitz Bernard holds it' (ibid.). But in a footnote Hall adds '*Johannes*, L.N., which adds in the text *cum filia Walteri Kaune*'. Thus this other source 'L.N.' gives the holder's name as *John* fitz Bernard rather than Walter fitz Bernard, and adds that he held the land 'with the daughter of Walter de Calne'. This footnote presumably inspired Lunan to comment, as we have seen, that information was 'added to the record later, in a different hand'—he does not identify the 'L.N.' of the footnote. But here and throughout Hall's footnotes it refers to the *Liber Niger*, the '(Little) Black Book of the Exchequer'—a shorter compilation, near but not quite contemporary with the Red Book. In this case, the alternative text of the Black Book is surely to be preferred—the holder of the property was *John* fitz Bernard, holding it jointly with his *wife* (Sibylla), the daughter of Walter de Calne. The Red Book presumably represents a later situation, when the land had been inherited from John and Sibylla by their son *Walter* fitz Bernard.[76]

Given, within two pages of Lunan's book, and those specifically addressing the 'breakthrough' in his search for the name and identity of the green girl, these basic errors, these misunderstandings and misreadings of the modern editions of medieval texts, one must ask whether it is worthwhile considering seriously the rest of his speculative reconstructions of family and political connections, and his revisions of English history (and indeed of both terrestrial and *extra*terrestrial history) in the twelfth and thirteenth centuries.

Who was 'Agnes Barre'? There is no reason to doubt the later presence of a lady called Agnes Barre in Aston (Warwickshire), as claimed by Lunan, and she may have descendants today; yet in the sense that Lunan uses the name, the green girl of Woolpit grown up, wife of Richard Barre and witness to scientific wonders and political turmoil, we must conclude that Agnes Barre did not exist.

Traditional motifs in a historical narrative

The story has ended on a domestic note, with its heroine—*not* called Agnes Barre—settled down and married to a man in King's Lynn. The framing narrative, to repeat Katharine Briggs's words, 'has a curiously convincing and detailed air' (Briggs 1967: 7–8). It would be difficult to conclude that it is wholly fiction. It is tempting to strip away apparent accretions in the hope of revealing a core of historical 'truth'—but 'accretions' and 'core' are confusingly integrated. We are left with a conviction that *something* happened, but an uncertainty as to exactly *what*.

The framing narrative seems an apparently straightforward account of an admittedly extraordinary occurrence. Yet traditional narrative elements and motifs are evident within this well-attested story, and there are far more present than merely Motif F233.1 'Green fairy' and Baughman's debatable Motif F103.1 as assigned to it by Briggs (1971: 1:263). We have already noted several; now is the time to consider others.

The whole story encapsulates a widespread migratory legend—ML6010 in Christiansen's classification: 'The capture of a fairy' (Christiansen 1958: 142–44). Both Ralph <R43> and William <W8> say the children were 'caught'. The children wept as they were led to the house of Richard de Calne <R12>, going unwillingly with the villagers who found them. If a version of 'The capture of a fairy' was known to our authors it may have influenced their narrative and their choice of vocabulary. Two of Thompson's motifs do *not* strictly apply, however—F329.4.1 'Lost fairy child found by mortals [...] It leaves with the remark "Ho! ho! ho! My Daddy's come!"' ('Colman Grey') and F329.4.3 'Fairy captured by mortal escapes' ('Skillywidden'), in both of which the fairy's parents come looking for their lost child. Both stories are quoted by Briggs (1971: 1:203 and 355–56).

'Colman Grey' otherwise has an odd resonance with our story. A farmer comes across a miserable-looking little creature, sitting alone in the middle of a field and suffering from cold and hunger; the farmer takes the child home, treats it kindly and feeds and warms it, until three or four days later when the fairy's father comes searching for it and calls his child by name, whereupon it vanishes.

However, the disparate fate of the two children seems to mirror the fate of fairies who have dealings with humans. The boy pined and died <R19, W24>: that is, Motif F329.4.2 'Lost fairy child found by mortals but it pines away'.[77] The girl became a household servant (if we interpret '*in ministerio*' thus) <R26>: one is tempted to cite Motif F346(a) in Baughman, 'Fairy helps mortal with housework of all kinds'—although this is more familiarly the role of a brownie. And/or she married a man with a home in a distant town <W27>, that is Motifs F300 'Marriage or liaison with fairy', F302 'Fairy mistress. Mortal man marries or lives with fairy woman' and F302.2 'Man marries fairy and takes her to his home'. And we note Ralph's report that members of Richard de Calne's household considered her 'very wanton and impudent'—often characteristics of such fairy mistresses. However, we miss the expected denouement, when by breaking some taboo the husband loses his fairy wife who returns to her own Otherworld home.[78]

An odd echo of other stories is the children's arrival among harvesters in the fields <W5, W42>. We shall consider below the important similarities to Gervase of Tilbury's story of the swineherd who made his way through Peak Cavern in winter to find himself in the harvest fields of the Antipodes (Gervase of Tilbury 2002: 642–45; Westwood 1985: 204–06; Westwood and Simpson 2005: 172). But we can also note that Ralph of Coggeshall's Malekin had been stolen from the edge of a field while her mother was helping with the harvest

(Ralph of Coggeshall 1875: 120–21; cf. Westwood 1985: 149; Westwood and Simpson 2005: 690–91).[79] And, according to a nineteenth-century report from Yorkshire, two children were similarly stolen by fairies from a field near Almscliffe Crag (near Harrogate) where their mother was harvesting—but were (unusually) returned when the mother wept at their loss (Young 2012: 228).[80] Simon Young recently compared Malekin's story with several other accounts of babies snatched by fairies from the harvest fields (S. Young 2023) and questioned whether these cases were coincidental, or whether harvest was a particularly dangerous time for mothers with children.[81]

Or does the harvest context suggest that we should, as Martin Walsh puts it, see in the Green Children 'a garbled account of an atavistic harvest ritual' (2000: 247)?[82] Probably not—see my comments elsewhere on Walsh's conclusions (Clark 2006b, especially 211). I see no reason to change my reaction to Walsh's theory.

The possible significance of the children's exotic clothing and language has been pointed out above. Yet neither is convincing evidence for the identification of the children as fairy-folk rather than as foreign strays. We have already noted both the symbolic associations of the beans eaten by the children and the slight evidence (in the tale of the monk Elidurus) of Otherworld inhabitants as vegetarians—or, rather, very particular about their diet. Yet the presence of traditional motifs or folkloric elements in a story cannot prove that it is fiction. For example, there must have been *some* wicked stepmothers in real life as well as in tradition (Motif S31, etc.). Yet there are many hints that the people who had met the Green Children were ready to identify them as 'fairies'—intruders from an Otherworld. It was an interpretation that both Ralph of Coggeshall and (reluctantly) William of Newburgh seem to have accepted.

However, this 'folkloric' interpretation of their story can be extended when we look at what purports to be the children's own account of their origins.

CHAPTER SEVEN

The Children's Story

'You must not tell us what the soldier, or any other man, said, sir,'
interposed the judge; 'it's not evidence.' Charles Dickens, *Pickwick
Papers*

What follows, then, purports to be the children's own story. As with our
Table 1, episodes common to both authors are highlighted in Table 2, and
are referred to in the text by a number in angle brackets thus: <29> (the
questioning of the children); where Ralph and William disagree, or one
includes an episode not found in the other, the number is accompanied by an
initial—for example <R32> (the information, only in Ralph's account, that
everyone and everything in the children's land was green) or <W30> (where
William identifies the children's land as 'St Martin's Land').

Persistent questioners

No matter what they do, who they are, or what they became, they
are perpetually figures of lurid interest. (Plumtree 2022: 223–24)

When we turn to the children's own story we are faced with narratives from
which our authors deliberately distance themselves. The accounts are supposed
to be those given by the children themselves, and Ralph and William both
hint at the circumstances in which they were recorded. Ralph tells us that the
girl 'was often asked about the people of her country' <R29>. In the circumstances it would not be surprising if the questions were not just persistent but
searching. William seems to confirm this when he refers to the questioners
as '*percunctantes*' <W44>. This word implies not simply asking questions but
'investigating' or 'questioning insistently' (Union Académique Internationale
1998: 338–40; Howlett 2006: 2194).[1] William has probably judged the
situation accurately.

Table 2. A further comparison of the two accounts

	William of Newburgh	Ralph of Coggeshall
29	(When they were asked who they were and where they came from, it is said they replied that)	(The girl was often asked about the people of her land. She said that)
30	they were people of the land of St Martin, who was highly venerated there.	
31	(Asked if Christ was believed in there, or if the sun rose, they replied that) the land was Christian and there were churches,	
32		all the inhabitants and all things there were coloured green.
33	but the sun did not rise there, and the light was similar to that before sunrise or after sunset in this world.	They never saw the sun, but the light was like that after sunset here.
34	However, a brighter land could be seen from their own, separated from it by a broad river.	
35	One day they were pasturing their father's herds	(Asked how they had come into our land, she replied that) when they were following the cattle
36		they came to a certain cavern and entered it.
37	when they heard a great noise like the bells of St Edmund's Abbey.	They heard the delightful sound of bells.
38		Enraptured by the sound they wandered through the cavern for a long time,
39		until they came to its mouth.
40	They were amazed and, as it were, driven out of their senses	They were struck senseless
41	by the sound,	.
		by the bright light of the sun and the unusual temperature, and were frightened by the noise of those who came upon them
42	and they suddenly found themselves in the field among the harvesters.	
43		They tried to flee, but could not find the entrance to the cave before they were caught.
44	(And they said many other things in answer to persistent questions.)	

Whatever experience the girl and her brother faced, it seems to have been traumatic. Much later, once they had apparently learnt enough English to communicate, the children (or the girl, after her brother's death) were asked where their home was and how they came to Woolpit.[2] Questions were repeated; the children were clearly under pressure to respond. They were distressed; some of their answers seem to have been incoherent <W40>. Accounts of the reactions of children put under similar pressure in modern times should warn us what to expect: a mixture of memories and imagination, all moulded by a desperate desire to tell the questioning adults the sort of story they were so obviously hoping to hear. The questioners would then be free to place their own interpretations upon the answers. It was these interpretations that entered the historical record. Jean La Fontaine's book on accusations of 'Satanic abuse' in modern Britain makes salutary reading (La Fontaine 1997— especially pp. 112–33, chapter 7 'Children's stories'). As she writes, 'These cases demonstrate without doubt that children can be put under pressure until they invent stories that support the allegations of adults and reflect their beliefs' (ibid.: 126).

Similarly, James Plumtree has compared the Green Children's situation to that of refugees in more modern times (Plumtree 2022: 210–12). Discussing the difficulty of interpreting the children's own accounts as reported by William and Ralph, he refers to the similar problems faced in checking the credibility of refugees' stories. And he concludes with a comparison to some of his own students, refugees from war in Afghanistan:

> Atop of displacement, they face—by no choice of their own—scrutiny and suspicion by official institutions and by individuals. Grouped into categories, their individuality is obscured. Repeatedly asked to retell their narratives, the content they provide is challenged, misconstrued, used by others for their own purposes, and, after their efforts to communicate, often disregarded. (Ibid.: 224)

Whether among abused children or refugees, leading questions, perhaps asked inadvertently and with the best of intentions, seem a common feature. William of Newburgh astutely hints at this sort of questioning <W31>. About their homeland, the children 'were asked whether Christ was believed in there or whether the sun rose'. Although it had been thought prudent to baptize the children <23>, it is very likely that someone would indeed try to discover if the land they came from was Christian—and that, if prompted, the children would say they were Christian. More interesting is the implication in William's text that the children's claim to have come from a sunless world <33> was not made independently, but was prompted by a question: 'they were asked [...] whether the sun rose there' <W31>.

William reports some of what the children said as if it were direct speech. However, he frequently enlivens his history with speeches and conversations that are more literary in inspiration than historical—'he takes considerable liberties with speeches' admits his editor (Howlett 1884: xxv). We cannot expect from him a transcript of the children's interrogation. But he seems to have made an honest attempt to record what he was told they had said.

Charles Oman, in a study chiefly of the folklore elements in Gervase of Tilbury's compendium of stories and anecdotes *Otia Imperialia*, also looked at the story of the Green Children and was forthright in his verdict. The girl had 'a love of notoriety' and had 'felt it necessary to concoct' her story of the sunless land and the route that had led the children into our world—although 'there is clearly some mystery behind it all, some story of drugging and kidnapping' (Oman 1944: 11–12). In the circumstances, he is surely wrong to blame the girl. If she 'concocted' a story, it was under pressure from adults, and probably she would come to believe it herself. However, we should not expect to find in her story either a coherent account of reality or a consistent adherence to the norms of a readily identifiable folktale or popular belief. And although there are features in the children's story that will be familiar to folklorists, there is much that remains puzzling—and provides material for both those who seek a 'down-to-earth' explanation and those who prefer an alternative 'extraterrestrial' hypothesis.

Differences between Ralph and William's accounts are more noticeable when they are recording what I have called 'the children's story' than in the framing narrative. This has the appearance of deliberate choice—William seems more interested in the children's claims about their homeland, Ralph in the route and the means by which they found their way to Suffolk. The accounts are in fact inconsistent—we cannot simply conflate them and hope to find a simple explanation in reality or a parallel in recorded Otherworld beliefs.

A green world?

It is Ralph alone who reports the startling assertion, attributed to the girl, that in her land everybody and everything was green like her <R32>: '*asserebat quod omnes habitatores et omnia quae in regione illa habebantur viridi tingerentur colore*'. Either William did not hear of this claim or has relegated it among the 'many other things' the children said in response to persistent questioners <W44>. Perhaps he felt that some of these 'other things' as well as being 'long to relate' were no more than childish imagination and not reliable evidence.

We note without comment Lunan's suggestion that, on the alien planet from which he proposes the Green Children came, edible food plants had been dyed or genetically modified to be green (Lunan 1996: 44; 2012: 380–81). And although Thompson and Cross provide an appropriate folktale motif (F178.2) for green as an Otherworld colour in Irish tradition, it does not seem to be widespread nor to imply a whole world of green. It is surely far more likely that the girl's assertion should be considered in the context of the questioning. Either she herself came up with the idea as a straightforward explanation to satisfy nagging questions about her coloration (and perhaps eventually came to believe it), or the questioners put words into her mouth or interpreted something she said in this way. It *may* reflect a contemporary belief that Otherworlds were green (although none of those we shall discuss here share that feature)—but it should not be used as evidence that such a belief existed.

The sunless land

> It was rather dark, because the sun did not shine there. The days were all overcast, as if by clouds, and the nights were pitch-black, for there was no moon nor stars. (Gerald of Wales 1978: 134)

Both our authorities agree that the land the children claimed to come from was a sunless one <33>:

> '[T]he sun does not rise among our people. Our land is scarcely illuminated by its rays; it gets only the amount of light that among you precedes sunrise or follows sunset.' (William of Newburgh)

> [T]hey never saw the sun, but experienced a sort of light like that which occurs after sunset. (Ralph of Coggeshall)

The similarity of the wording suggests that Ralph and William shared a common source—and we have already noted William's implication that one of the questioners might have inspired this concept: 'they were asked [...] whether the sun rose there' <W31>. About five hundred years later, in 1653, a Yorkshire white witch accused of using a powder supplied by the fairies to effect his cures replied in a similar way to a judge's question. When asked if it was light or dark inside the fairy hill he responded that it was 'indifferent, as it is with us at twilight' (Briggs 1976: 410). Christina Hole (1977: 49) noted the similarity to the Green Children's world—it remains unclear whether the similarity is significant of anything more than a temptation to reply to similar questions in a similar way.

In the seventeenth century, the questioner assumed that an underground world could not be lit by the sun. And perhaps one of the children's questioners made the same assumption. Yet it is never clear whether our authors believe the children's home to have been underground. Ralph in his chapter heading and William in his postscript <W28> remind us that the children 'emerged from the ground'. Their land was reached (at least in Ralph's version <R36–9>) through an underground passage, like the Otherworld visited by King Herla. But in Herla's Otherworld the light is 'not from the sun or moon, but from a multitude of lamps' (Map 1983: 28–29), and the presence of lamps presumably implies an underground cavern-like realm. Certainly such realms are well enough known in folklore and literature. Indeed, Thompson's Motifs F80–F100 equate 'Otherworld' with 'Lower World'.

But the children's land is perhaps more like that visited by young Elidurus in south Wales, reached through a cave from a hollow under a riverbank:

> [A] most attractive country, where there were lovely rivers and meadows, and delightful woodlands and plains. *It was rather dark, because the sun did not shine there.* The days were all overcast, as if by clouds, and the nights were pitch-black, for there was no moon nor stars. (Gerald of Wales 1978: 134; 1868: 75)

We are led to wonder whether there is a direct link between the Green Children's story, as it is reported, and that of Elidurus.

It was in 1191 that Gerald of Wales completed the first version of his account of the journey through Wales that he had made three years earlier (Gerald of Wales 1978: 38); but the story of Elidurus that he included was apparently one he had heard from his uncle David FitzGerald, bishop of St David's, who had died in 1176 (ibid.: 11). David himself had heard the story from Elidurus, who even in old age wept with regret when he recalled his boyhood visits to the Otherworld of the little people. If Elidurus was an old man when David FitzGerald heard his story, his adventures presumably took place in the 1120s or before. This seems to be confirmed by Gerald's dating of it 'somewhat before our own time'—he was born in 1145 or 1146 (ibid.: 9). There is, however, a hint in what Gerald writes that the story circulated independently of Elidurus (ibid.: 133): 'an odd thing happened in these parts. The priest Elidyr always maintained that it was he who was the person concerned.' A popular folktale, perhaps, that Elidurus claimed as his own?[3]

The story then, or variants of it, must have been circulating—at least in south Wales—in the first half of the twelfth century; could it have been known in Suffolk when the Green Children appeared in Woolpit? The concept of a sunless world reached through an underground passage could have been familiar to the children themselves or to their questioners—if not from the story of Elidurus then from whatever folklore may lie behind Elidurus's account. A hint from a bystander, as suggested by William of Newburgh, could have put words into a child's mouth. Or the sunless world could be a later accretion to the tale—an improvement made to the version that William and Ralph both used.

Purkiss (2000: 63) draws attention to the apparently 'liminal' nature of the light in the children's land, 'permanently in the state of the down-going of the sun'—caught, it seems, in a moment of change from day to night, a time of perpetual twilight. Yet this is not quite what William and Ralph tell us—rather that the sun did not rise or was not visible. The absence of the sun need not entail a lack of distinction between day and night. As we have seen, in the land visited by Elidurus the days were sunless and dim, the nights were moonless and black—yet day and night were clearly distinct. The children's land *was* a twilight one, but perhaps only during 'daylight' hours; we do not have to believe that that was its permanent state.

Yet we shall return to Purkiss's identification of the possible liminality of the children's world, a concept that it may prove fruitful to pursue.

St Martin's Land

> 'We are people from the land of St Martin—who is held in particular veneration in the land of our birth.' (William of Newburgh)

William of Newburgh alone records the children's claim to have come from '*terra Sancti Martini*' where St Martin (presumably St Martin of Tours) was particularly venerated and where there were Christian churches <W30–31>. Ralph of Coggeshall's omission of this claim is puzzling. It is, after all, one of the most unusual features of the narrative, distancing it as it does from any other description of an Otherworld—not, one would think, something easily forgotten. It is difficult to see why Ralph would have wished to censor this particular detail. Did it perhaps not accord with his own vision of the Otherworld? As we shall see, he may have improved upon the children's story of their journey from their homeland in the light of more familiar narratives of Otherworld travels. Was Ralph, already convinced that the children came from an Otherworld, unwilling to accept that such a land could be Christian, and so rejected any accounts of what the children had said about it? Was it simply not in the version of the story that he had heard—presumably from the de Calne household? Was it something William learnt from a source other than that which he had in common with Ralph? And if so, was it a recollection of something that the children actually said or a later embellishment?

Even if for the purpose of discussion we treat William's account as reliable, questions remain. In the context of the 'interrogation' of the Green Children, it is not clear how one should regard the reference to St Martin's Land. Should we take it at face value? Was it a real memory—but the name of the children's homeland perhaps garbled in translation from their own language? Was it misheard or misunderstood by the listeners? Was it prompted by one of the questioners, reflecting some local belief about the Otherworld? Or did the children, convinced by the questioners that they were indeed from another world, imaginatively relate their own concept of what such an Otherworld would be like?

Interpreters have floundered. Some have looked for a real 'St Martin's Land'—Fornham St Martin, just north of Bury St Edmunds (Rayner 1966: 341; Harris 1998: 93) (Map 2), or St Martin's Hundred in Kent (Harris 1999). Lunan (1996: 49; 2012: 135–36) notes that properties in Essex belonging to the collegiate church of St Martin-le-Grand in London were listed in the Domesday Book under the heading 'TERRA SANCTI MARTINI'. None of these identifications is convincing.

One might note in passing that if there was one land where St Martin of Tours *was* 'held in particular veneration' in medieval times it was *France*—with some 500 towns and villages bearing his name, and over 3,600 parish churches dedicated to him (Istituto Giovanni XXIII 1967: 1274 and 1277).[4] On the other hand, Harris (1999: 267), in support of his view that the children were of Flemish origin, reports that St Martin was—and is—'patron saint' of children in Flanders. Certainly St Martin's Day is an important occasion for young children in Belgium, and the Vatican's authoritative *Bibliotheca Sanctorum* refers to the belief that St Martin comes down the chimney to bring them gifts (Istituto Giovanni XXIII 1967: 1277). But the cult of St Martin was widespread throughout Europe, and Walsh (2000: 239–40) has confirmed its importance in England from an early date.

Fornham St Martin

The presence on modern maps of a village called Fornham St Martin, with a medieval church dedicated to that saint and only 8 miles (13 km) from Woolpit, has obviously proved a temptation to those trying to identify the 'St Martin's Land' from which (according to William of Newburgh) the children claimed to have come—given their reference to Christian churches in their land and to the veneration of St Martin there <W30–1>. Harris (1998: 94) cites local author Eric Rayner (1966) as perhaps the first to propose this identification.

'Fornham' comprises three contiguous settlements on either side of the River Lark, north of Bury St Edmunds, each of them already with a church at the time of the Domesday survey of 1086—though the dedication of only one, to St Genevieve, was recorded in the Domesday Book (Page 1911: 493, 498) (Fig. 18). The latter church survives only as a ruined tower; the medieval churches of Fornham St Martin and Fornham All Saints still stand.

The Green Children, however, with their incomprehensible language, unusual diet and strange clothing—let alone their green skin—were presumably not native-born residents of Fornham St Martin. Paul Harris (1998: 93) surmised that they were the children of Flemish immigrants who had settled in Fornham St Martin and were raising sheep (the children refer to their father's herds or flocks, although whether these were of cattle, sheep or other livestock is unclear <W35>) and perhaps were involved in a locally based immigrant cloth-making industry using wool from these sheep. Harris draws attention to the growth of a clothworking industry in the Lark valley, particularly fulling, the treatment of cloth after weaving, using power from water mills, which he suggests began in the twelfth century and might have been inspired by skilled clothworkers from Flanders settling in the area.[5]

There seems to be no evidence to support the concept of such local Flemish settlement, and although the use of waterpower for fulling was indeed a novelty in England in the mid-twelfth century (Munro 2003: 204–05), according to Mark Bailey (the source cited by Harris) East Anglian textile production in the twelfth and thirteenth centuries was concentrated in towns, including Bury St Edmunds, only later developing in rural areas (Bailey 1989: 170–71). Bailey notes that before the fourteenth century there are few references to fulling mills in East Anglia, although he cites records of mills at Sudbury by 1290 and Hadleigh by 1305 (ibid.: 172). Harris concluded on the basis of Bailey's work that 'Fornham St Martin was something of a centre for such [clothworking] activities' (Harris 1998: 93). Yet Bailey was referring to a much later period, when, for example, in 1384 and 1391 in Fornham St Genevieve one Robert

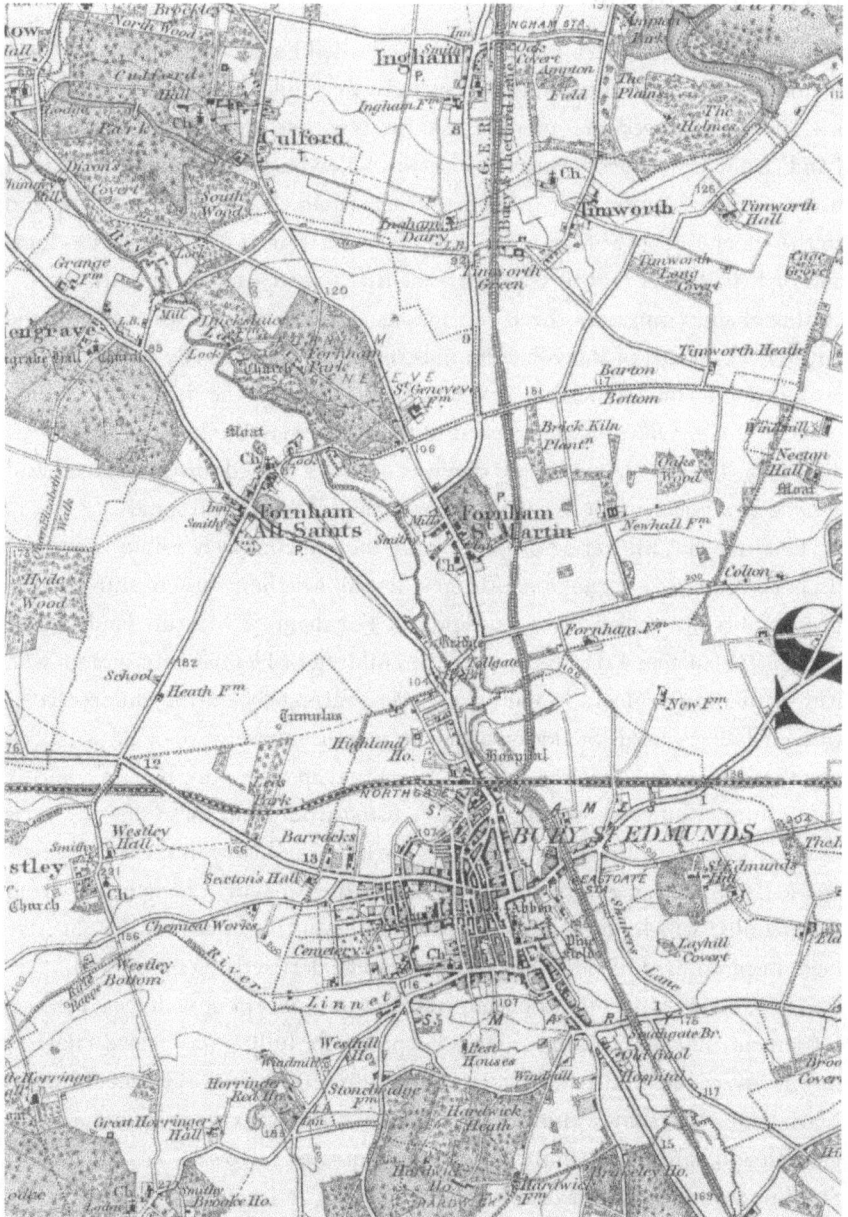

Fig. 18.   Bury St Edmunds and the Fornhams, 1898. The parishes of
Fornham St Martin, Fornham All Saints, and Fornham St Genevieve, in
the valley of the River Lark, north of Bury St Edmunds. The ruined tower
of St Genevieve's church stands in Fornham Park. Detail from Ordnance
Survey one inch to the mile Revised New Series map, Sheet 189 (1898).
Reproduced with permission of the National Library of Scotland.

Woolpit (an interesting local name!) was a spinner and weaver employing an apprentice and a female servant (Bailey 1989: 172). There were certainly fulling mills on the River Lark in the late fourteenth century, and indeed one at Fornham St Martin is mentioned in 1385 (ibid.: 176–77). But one should not attempt to read back into the twelfth century the evidence that Bailey provides from a meticulous study of the copious documents surviving from the very different world of the fourteenth and fifteenth centuries.

Fornham plays a further important role in Paul Harris's reconstruction of events (Harris 1998: 91), for in 1173 it was the site of a decisive battle in the civil war between supporters of King Henry II and those of his son 'Young King Henry'.[6] As we have noted above, in support of the rebels Robert de Beaumont, Earl of Leicester, had sailed to England with a force that included several thousand Flemish mercenaries. Landing at Walton, Suffolk, he joined forces with Hugh Bigod, Earl of Norfolk (Bartlett 2000: 55–56, 257–58). After a number of local engagements, and apparently some plundering by the mercenaries, the Earl decided to march across country to his own stronghold in Leicester, which was threatened by royalist forces.

On 17 October 1173 his army attempted to cross the River Lark at Fornham St Genevieve, but was intercepted and destroyed by forces loyal to King Henry II, including levies from Bury St Edmunds bearing the banner of Saint Edmund himself.[7]

The Earl and his wife and other rebel leaders were taken prisoner. Those Flemings unlucky enough to be on the losing side were treated more harshly. Of those who were not killed in the battle, some drowned in the river, others were taken into captivity and, we are told, starved to death (apart from two whose persistent prayers to St Edmund and to St Thomas Becket led to their survival and eventual freedom). Others, fleeing from the battlefield, were set upon 'with pitchforks and flails' by the local peasants and beaten to death (Roger of Hoveden, 1853: 1:375; 1869: 55; Diceto 1876: 1:377–78; Arnold 1890: 364–65; Fantosme 1981: 78–79; Bartlett 2000: 257–58).

In connection with the Battle of Fornham and possible subsequent violence against Flemish settlers, Harris (1998: 91) reports the discovery of 'a bizarre circle of skeletons, the remains of a group of Flemings' at Fornham All Saints. This discovery was made in 1826, in a mound close to the ruined church of Fornham St Genevieve rather than at Fornham All Saints (which lies on the other side of the River Lark). John Hosler (2017: 44) has traced what seems to be the earliest reference to this discovery in a note in the *Gentleman's Magazine* in 1827. The story was taken up by J.G. Rokewode in the notes to his edition of Jocelin of Brakelond's chronicle of Bury St Edmunds Abbey, in which the battle was mentioned (Jocelin of Brakelond 1840: 106). More than forty skeletons, says Rokewode—hundreds, according to the *Gentleman's Magazine*—in several layers, were arranged radially with their feet to the centre (their heads to the centre according to the *Gentleman's Magazine*), and some were said to show signs of violent death; these were interpreted as the bodies of some of those who died in the battle. No weapons were found. It is possible that such a mass burial is a battlefield grave, although its peculiar arrangement is unexplained; however, there is clearly no evidence to confirm the date, the identity of the bodies as Flemings or indeed any relationship to the battle.

Since it was unlikely that the mercenaries in Leicester's army had brought their children with them, Harris's hypothesis was that the violent treatment of the Flemish mercenaries by local people escalated into a pogrom against Flemings settled peacefully in the area, among them the Green Children's family, and that the children had fled when the family and their Flemish neighbours were attacked (Harris 1998: 93, 95). Although Oksanen (2012: 219–50) confirms the unpopularity of Flemings—particularly Flemish mercenary soldiers—in England in the later twelfth century, in the absence of evidence for violence against Flemish settlers (or indeed for the existence of any Flemish community in the vicinity of Fornham) it is hard to accept this reconstruction of events.

St Martin's summer

If we accept that St Martin's Land was not Fornham, with its very real church dedication to St Martin, attempts to find a symbolic or folkloric link with St Martin have also failed. There seems to be nothing to indicate that St Martin had particular Otherworldly connections, although Anne Witte (1988) has argued that St Martin, or rather the November festival associated with his name, had strong links with the dead—that Martinmas originated as a Feast of the Dead. She draws attention to the celebration of All Saints' Day on 1 November, identifying this and the subsequent All Souls' Day as the Christianization of a Celtic Feast of the Dead, and suggests that many of the features of this supposed pagan feast are repeated in traditional activities associated with St Martin's own festival a few days later (ibid.: 65–6). Most of her evidence comes from German sources, strangely for a supposed 'Celtic' festival (Hoffmann-Krayer and Bächtold-Stäubli 1927–1942: 5:1708–22): *Martinsfeur* bonfires; a children's visiting custom involving the singing of *Martinslieder*; gifts of cakes, particularly horseshoe-shaped *Martinshörner*—which Witte identifies without authority as soulcakes; divination; the nocturnal activities of ghosts and other supernatural beings.

Witte's conclusions are interesting but debatable. However, Martin Walsh also brought the Green Children into his wide-ranging discussion of the festival of Martinmas:

> What is particularly germane to our inquiry is the harvest season (whose endpoint is marked by Martin's feast), the magic bean-food, and the green-hued wanderers among the sheaves. We appear to have a reference to the transposition of seasons between Faerie and Middle Earth with these very green children, younger cousins of Gawain's nemesis, in the golden harvest fields, a reversal that is also recalled in the weather expression 'St Martin's Summer'. (Walsh 2000: 247)

There is much to give us thought here.[8] But a link between the high summer of the children's appearance in the harvest fields and the 11 November date of St Martin's feast is difficult to argue convincingly.

Walsh sees significance in a contrast between the springtime green of the Green Children and the autumnal end-of-harvest festival of Martinmas. However, an exact 'transposition of seasons' would require that, to arrive in Woolpit at harvest time (and early in the season, when they could eat freshly plucked beans) as they did, the children must have left their homeland in its winter season. And there is nothing in the text of either Ralph of Coggeshall or William of Newburgh to suggest that it had been wintertime in the children's land when they left it. Indeed, they were 'pasturing' their father's cattle <W35>—'pecora patris nostri in agro pasceremus'—surely a summer activity, not a winter one. In this context, however, we may recall that St Martin had *another* feast day, in summer—on 4 July, the anniversary of his consecration as bishop of Tours (Attwater 1965: 234). Perhaps the reference to St Martin was inspired by no more than the date of the Green Children's arrival in Woolpit.

Walsh continues:

> Martin's patronage over the *viridi* [*virides*] *pueri* is extremely significant. The saint's position in the liturgical calendar apparently did coincide with other, older and deeper calendars, allowing him to sink, as it were, into the realm of Faerie and rule over at least its outer province, the Land of Cockaigne. (Walsh 2000: 247)

But however strongly Walsh may argue on other evidence that in St Martin we can see a disguised Germanic or Celtic deity, the story of the Green Children in itself lends no support to his argument (Clark 2006b).

Perhaps more promising is the suggestion by Purkiss (2000: 63) that the 'liminality' of St Martin's Land lies not only in its twilit landscape, ever caught in transition from day to night (if that is how we interpret it—above), but also in its name, which reminds us of St Martin's summer, those final warm days in late autumn before the onset of winter cold. And Walsh, as we have seen, brings St Martin's summer into his argument about 'the transposition of seasons between Faerie and Middle Earth' (above).

However, can it be shown that the concept of St Martin's summer was known as early as the twelfth century? The *Oxford English Dictionary* cites no mention of St Martin's summer in English any earlier than that in Shakespeare's *Henry VI, Part 1* (I. 2. 131) noted by Walsh (2000: 236). Edward Burns, editing the play, derived the belief from legend: 'it is said that, when [St Martin's] coffin was carried back to Tours along the Loire for burial, trees and flowers bloomed in a second spring' (Shakespeare 2000: 139). But a twelfth-century account—a letter from the treasurer of Tours cathedral to Archbishop Phillip of Cologne (1167–1194)—makes it clear that this miracle was believed to have occurred *not* on 11 November, the date of the saint's burial in Tours, but on the 'Reversion' of St Martin, 13 December 885 (Lecoy de la Marche 1881: 444–45; Smedt et al. 1884: 241). This was the date on which, after some thirty years during which it was removed from Tours as Viking raiders ravaged the region, the saint's body finally returned to its original resting place. This story may of course have influenced the application of St Martin's name to a warm spell around his better-known *November* feast-day—but presumably not as long as it was associated with the annual Reversion celebrations held in Tours on 13 December.

Of course, French 'l'été de la Saint-Martin' (which, like the English phrase, seems not to be recorded early: a 1611 occurrence is cited by Alain Rey (1993: 737)) takes its name from the *feast* of St Martin ('la Saint-Martin') not from the saint. And it is not clear that St Martin himself was thought to be responsible for the unseasonably good weather. Alternative English names for autumnal warm spells such as 'All Saints' summer' (around 1 November) or 'St Luke's little summer' (around 18 October) suggest that there was no essential association with any particular saint, simply with a date in late October or November (Room 1999: 24 and 723).

On the other hand, even if St Martin's summer cannot supply the missing link between the saint and the Green Children's land, it seems clear enough

from Walsh's work (2000: 237–38, 240–41) that (at least by later medieval
and Tudor times) the feast of Martinmas was regarded as the first festival of
the winter season—and at the same time the last opportunity for outdoor
entertainments such as tournaments (ibid.: 243). 'Martinmas became a kind
of threshold holiday, both the last harvest festival and the first winter revel'
(Walsh in Lindahl et al. 2000: 663). As Walsh's use of the term 'threshold'
implies, Martinmas was itself liminal. It was the point in the year's round,
perhaps, that could be seen as equivalent to the setting of the sun each day.
For the Green Children's land, if it really was caught in an endless twilight,
it provides a most poetic and appropriate name. Yet it is perhaps *too* poetic
a conceit—to whom do we attribute the train of thought that led from
the setting of the sun to the fall of the year, to St Martin's feast and so to
St Martin's Land?

Little Martins

In a different approach, when discussing the Green Children's 'St Martin's
Land', folklorist Katharine Briggs (1967: 8) comments that 'witches' imps were
often called Martins or Martinets'. The relevance of this remark is unclear and
in its use of the word 'often' it is surely ill founded.

Although Briggs's immediate source was probably later, the information
seems to originate with Paulus Grillandus, the Italian judge and legal authority
whose *Tractatus de Hereticis et Sortilegiis*, published in 1536, was one of the
basic texts of the European witch-craze (Lea 1939: 395). Grillandus quotes
(without comment on the name) a case where a witch used to address the
demon that summoned her and (in the form of a goat) carried her through
the air to meetings as '*magisterulus*' ('little master'), '*magister Martinettus*' or
'*Martinellus*' ('little Martin') (Grillandus 1536: Bk II: vii, no. 26, fol. xlii r).
In the seventeenth century both Ben Jonson, in one of his notes to his *Masque
of Queens* (1975: 529), and Thomas Heywood, in *The Hierarchie of the Blessed
Angells* (1635: 475), credited Grillandus for information on the witches' 'little
Martin'. Briggs drew on the works of both Jonson and Heywood in her books
The Anatomy of Puck (1959) and *Pale Hecate's Team* (1962)—although with no
specific allusion to these particular passages from Grillandus. Whereas Jonson
summarized Grillandus and correctly ascribed the names to the summoning
goat-demon, Heywood applied them generally to witches' familiar spirits. Thus
Briggs's 1967 use of the word 'imps' may suggest that it was to Heywood she
owed the immediate reference.

In any case, it is surely unwise to bring into a discussion of twelfth-century Suffolk folklore the reported practices of witches in sixteenth-century Italy, even though they may be quoted as if universally true by two seventeenth-century English playwrights.

The sundering river

William's account of the children's home differs also from that of Ralph in his report, cast as if in the children's own words: 'one can see a bright land not far from ours, with a very broad river separating the two' <W34>. This physical 'limen' separating St Martin's Land from another provides at least a verbal link with Celtic tales of Otherworld voyages: in the *Adventure of Saint Columba's Clerics*, for example, dated probably to the tenth century, the travellers saw 'a wondrous realm facing them on the southeast, with a veil of crystal between them and it' (Patch 1950: 34).

Otherworld rivers are recorded in the motif indexes (Motif F162.2, etc.), yet they are usually very different (rivers of milk, honey or fire, for example) from the ordinary, if large, river described by the Green Children. But the dividing river appears in a number of the early medieval accounts of visits to another world (usually taking the form of 'visions') discussed by Patch (1950: 80–133) and Le Goff (1990: 107–22, 177–203 and *passim*). In these the Otherworld is the *afterlife*, containing the regions of the damned and the blessed and of Purgatory—not the mundane pastoral land described by the Green Children. In such visions, the river, usually fiery or otherwise perilous and crossed by an equally perilous bridge (Dinzelbacher 1986: 76–77), separates two regions of the afterlife. Thus in the vision of a monk of Wenlock, recounted by Saint Boniface (680–754) in a letter to the Abbess of Thanet:

> He sees a pitchy river boiling and flaming, over which was placed a piece of timber for a bridge. Over this the holy and glorious souls strove to pass [...] Beyond the river were walls shining with splendour, great in length and height—the heavenly Jerusalem. (Patch 1950: 101; Sims-Williams 1990: 262–63)

Another divided world, one part dark, the other bright, is found in the vision attributed to Charles the Fat (c.885). This however contains no river, but a valley 'on one side dark, burning with fire like an oven; and on the other side so delightful and glorious that I can no way describe it' (Patch 1950: 106–07).

In a short review of the similarities between such early medieval Christian visions of the afterlife and the Otherworld of folklore, Jacques Le Goff (1984: 31) notes that 'the essential process is that of Christianization [...] substituting Christian motifs for pagan elements and conceptions'. For example, the narrator is led into the Otherworld not by an animal (Thompson's Motif N773—exemplified in the story of the Green Children <R35–36>), nor by a grotesque figure like Herla's pygmy king, but by an angel or saint. Thus in the vision seen by Thurkill of Stisted, probably recounted by Ralph of Coggeshall himself, Thurkill is guided into and through the world of the afterlife by St Julian and St Domninus (Ward 1875: 426, 431; Ralph of Coggeshall 1978: 6, 11; Schmidt 1978: 56–59).

However, it would be an oversimplification to regard the influence as totally one way. Indeed, elsewhere Le Goff comments: 'The reciprocal borrowings and symmetrical approaches of high culture and folklore are clearly in evidence' (Le Goff 1990: 295). The divided Otherworld of the afterlife is surely a Christian concept—or at least had become one by the twelfth century, as Le Goff demonstrated in his study of *The Birth of Purgatory* (1990). When in William's version of the story of the Green Children we find an Otherworld divided into 'dark' and 'light' regions by a river, we may suspect the influence of the Christian afterlife visions that would have been familiar to William and his monastic contemporaries.

Indeed, the fact that an Essex peasant such as Thurkill of Stisted could apparently give an account of the afterlife that was broadly consistent with those of earlier visionary clerics suggests that such concepts circulated quite widely among the laity as well—an issue discussed by Schmidt (1978).[9]

But if concepts such as those found in afterlife visions lie behind the children's story, they seem to have been rationalized and stripped of their more horrific features. Compared with that seen by the monk of Wenlock, St Martin's Land with its flocks and pastures is, although gloomy, not an unpleasant place. Perhaps after all this was no more than a real childhood memory of the view across a river from a shaded, perhaps wooded, area to sunlit meadows on the other side—as Harris has suggested (1998: 92–93).

'By passages under the ground'

Ralph and William agree that it was when the children were herding cattle ('*cum pecora sequerentur*' and '*cum quodam die pecora patris nostri in agro pasceremus*') <35> that the adventure that brought them to our world happened. But it is Ralph who attributes to the green girl the more coherent story of what followed <R35–43>. It is in several ways a familiar, indeed traditional, tale. The children followed the cattle and entered a cavern <R36> (Thompson's Motif N773: 'Adventure from following animal to cave (lower world)'), which eventually led them into our world 'by passages under the ground' as William Camden's translator put it <R36–39> (Motif F92.6: 'Entrance to lower world through cave'; Motif A671.0.3, with exemplars from Ireland in which a cave forms the gate to *Hell*, is also apposite).

At first sight naturally occurring 'caves' and 'passages under the ground' are alien to the landscape of central Suffolk. However, the underlying geology is chalk, and historic chalk-pits and chalk mines (and the associated lime kilns) are certainly widespread, particularly in the south and west of the county (Suffolk Historic Environment Record 2023: search term 'chalk pit').[10] Most of the recorded sites, often surviving as place- or street-names, are undated or relatively modern, and there are none within the immediate vicinity of Woolpit. However, there are certainly artificial caverns and labyrinthine passageways in the chalk underlying Bury St Edmunds (Taylor 2022: 32–44). The most elaborate are probably eighteenth- or nineteenth-century in date, but the flint, chalk and lime mortar employed in the building of the medieval abbey must have come from local sources.

Yet caves and passages under the ground may be more common and more significant in folklore than they are in reality.

This, then, is a typical Otherworld journey—and one recounted from the viewpoint of the Green Children. In a typically perceptive insight, Diane Purkiss (2000: 63) says:

> [T]he children's experience might be a way of telling in a reverse-angle shot what it might be like for a human child to visit fairyland. The children cannot eat human food, just as we must never eat fairy food. They are lonely, heartbroken, crying, They are frightened by difference.

The world of humankind is the Otherworld, and the cave to which their father's cattle led the children is its entrance—in spite of Baughman's identification of the wolf-pits themselves as 'Pit entrance to lower world' under Motif F92.6 (1966, 203). In this mirror image of the standard story, the Green Children are unusual among Otherworld inhabitants in finding their way into our world *accidentally*. It seems generally to have been assumed that such beings are well aware of the human world that exists alongside theirs, and make deliberate excursions into it. However, it is unclear whether fairy children such as 'Skillywidden' (Briggs 1971: 1:355–56), found sleeping on a sheltered bank, or 'Colman Grey' (ibid.: 203), found by a farmer 'starving with cold and hunger', had wandered alone from their homeland, or had first been brought by their parents into the world of mankind and only thereafter become separated from them. Humans, on the other hand, may be invited or abducted into the fairy realm, or they may find their way there by cunning or by accident—and the last seems to be the model for the Green Children's misadventures.

Charles Oman (1944: 10) writes of the late twelfth century: 'Tales of mysterious lands reached through caverns seem to have been particularly rife in England about this date.' We have already noted several. William Peverel's swineherd of course journeyed for a long time through famous Peak Cavern ('*foramen Pech famosum*') until 'at last he came out of darkness into a bright place, a wide expanse of fields' (Gervase of Tilbury 2002: 644–45). To reach the home of the pygmy king, Herla and his followers 'entered a cave in a high cliff, and after an interval of darkness, passed, in a light which seemed to proceed not from the sun or moon, but from a multitude of lamps' (Map 1983: 28–29). Young Elidurus was led from his truant hiding place 'under the hollow bank of a river' by two tiny men, 'first through a dark underground tunnel and then into a most attractive country' (Gerald of Wales 1978: 133–34; 1868: 75). And these stories (or their prototypes) were already in circulation at the time of the reported appearance of the Green Children.

Rather later, in the fourteenth-century poem *Sir Orfeo*—a medieval retelling of the story of Orpheus and Eurydice that has been thought to represent 'an instance of the Celtic Other World which replaces the classical Hades' (Patch 1950: 243)—the hero enters a 'rock':

> When he was in the roche y-go,
> Wele thre mile other mo,
> He com into a fair cuntray,
> As bright so sonne on somers day,
> Smothe and plain and al grene. (ll. 349–53: Shepherd 1995: 183)[11]

Several medieval parallels exist, then, for the Green Children's claim to have wandered through a cavern for a long time before coming out into the bright sunshine of Woolpit's fields (<R38> '*per cavernam diutius errando incedebant*'). But of all these it is Gervase of Tilbury's account of the adventures of William Peverel's swineherd that is the most similar—perhaps suspiciously so.

The land of the Antipodes

> [T]hey had made along journey by passages under the ground, from
> out of another world from the *Antipodes* and Saint *Martins* land.
> (William Camden 1610: 463–64)

Reversed or unsynchronized seasons are to be found in some Irish accounts
of Otherworlds cited by Cross (1952: 236) under his Motif F161.2 (and by
Thompson as Motif F161.1.1). Thus, for example, the adventurer Nera,
returning to this world at Halloween time, could bring back summer fruits
from the Otherworld to prove his story (Carey 1989: 6; Meyer 1889: 220–21).
And the fourteenth-century Welsh poet Dafydd ap Gwilym suggests that
in wintertime Summer goes to Annwn, the (usually subterranean) Welsh
Otherworld:

> [Summer speaks:] 'To escape the winter winds I go
> To Annwn from this world'. (ap Gwilym 2001: 60: 'In Praise of
> Summer', ll. 39–40)

This is perhaps 'the transposition of seasons between Faerie and Middle
Earth' that Martin Walsh refers to (Walsh 2000: 247). And transposition of
seasons is a feature of the story told by Gervase of Tilbury of the swineherd who
ventured through Peak Cavern (Fig. 19) in search of a lost and pregnant sow
(Gervase of Tilbury 2002: 642–45; see also Oman 1944: 10–12; Westwood
1985: 204–06; Westwood and Simpson 2005: 172). Returning (with the sow
and her new piglets) from the Otherworld he found beyond the cavern, the
swineherd reported that the seasons were reversed there, for he had left winter
in Derbyshire to find himself in summer Otherworld fields, returning only to
find it was still winter in his own land.

Gervase himself suggests a rational scientific explanation, however, for
he calls the land the swineherd visited 'the land of the Antipodes' (Gervase
of Tilbury 2002: 642; Gautier Dalché 1989).[12] Gervase is referring to the
people who walk with their 'feet opposite' ours ('anti-podes')—that is, on the
opposite side of a spherical earth—rather than the monstrous race of people
with 'feet back-to-front' believed to live in India (or perhaps Libya) who were
sometimes designated by the same name (Wittkower 1987: 60–61; Gautier
Dalché 1989: 109).

Whether there was an antipodean or southern continent, separated from the
known world by the heat of the equatorial zone, and whether it was inhabited,

Fig. 19.   The entrance into Castleton Cave (Peak Cavern,
or 'the Devil's Arse'), Derbyshire. Anonymous watercolour, 1782.
© The British Library Board, Maps K.Top.11.26.

were much-debated questions in the Middle Ages (Wright 1925: 55–57;
159–61; 385–6; Gautier Dalché 1989: 111–13; Hiatt 2008: 38–144). Gervase
was well aware of the concept, for in the part of his *Otia* devoted to geography
he mentions the existence, between the Red Sea and Ocean, of a torrid zone
'on the borders of which the Antipodes are said to live' (*'in cuius finibus antipodes
esse dicuntur'*) (Wright 1925: 427; Gervase of Tilbury 2002: 216–17).

   The swineherd claimed, according to Gervase, that although it was winter
when he left Derbyshire and still winter when he returned, he had on his
journey found harvesters in the summer fields of the Otherworld. According
to twelfth-century geographers, who recognized the significance of the annual
change in the sun's apparent course through the heavens, such a reversal
of seasons was to be found in that hypothetical (and inaccessible) southern
continent on the other side of the world, the supposed actual home of the
Antipodes. For example, a mid-twelfth-century *mappa mundi* (world map)
shows the southern continent with the legend 'philosophers say the Antipodes
dwell here; who they assert differ from us in the difference of seasons. For

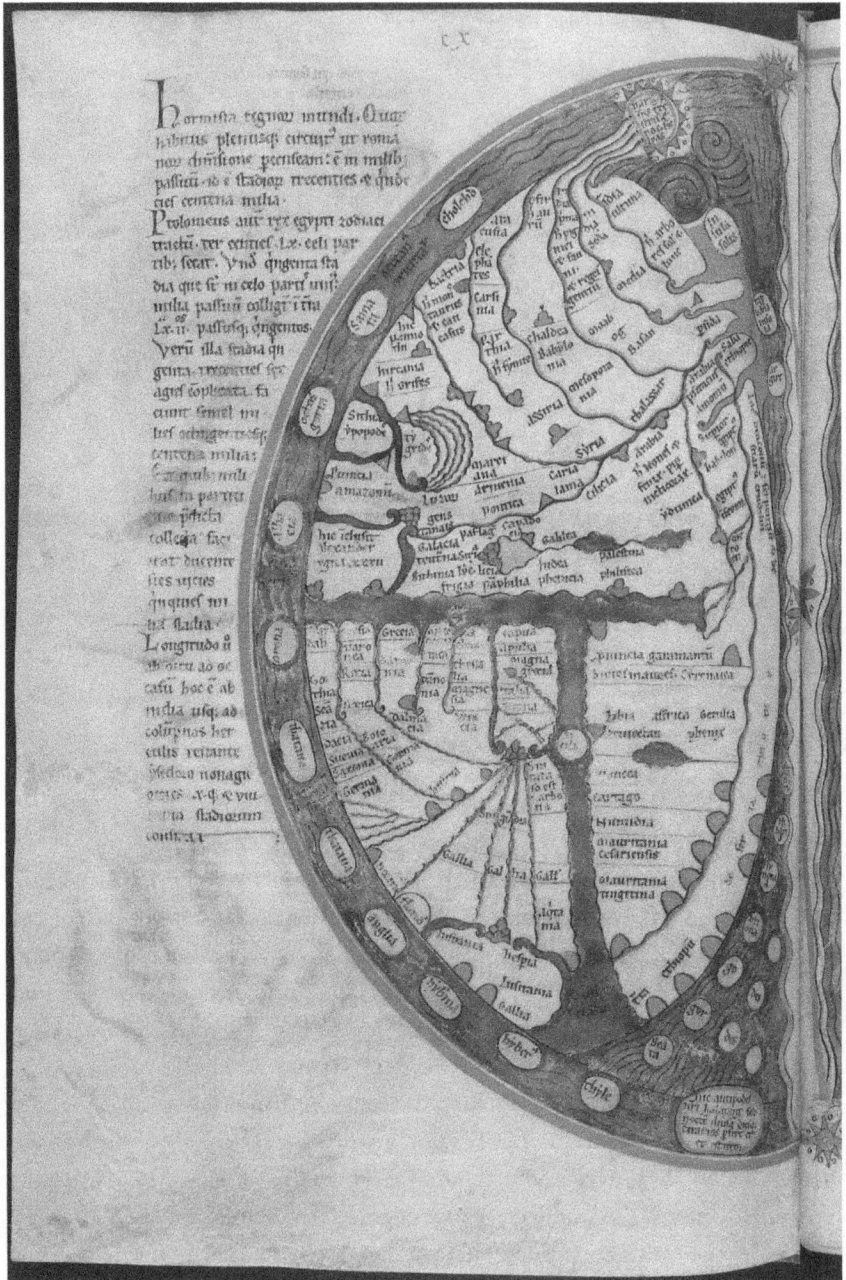

Fig. 20.   *Mappa mundi*, c.1150, in a copy of Lambert of Saint-Omer's *Liber Floridus*. In the north (left) the known world of Europe, Asia and Africa, separated by a torrid zone from a great continent in the south (right) where the Antipodes are said to live. Courtesy of Herzog August Bibliothek Wolfenbüttel: Cod. Guelf. 1 Gud. lat., ff 69v/70r (public domain).

Auster.

Plaga austral' temperata .f. f; filijs
ade incognita: nichil prinens
ad nrin gen̄. Mare naq; medi
tranen qd ab ortu solis ad occi
dente defluit. & orbe tre diuide
human oculr n̄ inscit: qm soli'
ardore semp illustrata qm desup
p̄ lacteu currit circuli: accessus
repellit hominū: nee ulla rati
one ad hanc zonā pumittit tra
situs. Hanc inhabitare phy
losophi antipodes auruniat: qd
a nob dinisitate tepor diuisos
asserit: na cū estare torrem: illi
frigore congelant. Soli u sep
tetrionalia sydera cernere per
mittū: e̅ & illis penit' denega
tū. Nulla alia astra st que il
lon obturib; denegens. & que
simul cū illis oriunt simul
neniunt in occasu. & dies no
clesq; sub una longitudine pa
tiunt. Solstici; aut celertas
& sol p brina aperando re
itteris. bis hyemem per illos
inducit.

Zona austra
lis frigida in
habitabilis inte
penta.

Spera Geometrica aiarciam hu
uies felicis capelle affri cartagini
sis. et figura rotunda. & globosi.
magintudinis tre eiusq; diuersa
diuisio. & gemin̄ occeani circa orbe
ambit'. Occeani igit̄ poc corona. 20
nam tre calida emgit undiq; :
Ab oriente duos sin̄ resudit.
unū ad septetrionē alterū
ad austrū. et ab occidente
ii. Qd ad ambas extrema
tes resusi. occurret ab ori
ente. muiceinq; feriunt.
& ex ipsa aquarū colli
sione nascit' illa famo
cū occeani accessio et
refusio. & ubicumq;
seu in frets uel in
angustis locis siue
in nro maraeon
tingit: uel in pla
nis littorib; . ex
ipsis occeani fini
bus semper eue
niunt.

when we are heated by summer, they freeze with cold' (Miller 1895: 46 fig. 8; 50; Wright 1925: 158; Hiatt 2008: 107–09, pl. 1) (Fig. 20).[13] Gervase has this land in mind when he retells the swineherd's story. Indeed, he explicitly contrasts the seasons in the land reached through Peak Cavern with conditions prevailing 'in our hemisphere' ('*in nostro emisperio*') (Gervase of Tilbury 2002: 644–45; Gautier Dalché 1989: 105).[14]

The reversal of seasons may well have been an original part of the swineherd's story—reflecting the folkloric belief noted by Cross. If so, Gervase interpreted it in purely geographical terms. Indeed, it would surely be this alternation of seasons that prompted his identification of the land reached through Peak Cavern as that of the Antipodes. Carey (1989: 6) and Loomis (1941) note other apparent instances of medieval authors identifying Otherworlds with the land of the Antipodes. Loomis concludes (1941: 303): 'What could be more plain than that [...] our clerical authors have been treating lay traditions, many of them of Celtic origin, and have given them a learned slant by harmonizing them with the best geographical science available.'

Gervase of Tilbury was born in the 1150s or 1160s (Gervase of Tilbury 2002: xxvi). His name indicates that he was a native of Essex—as was, presumably, Ralph of Coggeshall. But Gervase was widely travelled, being educated in Bologna and spending time in Naples and Venice. He served King Henry II and his son 'Young King Henry' both in England and abroad, and in 1209 he became a member of the court of the new German Emperor Otto IV. For Otto he wrote a book of 'Imperial Entertainments'—*Otia Imperialia*. Part III of this compendium of geographical and historical information and interesting tales is devoted to 'wonders'.

The *Otia* was completed in about 1215 (Gervase of Tilbury 2002: xl). However, it clearly includes material Gervase had gathered over many years. Indeed, already before 1183—while in service with 'Young King Henry'— Gervase had composed a *Book of Anecdotes* (*Liber Facetiarum*), now lost, that must have contained much similar material (ibid.: xcii). The story of the swineherd's adventure (Gervase of Tilbury 2002: 642–45) was certainly one that Gervase had collected earlier, since he tells us that he heard it from Robert, prior of Kenilworth ('a native of the [Peak] district')—and Robert was prior of Kenilworth only from about 1160 to 1186 (Gervase of Tilbury 2002: 643 n.2). The events are said to have happened even earlier, at the time that William Peverel held Peak Castle—that is, before William lost his lands to Ranulf, Earl of Chester, in 1153, and afterwards in 1155 fled when he was accused of poisoning Ranulf (E. King 2004). Thus whatever the origins of this story—and Charles Oman characteristically regarded it as a fabrication by a servant covering up his failure to take proper care of the valuable beast in his charge (although, he admitted, a fabrication 'full of interesting folklore') (Oman 1944: 12)—it would seem to have been in circulation by the mid-twelfth century.

Ralph of Coggeshall could have come across the story independently, but there may be a more direct connection. Ralph knew Gervase of Tilbury personally. Within two pages of his account of the Green Children Ralph turns to a long and detailed narrative of extraordinary events that took place in Rheims when Gervase of Tilbury was in service there with William of Champagne, the archbishop (Gervase of Tilbury 2002: xxvii–xxviii). Wakefield and Evans (1969: 251–54) usefully provide a translation of Ralph's account of this case of heresy and sorcery, also discussed by Freeman (2002: 202–05). Ralph tells us that Gervase himself was involved in the events; Ralph had heard the story from Gervase's own lips—'sicut ab eius ore audivimus postea' (Ralph of Coggeshall 1875: 122). Is it possible that, at the time he was putting the final touches to the story of the Green Children a few pages earlier, Ralph's mind was already turning to his acquaintance with Gervase and stories he had heard from him?

We cannot prove that Ralph of Coggeshall knew of the swineherd of Peak Cavern, either from Gervase or from some other source; we cannot show that he had come across other tales of adventurers who had followed a farm animal through a cavern to an Otherworld. Yet in the absence of confirmation from William of Newburgh that this was an original element in the story as told by the Green Children there must be a strong suspicion that Ralph has here improved upon what he had heard from the de Calnes. Whatever its significance as folklore, this episode should not be considered an integral part of the story of the Green Children.

On the other hand, Ralph adds a detail of the children's adventure that cannot be matched in Derbyshire—indeed it would have no place in the swineherd's narrative. It is by following the sound of bells through the cavern that the children eventually come out into the sunlight <R37–38>. Thompson seems to provide no motif for the theme of 'lost travellers follow the sound of church bells'— although it is common in English local legends. Jennifer Westwood (1985: 177–78) listed examples of such stories from Ashby Folville (Leicestershire), Newark-on-Trent (Nottinghamshire), Cudworth (Warwickshire), Barton-upon-Humber (North Lincolnshire) and Stamford Bridge (East Riding of Yorkshire). Later, she and Jacqueline Simpson (Westwood and Simpson 2005: 51, 318, 420, 605, 607, 677 and 736) added Wingrave (Buckinghamshire), Aymestrey (Herefordshire), Glenfield (Leicestershire), Langham and South

Luffenham (Rutland), Uttoxeter (Staffordshire) and Rodmell (Sussex) to this tally. Indeed bequests have actually been made to pay for church bells to be rung on winter nights to guide travellers.

Bells do seem to have played a part in the children's original story—in William's account they had heard a great noise they liken to the sound of the bells of St Edmund's Abbey <W37>. Perhaps here we can identify an elaboration on the part of Ralph (or his source), when he draws on a known concept to provide a rational explanation of the role of the bells that in William's version merely serve to confuse and astonish the children.

'We found ourselves amongst you'

Ralph's story of how the Green Children found their way into the Otherworld of humankind is almost certainly apocryphal, in spite of (or perhaps because of) its coherence. By contrast, William's version of the children's account of their adventures is incoherent enough to be believable in the context. The children explain that they simply do not know how they came to our land:

> We heard a loud noise—such as now we usually hear at St Edmund's when the bells are said to be sounding. We were amazed by the noise, and when we were intent on it, suddenly it was as if we were driven out of our senses, and we found ourselves amongst you in the field where you were harvesting. <W37, 40–42>

Stith Thompson provides nothing more similar than 'Journey to otherworld with magic speed' (Motif D2122.0.1) as a narrative element. However, the concept was familiar to Charles Fort, who reported a number of well-attested instances in modern times of such apparent 'instantaneous' transport, by which inadvertent travellers arrive confused and with no awareness of their journey or the passage of any time. Indeed Fort coined a word for the phenomenon: 'teleportation' (Fort 1974: 571; Gardner 1957: 313). This he applied—although coining a word is hardly an explanation—to the sudden appearances and disappearances, and occasionally apparent instantaneous translocations, of people, animals and things that he found in newspaper reports. Among such occurrences he records no fewer than six people found wandering in or near the town of Romford, Essex, between January 1920 and December 1923, 'unable to tell how they got there, or anything else about themselves'—and what he terms an 'outbreak' of ten 'wild men' who appeared in different parts of England in the winter of 1904–1905 (Fort 1974: 688–91). One of these latter, Fort says, spoke a language that nobody could understand and carried a book with writings that could not be identified. The book was sent to Scotland Yard, where an expert commented:

> It is not French, German, Dutch, Italian, Spanish, Hungarian, Bohemian, Greek, Portuguese, Arabic, Persian, or Turkish. Neither is it Hebrew or Russian.[15]

Students of fortean phenomena are well aware of their habit of clustering in time and/or place, and will not be surprised that this last incident occurred in Suffolk. But, not unexpectedly, on closer investigation it proves much less mysterious than Fort's account would lead us to suppose. Scotland Yard's conclusion (omitted by Fort) that 'The writer appears to be mad' seems sadly convincing.

As if these 'wild men' were not sufficiently reminiscent of the Green Children, Fort goes on—by way of the 'wolf children' of India—to describe the well-known case of young Kaspar Hauser. Hauser's sudden arrival in the streets of Nuremberg, Germany, in May 1828, speaking only two sentences of German and apparently 'unacquainted with the commonest objects and experiences of everyday affairs of human beings', seems to have caused as much excitement in the German city as the appearance of the Green Children did in Woolpit (ibid.: 700–10).

Kaspar's own story, when he came to tell it, was as mysterious in its way as that told by the Green Children. But there is no suggestion in it of instantaneous transport from one place to another, except in Fort's interpretation of events. For a clearer case we need to turn to Fort's account of Leonard Wadham, who in September 1920 found himself near Dunstable, 30 miles from London, with no recollection of how he got there from his home in Walworth, south London (ibid.: 684). Fortean investigators have noted other such occurrences (Michell and Rickard 1979: 7 and 102–03), though the more sceptical among them have thrown considerable doubt on some of the most extravagant claims ('Mr X' 1989).

In the case of Leonard Wadham, today's medical profession would probably have little hesitation in diagnosing some form of amnesiac episode (Miller 1997: 68). The accident victim who wakes up in hospital with no memory of the accident or of events leading up to it is a commonplace of journalism. But the trauma that causes a loss of short-term memory need not be physical: 'A shocking or unacceptable situation may be too painful to remember.'

When amnesia results from a single physical or psychologic incident, such as a concussion suffered in an accident or a severe emotional shock, the victim may forget only the incident itself; the victim may be unable to recall events occurring before or after the incident or the order of events may be confused. (Ibid.)

This could be what, according to William of Newburgh, the children were trying to describe: 'We don't know. We only remember this: [...] suddenly it was as if we were driven out of our senses, and we found ourselves amongst you in the field.' Nancy Partner warned us against 'worrying over the suggestive details of these wonderfully pointless miracles in an effort to find natural or psychological explanations of what "really", if anything, happened' (Partner 1977: 122). Yet here, surely, William's story rings true—this is no 'pointless miracle' but an honest account of an understandable psychological reaction to unbearable circumstances.

But if there was a 'single physical or psychologic[al] incident' that triggered amnesia in the children we shall never know what it was, nor the significance of the great noise like the sound of the bells of St Edmund's, which seems to have been associated with the event in some way.

CHAPTER EIGHT

Excursions

Merlin's Precinct

'Well,' replied the Parson, 'I expect it is quite as good an explanation as you will find, so mind you put it in your book.' (Maxwell
1926: 108)

To this point, our main concern has been to summarize, critique and
(sometimes) attempt to confute the many plausible and implausible theories that
have been put forward in the past about the Green Children. Before reaching
any conclusions of our own, it is perhaps time to venture into uncharted waters
and consider some other concepts that, as far as I'm aware, have not so far been
applied in this context.

For example, there is one, perhaps unlikely, identification of the children's
'St Martin's Land' that seems not to have been discussed seriously or in any
detail. The redoubtable M.R. James (1862–1936), medievalist, author of
ghost stories, provost of King's College, Cambridge, and of Eton College, in a
guidebook to the historic buildings of Suffolk and Norfolk gives a brief account
of the Green Children: he reports that they 'said they lived underground in
St Martin's land (query Merlin's)' (James 1930: 75–76). He does not enlarge
on this identification of Martin with Merlin. Harold Wilkins, amid his speculations that the Green Children were 'teleported' to our world from another,
also provides the same alternative name for that world: 'St Martin's Land,
or *Merlin's Land*, was the land of "gramarye" or necromancy' (Wilkins 1959:
191). He quotes no authority for this—it is presumably conjecture. The name
'Merlin Land' was also adopted by Adrian Mitchell, no doubt independently,
in his children's story *Maudie and the Green Children* (1996: unpaginated). When
Mitchell's narrator, the village girl Maudie Hessett, reports that the children
said they came from 'somewhere called Merlin Land' it is easy to dismiss it as
an understandable mistake (after all, 'Some call me simple,' she says). However,
if so, it is a fruitful mistake—at least in inspiring some speculation of our own.

Merlin ('Merlinus') was introduced, under that name, in Geoffrey of Monmouth's *Historia Regum Britanniae*, written in about 1136 or 1138. Although there has been much debate about Geoffrey's sources, there is little doubt that the 'very ancient book written in the British language' he claimed to be translating had no existence outside his own imagination. His actual sources included elaborations upon (and apparently deliberate distortions of) earlier historical writings, Welsh mythology and genealogies, local folktales, the works of Virgil and plenty of creative thinking (Tatlock 1950). Yet Geoffrey's 'British History' was for over four hundred years generally accepted as a true account of Britain's past. His story of the glorious but ill-fated reign of King Arthur became the basis of Arthurian legend; his kings Kimbelinus (Cymbeline) and Leir (Lear) are still familiar to us from the plays of Shakespeare (Kendrick 1950).

The 'Prophecies of Merlin' form a free-standing central chapter in the book (Geoffrey of Monmouth 2007: 142–59), while Merlin is also credited with transporting the stones of Stonehenge from Ireland and re-erecting them on Salisbury Plain, and brings about the conception of the future King Arthur, using his magic (or rather scientific) skills to help King Uther Pendragon seduce the wife of Gorlois, Duke of Cornwall (ibid., 170–75, 186–87; Tatlock 1950: 171–77, 403–21). Geoffrey went on to write a poetic *Vita Merlini* (*Life of Merlin*), drawing on further Welsh traditions (Geoffrey of Monmouth 1973). Merlin faded out of Geoffrey's *Historia* before the birth of Arthur, but was to play a much more extensive role in later romances. He is characterized in *The Arthurian Encyclopedia* as 'one of the most ubiquitous characters in Arthurian romance' (Lacy 1988: 382–85; and see also Peter Goodrich in Lindahl et al. 2000: 654–58). But he was, in origin, Geoffrey of Monmouth's transformation of a legendary Welsh seer or bard *Myrddin* (the -*dd*- pronounced like English *th* in 'then')—perhaps renamed merely to avoid the unpleasant connotations of the Norman French word '*merde*' ('shit') and its Latin equivalent that would have been evident in 'Merdinus' (Tatlock 1950: 175).

The 'developed' Merlin of Geoffrey's *Historia* and *Vita Merlini* seems to conflate a number of characters: an eponym of the south Welsh town of Carmarthen (Welsh *Caerfyrddin*, as if from *Caer* plus *Myrddin*, 'the fortress of Myrddin'), possibly already with a local reputation as a sage or prophet; a 'fatherless boy' named Ambrosius, who according to the ninth-century *Historia Brittonum* was able to explain to King Vortigern the reason why the fortress he was trying to build in north Wales continually collapsed during the night, and the prophetic significance of the two worms or dragons found beneath the foundations; and a legendary figure from the lost British kingdoms of the

Celtic North known as *Lailoken*, a 'wild man' with prophetic powers (Jarman 1960; 1991). Jarman concluded that the first and last of these had already become associated before Geoffrey's time. More recently Oliver Padel (2006) has argued that the whole of this conflation, and its further elaboration, could be attributed to Geoffrey.

It was, of course, in south Wales that Gerald of Wales sets the story of the monk Elidurus and his childhood adventures in a twilight Otherworld, which (as we have seen) has a strange affinity to that of the Green Children. He includes it as a digression in his account of an overnight stay in Swansea Castle during his journey through Wales in 1188, as something that had happened many years before 'in these parts' (Gerald of Wales 1978: 132–33). Two days later his party arrived in Carmarthen, *Kairmerdin*, which, he writes, 'means the town of Merlin [*urbs Merlini*], because according to the British History [that is, Geoffrey of Monmouth's *Historia*], Merlin was discovered there' (Gerald of Wales 1868: 80; 1978: 138).

In his novel reworking of the story of the Green Children and other medieval tales *The Girl Green as Elderflower* Randolph Stow has the green girl herself categorically identify St Martin and Merddin (so spelt; Stow 1980: 131). As the spelling of 'Merddin' suggests, and as he later notes (Stow 1980: 143), Stow is here alluding to the eccentric views expounded in Algernon Herbert's revisionist history of *Britannia after the Romans* ([Herbert] 1836–1841). In the course of this extraordinary work Herbert had not only identified Merlin/ Merddin with St Martin of Tours, but had seen in him a sinister figure who, in the guise of a Christian mission, restored the evils of Druidic paganism to post-Roman Britain: 'Martinism was at the bottom of the defection [from Christianity] that happened in these islands' ([Herbert] 1836–1841: 2:41–50 and *passim*). We have already reported Herbert's view that the Green Children were high-status members of this Druidic cult: 'The legend in my opinion relates to the secret orgies of the "virides Britanni" and the mysteries of Manogan and Brithan' ([Herbert] 1836–1841: 1:lx).

A suggestion of a link (although a negative one) between the names of Merlin/Myrddin and St Martin has also been made by a more reputable authority. J.S.P. Tatlock, a leading commentator on the works of Geoffrey of Monmouth, noted in 1950 that the prophet's name was spelt *Myrtin* or *Mirtin* in a twelfth-century Welsh poem, and pondered why Geoffrey had not chosen to call him 'Mertinus'. Was it, he asked rhetorically, because such a name might be confused with that of St Martin of Tours (Tatlock 1950: 175–76, and note 18)?

No one else seems to have commented on the similarity of names—not surprisingly, since there is no obvious likeness between the figures that would lead one to look for a connection.

However, once M.R. James and Maudie Hessett have drawn our attention to Merlin, we may find an analogue for the Green Children's 'St Martin's Land' in another Welsh tradition. A Welsh text *Enweu Ynys Prydein* ('The Names of the Island of Britain') lists three names that Britain once had. The first, before the land was settled, was 'Clas Merdin'—apparently 'Myrddin's Precinct' (Bromwich 2006: 246–48). The word *clas* has a variety of meanings, including a monastic community, an enclosure or the 'people of the same country' (Thomas et al. 1967–2002: s.v.).

Although *Enweu Ynys Prydein* first appears in a manuscript of about 1350 (the *Llyfr Gwyn Rhydderch*, or White Book of Rhydderch) (Bromwich 2006: xx), its content seems much more ancient—Bromwich (ibid.: cii) concludes that 'the text originates in a milieu more archaic than that of the twelfth century'. Certainly the three names of Britain that the author gives us—'Myrddin's Precinct', 'the Island of Honey' and ('after it was conquered by Prydein son of Aedd the Great') 'the Island of Prydein [Britain]'—show no influence from Geoffrey of Monmouth, who credits the settlement of Britain and the origin of its name to Brutus, a descendant of Aeneas of Troy (Geoffrey of Monmouth 2007: 6–29). Thus Bromwich notes that the story 'bears no relation whatever to the fiction of the Trojan origin of the Britons, which Geoffrey adopted from HB [*Historia Brittonum*]' (Bromwich 2006: ciii), and suggests that Prydein son of Aedd 'belonged to a genuine pre-Geoffrey antiquarian tradition preserved by the poets' (ibid.: 484–85). Indeed, since the story of the settlement of Britain by Trojan Brutus (or Britto), descended from Aeneas, was known to, and probably invented by, Welsh historians (the *Historia Brittonum*) in the ninth century (Faral 1929: 3:6–11; Lot 1934: 153–55; Clark 1981: 141–42), this alternative story of Prydein son of Aedd—and thus the 'earlier' name 'Myrddin's Precinct'—may be very early indeed.

The phrase 'Myrddin's Precinct' is strangely reminiscent of the Green Children's 'St Martin's Land', and one should not forget that in his wide-ranging study *The Quest for Merlin* Count Nikolai Tolstoy suggested that there were links between the Merlin figure (or figures) and Otherworlds and Otherworld journeys (Tolstoy 1985: especially 160–70). However, Tolstoy's conclusion reflected his identification of Merlin/Myrddin as a shaman and druid, with parallels in Classical and Scandinavian mythology. His case has not been widely accepted—although Peter Goodrich (in his entry on 'Merlin' in Lindahl et al.

2000: 658) refers in passing to 'the Merlin figure's pre-Christian shamanistic origins'. None of the Welsh references to Myrddin quoted by Rachel Bromwich (2006: 458–62) imply Otherworld connections—apart perhaps from very late (fifteenth- and sixteenth-century) allusions to Myrddin's mysterious 'House of Glass' (*Tŷ Gwydr*) to which he retired and where he safeguarded the Thirteen Treasures of the Isle of Britain (ibid.: 462 and 261; Tolstoy 1985: 118, 249). And there seems to be no reason to suppose that the term 'Clas Myrddin' itself was ever applied to any of those Otherworlds familiar in Celtic literature and folklore (Patch 1950).

Myrddin of Carmarthen, like his near neighbour Elidurus, may lead us into a search for influences from south Wales on the beliefs of Suffolk villagers or their Anglo-Norman lords, or a common survival of Celtic traditions in both areas. However, if the personal name Myrddin began as an explanation of that of the town of Carmarthen it could hardly have done so as long the original Brythonic name of that place, *Moridunon*, readily construed as 'Sea-fort', survived. Jarman suggests that the explanatory eponym developed 'by the end of the sixth century, but possibly later' and that only afterwards were the prophetic powers of the northern Lailoken attached to this mysterious Welsh Myrddin (Jarman 1991: 138). If so, we are dealing with a late Welsh invention, not a name that had survived since the time when East Anglia and Wales shared common and easily communicated Celtic beliefs, language and culture.

Alternatively, of course, we may follow the lead of those who, like Harris (1998), have sought a 'down-to-earth' explanation and have identified the children as foreign, perhaps Flemish, strays. We may suggest, rather, that the Green Children were themselves *Welsh*. Having been convinced by their 'persistent questioners' that they must indeed come from some other world, they responded by expressing as well as they could concepts of Otherworlds that they knew from tales they had heard at home in Wales, and by recognizing a familiar name *Myrddin* as the villagers' *Martin*.

Although an intriguing concept (it does not of course explain their colour or their fondness for beans!—or indeed what they were doing so far from home), this is as inconclusive as the other suggestions recorded here. There is as yet no satisfactory explanation for the involvement of St Martin—or indeed Merlin— in the Green Children's story, no convincing source for the name of St Martin's Land in folklore or legend or even geography. The search may be fruitless. We must allow for the possibility that the name of the children's homeland in their own language simply sounded like or was misinterpreted as 'St Martin'.

Rite of passage?

We have seen in how many ways the story of the Green Children embodies traditional narrative motifs and attitudes to the Otherworld. Another concept familiar to folklorists may now be considered—that of *liminality*. Diane Purkiss (2000: 63) viewed St Martin's Land as 'liminal' because of what she took to be its 'frozen' twilight state, caught in transition from day to night, and the anomalous seasonality of St Martin's summer expressed in its name. Though there is reason, as indicated above, to doubt both these interpretations, the concept of liminality cannot be ignored when discussing the Green Children's Otherworld.

In anthropology and folklore studies the term 'liminality' (from Latin *limen*—'threshold') is integral to the concept of 'rites of passage' first set out by Arnold van Gennep in 1909: 'a category of rituals or rites that accompany change of place, state, social status and age' during an individual's life (Gennep 1960; Green 1997: 732–33). The central phase in any such ritual is transitional or 'liminal'—'an abnormal condition, beyond society and time' (Green 1997: 501–03). It can be a dangerous condition for those involved, and, if protracted, can bring dangers for society as a whole—the returning ghosts, for example, of the restless dead who died without the proper ceremonies and reconciliation (Lindahl et al. 2000: 833–34). To the many interpretations of the story of the Green Children by folklorists and others that we have already considered, can we add another, and identify their experience as a rite of passage?

A simple interpretation of the Green Children's memory of what had happened to them—emerging from a dark passage into a bright and noisy world, surrounded by frightening strangers—would see it as a memory of the process of birth; and it seems appropriate that the children's first reaction was to cry <R12>. Perhaps the villagers regarded the occurrence in this way, for, as we have seen, it was decided that the children must be baptized <23>. And baptism is itself a rite of passage, a ritual to integrate the baby into the society of the living and the community of Christians.

From the children's viewpoint, their experience takes on a different aspect, yet still one that can be seen in terms of van Gennep's formula. Removed from their childish task of herding their father's cattle, they undergo a terrifying ordeal, and find themselves in strangely different circumstances, where people look and behave differently, where they have to learn a new way of speaking, eat unfamiliar food and wear strange clothing. The transition they face is that from childhood to adulthood, the rite that of initiation into the adult world (Green 1997: 463–64). And the children face, separately, two possible conse-quences of that initiation—death for the boy and marriage for the girl.

Woolpit on the edge

> Therefore to cross the threshold is to unite oneself with a new
> world. (Gennep 1960: 20)

Liminality, however, has an obvious spatial as well as a temporal sense. In his
contribution to a volume of essays on fairylore, Peter Narváez (1991b: 337–38)
adapted the usage to 'a spatial understanding of areas between known space
(purity) and unknown space (danger)'—or perhaps reclaimed for it this sense,
given the original meaning of *limen*, the threshold between the safety of home
and the perils of the outside world. He quotes van Gennep's own observation:
'whoever passes from one [zone] to the other finds himself physically and
magico-religiously in a special situation [...]: he wavers between two worlds'
(Gennep 1960: 18); indeed this quotation is from the short introductory
chapter that van Gennep devoted to 'The Territorial Passage' (ibid.: 15–25).
Narváez argues that marginal lands, on the fringes of small communities, are
liminal spaces, thought to be inhabited by fairies, who are themselves liminal
beings (1991b: 338). And other contributors to the same volume of essays make
similar points about the liminality of the fairies and their world (Lysaght 1991:
44 n.39; Ó Gilláin 1991: 200–01).

To the Green Children the world beyond the *limen* is the bright land across
the broad river <W34> or the summer fields of Woolpit reached through the
cavern <R36–39>; to the villagers of Woolpit it is the sunless land from which
the children come. To each it is a place of wonder and fear. In his discussion
of the role and significance of the literally marginal images to be found in
early medieval manuscripts, Michael Camille comments on the dangers that
medieval people saw lying beyond 'the safe symbolic spaces of hearth, village
or city' and the importance of recognizing their boundaries (1992: 14–16).
The margins were dangerous, but also places of power.

And in a real sense, the village of Woolpit itself *was* liminal, a marginal
territory. But in the heart of agricultural Suffolk, its neighbours were not the
'muskeg bogs, barrens and marshlands' of Newfoundland (Narváez 1991b:
338) or 'the untamed world of mountain, moor and sea' of the Irish fairies
(Ó Gilláin 1991: 201). Instead, Woolpit's boundary was a geopolitical and
symbolic one. Woolpit was the most easterly parish in the Liberty of St Edmund,
that part of the county of Suffolk under the jurisdiction of the abbot of Bury
St Edmunds. On its eastern edge lay the Franchise Bank, a functional *limen*,
marking the limit of the abbot's power. This mysterious ditch might have been
thought by some to be the original 'wolf-pit' that gave the village its name; and

the Green Children may even have first appeared to the villagers climbing out of the same ditch.

Moreover, in a medieval society that was so aware of its hierarchies and feudal obligations (Camille 1992: 16), Woolpit's situation at the time of the appearance of the Green Children was anomalous. We have noted that the village's relationship with the Abbey of St Edmund was, in the period before Abbot Samson was able to reclaim rights over its church, a doubtful and contested one (Arnold 1890: 252–54; Jocelin of Brakelond 1989: 43–45). A spirit of independence from abbatial control may be read into the later dispute between the incumbents of Woolpit church and the Abbey about church revenues (Arnold 1896: 78–114). In such circumstances, the people of Woolpit might well have been aware of the 'marginality' of their community. Brushes with a liminal Otherworld could even be expected.

The story of the Green Children is a rich mine—there are probably seams as yet untouched. We can read anthropological liminality into it, just as we can find the standard narrative motifs of folklore studies or evidence of alien intervention in earthly affairs. Yet in the end we may be left unsure of the essential nature of the story.

Ostensible fairies?

> "Come, listen, my men, while I tell you again
>   The five unmistakable marks
> By which you may know, wheresoever you go,
>   The warranted genuine Snarks." (Carroll 1962: 59)

No medieval author provides a checklist by which his/her contemporaries could recognize a warranted genuine 'fae' or fairy. Indeed, there would have probably been no consensus, although, as we have seen, Ronald Hutton (2014: 1138–39) listed six features that might be attributable to early medieval fairies.

But there seems little doubt that those who met the Green Children, those who heard of their strange first appearance and then of their own story of their homeland, all those who read the accounts by William of Newburgh and Ralph of Coggeshall, would have considered that (if there was any truth at all in the story) the children were strays from an Otherworld, a twilight land for which there were parallels in current stories of similar status and believability.

The evidence, apart from the children's own strange story, is reviewed here once more:

- Their appearance in a 'pit'—possibly an entrance to a subterranean Otherworld.
- Their green skin—not because green was a 'fairy' colour, but because it was obviously not a natural coloration for a human being.
- Their strange clothing—again not conclusive, but surely a sign of 'otherness'.
- Their incomprehensible language—also a sign of 'otherness'.
- Their refusal to eat bread or other ordinary 'human' food.
- Their diet of raw beans—possibly because of the 'magical' or Otherworldly connotations of the faba bean, but also simply because it was not, eaten raw, a normal human foodstuff.
- The later reputation of the green girl as 'wanton', like a typically seductive fairy mistress.

No one of these was the 'unmistakable mark' of a fairy, but together they may have seemed convincing evidence. Yet once the children started eating 'normal' food and their green colour faded there must have been some doubts. 'At last, as the nature of our food prevailed, they gradually changed their colour and became like us', as William puts it, or as Ralph says of the green girl 'she gradually *recovered* the ruddy appearance of her whole body'. Their colour and their preferred diet were both temporary. And to anyone familiar with any versions of stories of the 'Colman Gray'/'Skillywidden' type, the apparent failure of the children's parents to come looking for them and calling their names would have been a disappointment!

But after the children (or the surviving girl) had learnt enough English to tell their own story their Otherworldly origin would surely have been confirmed. William and Ralph provide very different accounts. Both writers tell us the children came from a twilight world, but Ralph seems to emphasize the Otherworldly characteristics: everybody and everything there was green <R32>; it was reached by a long journey through a cavern <R36–39>; the children had followed animals into a cave from their home world <R36>; they had followed the sound of bells to come out in Woolpit <R37–38>. And Ralph's reference to the girl's reported wantonness in later life <R26> suggests, as we have noted, that he and his informants were ready to see in the girl's behaviour the traits of the fairy temptresses who were familiar from romances and popular tales.

Here, then, is surely an example of the folklorists' concept of 'ostension', the apparent occurrence in real life of events described in a pre-existing legend (Dégh and Vázsonyi 1983), or more specifically in this instance 'quasi-ostension': 'in this case the subject of ostension is only imaginary', 'a

misinterpretation of naturally occurring events in terms of an existing legend'
or 'the observer's interpretation of puzzling evidence in terms of narrative
tradition' (ibid.: 19–20; Ellis 2001: 163, 224). We glimpse in our authors'
accounts of the Green Children's home and their strange journey such quasi-
ostension in action—the supposed words of the Green Children themselves
mediated through their questioners and by the chroniclers, all within a
framework of perhaps conflicting or incoherent understanding of Otherworlds
and how their inhabitants might behave.

William's comment that 'They are reported to have said these and
many other things, too long to relate, in answer to inquisitive questioners'
<W24> may suggest he was deliberately omitting material he considered
was unbelievable, or he felt had perhaps been prompted by over-enthusiastic
'inquisitive questioners' of the children. His own account of the overcast land
of St Martin with its Christian churches sounds nearly plausible as a 'foreign'
country, and different from any other contemporary Otherworld.

A question of belief

Clearly, the whole story caused William of Newburgh some misgiving. We have
noted his reluctance to include the story in his *Historia* at all: 'Certainly I long
hesitated about this matter, although it is spoken of by many people' <W1>. He
returns briefly to the subject in his next chapter on 'wonders': of the abilities of
demons to mislead humanity through illusions he concludes <W28>:

> [I]ndeed, when they are allowed to, these evil angels can very easily
> do things by which people are dreadfully misled. But the expla-
> nation of those green children who are said to have emerged from
> the ground is more puzzling; certainly our small intelligence is
> insufficient to solve the problem.

We note, perhaps, a touch of scepticism—the children '*are said to have
emerged* from the ground'. Though the Green Children were not, in William's
view, a diabolical illusion, he admits his failure to come up with rational explanation—'*abstrusior ratio est*'. Although, even in the story as he told it, there is
little doubt the children themselves claimed to have come from the twilight
St Martin's Land, which has every appearance of being an Otherworld (and
were almost certainly viewed by those who knew them as visitors from such
a world), William seems to have been reluctant to accept the existence of
such a land, at least one accessible by way of a pit or cave in a small village in

the heart of rural England. As we have noted, Jeffrey Jerome Cohen (2008: 84–91) concluded that William was reluctant to concede the existence of such 'otherness' in the heart of a unified 'England', rather than safely placed beyond the bounds, in barbaric Wales, Ireland or Scotland.

By contrast, Ralph of Coggeshall seems to have been happy to tell the story as he heard it, to accept the existence of the Otherworld reachable through caverns from Woolpit, and possibly, as we have seen, to enhance the tale in this light. We should, however, rely for 'local' details—the villagers' journey with the children to Wykes, the involvement of Richard de Calne, the later life of the girl in his household—on our local author, Ralph, and his contacts. These details might seem unimportant to William in distant Yorkshire.[1]

Can we then give more credit to one of our sources than the other? Can we envisage circumstances that would allow us to assign 'priority' to one author's text? I have suggested above that Ralph might have written a first version of the story that he had heard from Richard de Calne, perhaps soon after—or even before—Richard's death in about 1187; that this ur-text could even have travelled by way of the Cistercian 'network' linking Coggeshall to Byland and Rievaulx Abbeys in far-off Yorkshire; and that it might have come to the attention of William in neighbouring Newburgh Priory. Such a scenario would account for those similarities between the texts that we have noted—'the same substance though in different though equivalent words'. Ralph's lost text would be the primary version; William would have used it, but would have recast it in his own words and balanced it against those other versions that he heard 'spoken of by many people'—and perhaps stripped it of some elements that he felt he could not credit.

Yet even Ralph's story as it has come down to us in manuscripts is not itself the original text that I envisage. Consciously or unconsciously, Ralph must have developed and improved the tale over the years after he was first told it by Richard de Calne. He had heard the story 'often' from Sir Richard and his family; it seems unlikely that he would fail to recount it himself equally often in later life. As we have seen, it has been suggested that the main section of Ralph's *Chronicon*, covering the years from 1195 to 1200, which includes the account of the Green Children, was written soon afterwards, perhaps by 1201 (Carpenter 1998: 1216). That would have been more than ten years after the death of Richard de Calne, time enough for Ralph to have been influenced by remembered tales of Otherworld adventures (like those of young Elidurus or William Peverel's swineherd) or motifs from traditional narratives—or he may have incorporated elaborations simply to make a good story.

Neither text can claim priority; nor can we reconstruct our hypothetical Coggeshall ur-text. Each surviving version must be considered in its context. The folklorist may well prefer to find unashamed folklore in Ralph's account; the 'rationalizer' may seek historical, medical and psychological explanations for the events as they are described by William. But neither folklorist nor rationalizer can afford to ignore the other text.

'Folktale' or 'memorate' or 'legend' or 'classic of forteana'?

The status of the medieval 'folktale' has been questioned. According to Bruce Rosenberg:

> The folktale's existence in the Middle Ages is somewhat hypothetical, since the only evidence we have of it is in written narrative—in a form, in short, which is not folklore—and in analogous folktales collected recently. (Rosenberg 1981: 441–42)

Is the story of the Green Children a 'folktale'?

> In the broad sense it [the term 'folklore'] applies to all prose narratives following traditional story lines, which were told orally, or were so told in previous generations. (Simpson and Roud 2000: 132)

And we have seen that the story was circulating orally—that is how it came to the attention of Ralph of Coggeshall. The fact that he wrote it down as a record of an actual event is irrelevant to its original form. And Rosenberg is right to question how far we are justified in comparing such medieval stories with tales collected directly from oral tradition in modern times. More recently Jürgen Beyer has commented:

> In the beginning, oral prose tales (which later came to be called legends or fairytales) were not told as fiction but as real events. Tales about supernatural beings, although containing well-known motifs and types, were told as memorates. (Beyer 1999: 39)

A *memorate* is defined by one recent authority as 'a description of a supranormal experience undergone by the narrator or a person close to him or her' (Green 1997: 553). Ralph of Coggeshall never met the surviving child;

but if we trust his story he had spoken to Richard de Calne and others who had known her well (well enough at any rate to comment on her 'wanton and impudent' nature <R26>). Some of these people were presumably present when the villagers of Woolpit brought the weeping children to the de Calne house. Even though they were not witnesses to the first discovery of the children in Woolpit, they could certainly report what the villagers had said, as well as the children's strange appearance and behaviour and their later account of themselves. Ralph then is indeed recording a memorate, although one may question whether the Green Children were regarded at the time as 'super-natural beings' in Beyer's terms—Otherworlds were not supernatural. Nor is there any doubt that both Ralph of Coggeshall and William of Newburgh received and transmitted the story as a 'true' account of a real event. And yet, as we have seen, it embodies a number of now well-known narrative motifs.

Ralph's claim to have heard the story 'frequently' from Sir Richard and members of his household suggests that it was circulating in oral form locally, or at least within the family, several years after the event. How it reached William of Newburgh 160 miles (260 km) away in Yorkshire is not clear. I have suggested possible routes; if we trust William, it reached him from several sources or by a number of different channels, written or oral.

In compiling his *History* William seems to have taken great care to track down witnesses to the events he describes. In the case of the Green Children, he credits no particular one source, rather the weight of the testimony of so many good witnesses ('*tantorum et talium pondere testium*'). Partner notes that 'in the twelfth century the evaluation of testimony rather than laws of proba-bility was central to the problem of authenticating prodigies' (Partner 1977: 116–17).[2] It was clearly the difficulty he found in evaluating the evidence for the Green Children—but perhaps also his uncertainty about how 'probable' their story was—that made William, as he says, hesitate for a long time before deciding to include the story in his *History*. And although he confesses that he cannot *explain* what happened, he seems eventually to have been convinced of its status as an actual occurrence. Modern fortean investigators of anomalous events would perhaps be less likely to accept eyewitness reports at their face value, but we cannot fault William for his adherence to the historical method-ology of his time.

The story seems to have circulated widely—either in written or in oral form. It reached William in Newburgh by (it seems) more than one route. The story must have been around long enough when he wrote in the 1190s for him to accept that it had happened forty or fifty years earlier in the time of King Stephen. Whether by the time it reached William we call it a memorate or a folktale, it seems certainly to fall within Katharine Briggs's definition of a 'folk legend'. It was traditional (for a generation or so at least), and it was told with the expectation of being received as fact (Briggs 1971: 1:vii–viii). And we can consider it in the light of other definitions of 'legend'—for example, those in two dictionaries of folklore: 'a story that treats its unusual, extranormal, metaphysical or supernatural topics from the vantage point of the real world of its tellers and audiences' (Green 1997: 485) and 'even when it recounts a supernatural or highly unusual event, this is claimed to have occurred in real life' (Simpson and Roud 2000: 212).

But we have seen similarities between the story of the Green Children and cases reported by Charles Fort. And it has been, as we have noted, a staple of books on 'unsolved mysteries' and similar 'forteana'. Discussions of the Green Children have appeared in the magazine *Fortean Times* (Harris 1991) and the series *Fortean Studies* (Harris 1998 and 1999; Clark 1999). And in an entry on forteans in their *Dictionary of English Folklore*, Simpson and Roud (2000: 134) have noted that 'there is clearly a great deal of overlap with contemporary folklore studies, at least in subject matter if not always in approach'.

Perhaps, then, the story of the Green Children of Woolpit is best characterized as a folk legend, but one inspired by an event that today would have attracted the attention of those working in the tradition of Charles Fort. In the twelfth century it was accepted as a believable account of a visitation from a 'real'—perhaps subterranean or antipodean—Otherworld. In the seventeenth century it was brought into discussions, in fictional and non-fictional contexts, of the plurality of habitable worlds. The nineteenth century saw it as part of a primitive 'fairy mythology' and later folklorists stressed the parallels in documented folktales. But other writers in the later twentieth century and the early twenty-first century have set it alongside recent witness accounts of extraterrestrial incursions and alien abductions, and scientific speculations about 'vortices' in space and the possibility of the instantaneous transport of material objects or people.

The truth of the Green Children

> And no one yet has succeeded in explaining the story of the green children. (Staunton 2017: 127)

The 'legend' related by Ralph and William happened 'in real life' in 'the real world of its tellers and audiences' (Green 1997: 485; Simpson and Roud 2000:

212). It was firmly based in the geography and circumstances of medieval England.

If we are to believe anything it must be that an extraordinary event occurred in Woolpit that summer's day at (we think) the end of the reign of King Stephen, something that startled the eyewitnesses and those who later heard about it. There are elements of the story that cannot be regarded simply as the localization of a folktale or embellishment of folktale motifs.

If we take the 'reductionist' approach adopted by Harris (1998) and others, we may wish to identify a core of 'historical truth'. The Green Children existed; they *were* 'green' (however we interpret that colour and its cause or significance); they *were* found wandering in the fields of Woolpit; they *did* speak a strange language; they *did* eat only raw broad beans at first; and they gave a confused account of where they had come from. But it is surely dangerous to hypothesize a historical explanation for these events. Even less should we be prepared to invoke either the supernatural or the paranormal. The Green Children of Woolpit were surely not 'really' fairy-folk. They were not, we may take it, dwellers in the hollow earth, nor were they strays from an Otherworld or the land of the Antipodes—however plausible such an explanation might have appeared to their contemporaries. Nor, probably, were they extraterrestrial visitors, time-travellers or returned victims of abduction by aliens—however plausible such an explanation may appear today!

If they were aliens themselves, it was surely only in the down-to-earth sense of the Latin word—they were *alieni*, foreigners or strangers. And there are plausible explanations for the presence of a family of foreigners on the roads of East Anglia in the mid-twelfth century, from which the children may have strayed—pilgrims to the internationally known shrine at Walsingham, for example, or a party of merchants on their way between an east coast port and one of the great annual fairs (perhaps that at Bury St Edmunds). To go further and reach conclusions about their race or nationality as Harris (1998) notably did, with his hypothesis about a family of immigrant Flemish clothworkers, is to trespass beyond what the available evidence will permit.

But it is also clear that their story, as it has come down to us, has been influenced by contemporary views of an 'Otherworld' and by elements of 'folklore' perhaps known variously to Suffolk villagers, to a Norman landowner and his household, and to two clerical historians—and perhaps to the children themselves.

As we have seen, the story also provides material for the investigator of medieval attitudes to 'wonders' and the way in which they were incorporated into historical narrative by two different authors. It invites discussion of the relationships between memory, oral tradition and written history, and of the nature of the medieval 'folktale'. It provides some intriguing instances of the concept of liminality, and has led us to consider twelfth-century attitudes to baptism and the fate of unbaptized children. And in the attitudes of those involved in the event and of those who became aware of it, we can see striking parallels with twentieth- and twenty-first-century reactions to 'The Unexplained'.

CHAPTER NINE

Strangers in a Strange Land

> The power of the story comes in the end from our pity for these
> ultimate strangers in a strange land, these small, vulnerable ETs.
> (Purkiss 2000: 63)

> AGNES: I don't know what I am. That's the problem. But I don't
> think I want to be treated like some sort of monster in your book.
> (Nigro 2021: 81)

Perhaps it began as an adventure: the journey with their father to England.
There, at the great St James's summer fair at St Edmundsbury, their father
and other merchants would buy fine English wool and woollen cloth. The
excitement of the sea crossing. Landing at Ipswich town quay, the sights and
sounds of a different land. The oddly dressed people who spoke a strange
language. Hiring packhorses to carry the silks and fine textiles from the
ship that they hoped to sell, and the heavy bags of silver coins. Taking on
local guides and guards—there had been rumours about a Flemish merchant
robbed and killed in Kent. The dusty road through Stowmarket and Woolpit
Heath under the summer sun, harvesters in the fields staring at them. And
suddenly—

The children's own story, at least as reported by William of Newburgh,
suggests some dramatic event, a traumatic experience the children blocked
from their minds: 'it was as if we were driven out of our senses'. Robbery,
murder?

For here, at the end, we need to remember what the story was really
about—two lost, frightened and lonely children, taken in by strangers, and
caught up in a narrative over which they had no control.[1] As Diane Purkiss
(2000: 63) concluded: 'The power of the story comes in the end from our pity
for these ultimate strangers in a strange land.' In an interview in 2012 Kevin
Crossley-Holland talked of his lifelong fascination with the story, first told to
him by his father:

At once, I identified with this plangent tale of brother and sister who long to belong and, like all of us at one time or another in our lives, feel lost, feel like outsiders. In a way, they stand for all the refugees, all the homeless, all the people in camps, all the dispossessed, who walk across our Middle Earth. (Crossley-Holland 2012)

On these two little ones has been placed a great burden of interpretation and surmise, from the villagers of Woolpit and the household of Sir Richard de Calne who thought they were strays from a fairy Otherworld, to the medieval chroniclers who included them in their chapters on 'wondrous events', to seventeenth-century philosophers speculating about the plurality of inhabited worlds, to nineteenth-century folklorists seeking evidence in support of their theories of fairy origins, to twentieth-century investigators of extraterrestrial phenomena, and not least to the historians who have interpreted the story (or rather the chroniclers' use of it) in terms of the relations between the races of Norman Britain or the 'literature of trauma'.

We have compared the children and their treatment by 'persistent questioners' to reports of cases of so-called Satanic abuse in modern times: 'children can be put under pressure until they invent stories that support the allegations of adults and reflect their beliefs' (La Fontaine 1997: 126). Similarly James Plumtree has likened the treatment of the Green Children and the manipulation of their story to the experiences of refugees in modern society. He writes:

> The two mysterious children, appearing on the margins of a village, not only found themselves in the main text of two major chroniclers, but also found themselves endlessly scrutinized, slandered, misunderstood, manipulated, presented as proof for a range of speculative assumptions, and ultimately became minor walk-on characters in larger narratives in which they have no control. No matter what they do, who they are, or what they became, they are perpetually figures of lurid interest. (Plumtree 2022: 223–24)

Simon Young, in a perceptive article in *Fortean Times*, has also seen that it was the fate of the Green Children to become 'minor walk-on characters in larger narratives':

> What is most disturbing about the story for me is the way that the two (who I imagine were all too human) had walked into a fairy tale

not of their making. The locals understood the children to be fairy offspring who had stumbled into the human world. Their discovery was read in this way and the details of their discovery were put through a fairy filter. Then by the time that the only survivor, the girl, knew enough English to tell her story, she too seemed to believe that she had come from fairyland. Her past had been obliterated [...] There can be few horrors worse than becoming a bit player in a collective fantasy. (Young 2022)

In modern folklore terminology, the children were the subject of 'quasi-ostension': 'the observer's interpretation of puzzling evidence in terms of narrative tradition' (Ellis 2001: 224). If not fairies they were 'ostensible' fairies.

Yet, as Plumtree implies, playing a bit-part in 'a collective fantasy' was not just for life. It was to last long after the green girl's death. Academic folklorists have applied the 'fairy filter' and treated the children as examples of medieval fairy or Otherworld belief. Modern forteans have sifted the story for elements of 'down-to-earth' truth and discarded the rest. Their contemporaries in university history departments have, perhaps more cruelly, ignored the children and what happened to them to concentrate on how the medieval chroniclers used such stories and what messages might be coded within them.

It is easy to understand why the story has been so popular for so long with poets and children's authors, and why it attracted the attention of an American folk-rock band and a European electro-pop duo. Yet all these well-meaning retellers, interpreters and revisionists (and not least the present author) have themselves surely added to the burden of misunderstanding and speculation that attaches to these ostensible fairies. Their story continues to inspire writers and storytellers to tell it afresh for a modern audience. No doubt academic historians will find new ways to interpret the uses medieval chroniclers made of stories of wonders in their writings. Meanwhile, those who seek a 'down-to-earth' (or even an *extra*terrestrial) explanation of the events will find scope for endless speculation—but probably ultimate disappointment.

This book may itself have done nothing to lighten the burden borne on the slight shoulders of these two little twelfth-century waifs—although perhaps we have now clarified the nature of the load. We have at least warned of its unsteadiness and tendency to slip, and identified particular pieces of luggage that should now finally be discarded.

And yet we still don't know *where the children came from* or *why they were green* (Fig. 21).

Fig. 21.   Misty, resident witch and host of *Misty* magazine, ponders the mystery of the Green Children. *Misty* © Copyright Rebellion Publishing IP Ltd. All Rights Reserved.

Appendix: The Sources

After the publication, in the late nineteenth century, in the official Rolls Series, of good editions in Latin of Ralph of Coggeshall's *Chronicon Anglicanum* (Ralph of Coggeshall 1875) and William of Newburgh's *Historia Rerum Anglicarum* (Howlett 1884: 1885), scholars did not need, as Thomas Keightley did, to rely on rare and outdated printed texts. However, the lack of a complete English translation of Ralph's *Chronicon* hindered (and continues to hinder) discussion of the story, for the episode of the Green Children should be seen in the context of Ralph's attitude to the other such 'wonders' that he relates: see Elizabeth Freeman (2000) and Carl Watkins (2001, 2007). William of Newburgh has been better served, first with the appearance of the Rev. Joseph Stevenson's translation (1861)—which is widely quoted (but usually unattributed) on websites today—and more recently with editions by Walsh and Kennedy of the first two books of his *Historia* with the Latin text (from the Rolls edition) and an English translation on facing pages (William of Newburgh 1988, 2007). The 1988 volume includes William's account of the Green Children (1988: 114–17), as well as a number of other episodes of folkloric and/or fortean interest.

Randolph Stow also usefully provided his own translations of the relevant passages from both Ralph of Coggeshall and William of Newburgh in the appendix to his novel *The Girl Green as Elderflower* (1980: 147–50). In 1998 Paul Harris set out to provide definitive texts and translations as a basis for his own investigation of the problem of the Green Children (Harris 1998: 81–88). Sadly the texts and translations as printed contained minor errors—detracting from this laudable attempt to set study of the story on a firm footing (see Clark 1999: 270–71).[1] More recently Francis Young in his *Suffolk Fairylore* (2019: 119–23) has reprinted the text and translation of William of Newburgh's account from Walsh and Kennedy's edition (William of Newburgh 1988) and the Latin text of Ralph of Coggeshall from the Rolls edition (1875) with his own translation of it.[2]

British Library Stowe MS 62, a manuscript of William of Newburgh's *Historia Rerum Anglicarum* dating to about 1200, has been digitized and is available online: <https://www.bl.uk/manuscripts/Viewer.aspx?ref=stowe_ms_62_f002r>, with the story of the Green Children on ff. 24r–24v. Similarly, Ralph of Coggeshall's *Chronicon*, from Cotton MS Vespasian D X, is online at <https://www.bl.uk/manuscripts/Viewer.aspx?ref=cotton_ms_vespasian_d_x_f046r>, with the Green Children on ff. 91v–92r.

Here I reprint the stories from William and Ralph's texts as they appear in Latin in the Rolls Series—with some normalization of punctuation and use of capitals—alongside my own translations. The Latin texts will be found, respectively, in Howlett (1884: 82–84 and 87 (William of Newburgh)), and in Ralph of Coggeshall (1875: 118–20). In my translations I have not attempted to mirror the different styles and vocabulary of the two authors.[3]

William of Newburgh

Historia Rerum Anglicarum	The History of English Affairs

Cap. XXVII
DE VIRIDIBUS PUERIS

Chapter 27
CONCERNING GREEN CHILDREN

Nec praetereundum videtur inauditum a seculis prodigium, quod sub rege Stephano in Anglia noscitur evenisse. Et quidem diu super hoc, cum tamen a multis praedicaretur, haesitavi, remque vel nullius vel abditissimae rationis in fidem recipere ridiculum mihi videbatur: donec tantorum et talium pondere testium ita sum obrutus, ut cogerer credere et mirari quod nullis animi viribus possum attingere vel rimari.

Nor does it seem right to omit a wonder, unheard of by the ages, that is known to have happened in England in the time of King Stephen. Certainly I long hesitated about this matter, although it is spoken of by many people. It seemed to me ridiculous to take on trust a story that had either no rational basis or a very obscure one. At last I was overcome by the evidence of so many witnesses of such weight; so that I was forced to believe it, and to marvel at what, for all my strength of mind, I cannot grasp or fathom.

Vicus est in Estanglia quatuor vel quinque, ut dicitur, milliariis distans a nobili monasterio beati regis et martyris Edmundi. Iuxta quem vicum quaedam antiquissimae fossae visuntur, quae sermone Anglico Wlfpittes, id est, luporum fossae, dicuntur, et vico cui adiacent suum nomen indulgent.

There is a village in East Anglia four or five miles distant, it is said, from the noble monastery of the blessed king and martyr Edmund. Near that village can be seen certain very ancient ditches which are called *Wolf-pits* in English—that is, 'wolves' ditches'—and these give their name to the nearby village.

Ex his fossis tempore messis, et occupatis circa frugum collectionem per agros messoribus, emerserunt duo pueri, masculus et femina, toto corpore virides, et coloris insoliti, ex incognita materia veste operti. Cumque per agrum attoniti oberrarent, comprehensi a messoribus ducti sunt in vicum, multisque confluentibus ad tantae novitatis spectaculum per dies aliquot tenti sunt cibi expertes.

Out of these ditches, at the time of harvest when the harvesters were busy gathering the crops in the fields, there emerged two children, a boy and a girl. Their bodies were all green, and they were dressed in clothing of an unusual colour, made of unknown material. They wandered dazed through the field, and were caught by the harvesters. They were taken to the village, where many people gathered to see such a novel spectacle, and they were held for some days without food.

Cum ergo inedia iam paene deficerent, nec tamen aliquid ciborum, qui offerebantur, attenderent, forte ex agro contigit fabas inferri, quas illico arripientes, legumen ipsum in thyrsis quaesierunt, et nihil in concavitate thyrsorum invenientes amare fleverunt. Tunc quidam eorum qui aderant, legumen ex corticibus erutum porrexit eis, quod statim libenter acceptum comederunt.

Hoc cibo aliti sunt per menses aliquot, quousque usum panis noverunt. Denique colorem proprium, ciborum nostrorum praevalente natura, paulatim mutantes, et similes nobis effecti, nostri quoque sermonis usum didicerunt. Visumque est prudentibus, ut sacri baptismatis perciperent sacramentum, quod et factum est.

Sed puer, qui minor natu videbatur, post baptismum brevi vivens tempore immatura morte decessit, sorore incolumi permanente et nec in modico a nostri generis feminis discrepante. Quae nimirum postea apud Lennam, ut dicitur, duxit maritum, et ante annos paucos superstes esse dicebatur.

Sane cum iam nostrae usum loquelae haberent, interrogati qui et unde essent, respondisse feruntur: 'Homines de terra Sancti Martini, qui scilicet in terra nativitatis nostrae praecipuae venerationi habetur'.

Consequenter interrogati, ubinam esset terra illa, et quomodo exinde huc advenissent, 'Utrumque', inquiunt, 'nescimus. Hoc tantum meminimus: quia cum quodam die pecora patris nostri in agro pasceremus, sonitum quendam magnum audivimus, qualem nunc apud Sanctum Edmundum, cum signa concrepare dicuntur, audire solemus. Cumque in sonitum illum quem admirabamur animo intenderemus, repente, tanquam in quodam mentis excessu positi, invenimus nos inter vos in agro ubi metebatis'.

Now when they were almost dying of starvation but would not take any of the food they were offered, it happened that by chance some beans were brought in from the fields. They seized them and looked for the beans inside the stems; when they found nothing in the hollow of the stems they wept bitterly. Then one of those who were present took the beans out of the pods and offered them to the children. At once they took them happily and ate them.

They were nourished by this food for several months, until they learnt the use of bread. At last, as the nature of our food prevailed, they gradually changed their colour and became like us, and also learnt the use of our language. And it seemed good to prudent people that they should receive the sacrament of holy baptism, which was done.

But the boy, who seemed the younger of the two, lived only a short time after baptism and died an early death. His sister remained well, and was not in the least different from the women of our kind. Indeed, it is said, she later married a man at Lynn, and she was said still to be alive a few years ago.

Now when they had the use of our language, they were asked who they were and where they were from. It is reported that they replied: 'We are people from the land of St Martin—who is held in particular veneration in the land of our birth.'

Later they were asked where that land lay and how they had come here. 'We don't know where it is or how we came,' they said. 'We only remember this: one day when we were pasturing our father's cattle in the field we heard a loud noise—such as now we usually hear at St Edmund's when the bells are said to be sounding. We were amazed by the noise, and when we were intent on it, suddenly it was as if we were driven out of our senses, and we found ourselves amongst you in the field where you were harvesting.'

Interrogati utrum ibidem vel in Christum crederetur, vel sol oriretur, terram illam Christianam esse et ecclesias habere dixerunt. 'Sed sol', inquiunt, 'apud nostrates non oritur: cuius radiis terra nostra minime illustratur, illius claritatis modulo contenta, quae apud vos solem vel orientem praecedit vel sequitur occidentem. Porro terra quaedam lucida non longe a terra nostra aspicitur, amne largissimo utramque dirimente'.

Haec et multa alia, quae retexere longum est, curiose percunctantibus respondisse feruntur. Dicat quisque quod voluerit, et ratiocinetur de his ut poterit; me autem prodigiosum mirabilemque eventum exposuisse non piget.

When they were asked whether Christ was believed in there or whether the sun rose, they said the land was Christian, and there were churches there. 'But', they said, 'the sun does not rise among our people. Our land is scarcely illuminated by its rays; it gets only the amount of light that among you precedes sunrise or follows sunset. But one can see a bright land not far from ours, with a very broad river separating the two.'

They are reported to have said these and many other things, too long to relate, in answer to inquisitive questioners. Let anyone say what he likes and make what he can of this affair; but I am not ashamed to have related this wonderful and marvellous happening.

Cap. XXVIII
DE QUIBUSDAM PRODIGIOSIS

[...] qui nimirum mali angeli libentius faciunt, cum permittuntur, in quibus homines perniciose fallantur. Porro puerorum illorum viridium, qui de terra emersisse dicuntur, abstrusior ratio est, quam utique ostril sensus tenuitas non sufficit indagare.

Chapter 28
CONCERNING CERTAIN WONDERS

(extract)

[...] indeed, when they are allowed to, these evil angels can very easily do things by which people are dreadfully misled. But the explanation of those green children who are said to have emerged from the ground is more puzzling; certainly our meagre intelligence is insufficient to solve the problem.

Ralph of Coggeshall

Chronicon Anglicanum

DE QUODAM PUERO ET PUELLA DE TERRA EMERGENTIBUS

Aliud quoque mirum priori non dissimile in Suthfolke contigit apud Sanctam Mariam de Wulpetes. Inventus est puer quidam cum sorore sua ab accolis loci illius iuxta oram cuiusdam foveae quae ibidem continetur, qui formam omnium membrorum caeteris hominibus similem habebant, sed in colore cutis ab omnibus mortalibus nostrae habitabilis discrepabant. Nam tota superficies cutis eorum viridi colore tingebatur. Loquelam eorum nullus intelligere potuit.

Hi igitur ad domum domini Ricardi de Calne cuiusdam militis, adducti prae admiratione, apud Wikes, inconsolabiliter flebant. Panis ac caetera cibaria eis apposita sunt, sed nullis escis quae eis apponebantur vesci volebant, cum utique maxima famis inedia diutius cruciarentur, quia omnia huiusmodi cibaria incomestibilia esse credebant, sicut puella postmodum confessa est.

Tandem cum fabae noviter cum stipitibus abscissae in domo asportarentur, cum maxima aviditate innuerunt ut de fabis illis sibi daretur. Quae coram eis allatae, stipites aperiunt, non fabarum folliculos, putantes in concavitate stipitum fabas contineri. Sed fabis in stipitibus non inventis, iterum flere coeperunt. Quod ubi astantes animadverterunt, folliculos aperiunt, fabas nudas ostendunt, ostensis cum magna hilaritate vescuntur, nulla alia cibaria ex multo tempore penitus contingentes.

English Chronicle

CONCERNING A BOY AND A GIRL WHO EMERGED FROM THE GROUND

Another wonder also, not unlike the previous one, happened in Suffolk at St Mary of the Wolfpits. A boy was found, with his sister, by the inhabitants of that place, near the mouth of a certain pit that is situated there. In the shape of their whole bodies they were like other people, but they differed in the colour of their skin from all the mortal inhabitants of our world; for the whole surface of their skin was dyed with a green colour. No one could understand their speech.

So they were taken as a curiosity to the house of a certain knight, Sir Richard de Calne, at Wykes, while they wept inconsolably. Bread and other foodstuff was set before them, but they were unwilling to eat any of the food that was offered them, although they were tormented by great hunger for a very long time; for they believed all foodstuffs of this sort were inedible, as the girl later admitted.

At last when some beans, newly cut with their stalks on, were carried into the house, they made signs with great eagerness that some of the beans should be given to them. When the beans were brought, they opened the stalks, not the bean pods, thinking that the beans were contained in the hollow of the stalks. But when they didn't find beans in the stalks they began to cry again. When the bystanders noticed this, they opened the pods and showed them the naked beans. Once they were shown them, they ate them with great joy, and would touch no other food at all for a long time.

Puer vero semper quasi languore depressus infra breve tempus moritur. Puella vero sospitate continua perfruens, ac cibariis quibuslibet assuefacta, illum prassinum colorem penitus amisit, atque sanguineam habitudinem totius corporis paulatim recuperavit.

Quae postmodum sacri baptismatis lavacro regenerata, ac per multos annos in ministerio praedicti militis, sicut ab eodem milite et eius familia frequenter audivimus, commorata, nimium lasciva et petulans exstitit.

Interrogata vero frequenter de hominibus suae regionis, asserebat quod omnes habitatores et omnia quae in regione illa habebantur viridi tingerentur colore, et quod nullum solem cernebant, sed quadam claritate fruebantur, sicut post solis occasum contingit.

Interrogata autem quomodo in hanc terram devenisset cum puero praedicto, respondit, quia cum pecora sequerentur, devenerunt in quandam cavernam.

Quam ingressi, audierunt quendam delectabilem sonum campanarum; cuius soni dulcedine capti per cavernam diutius errando incedebant, donec ad exitum illius devenirent.

Qui inde emergentes, nimia claritate solis et insolita aeris temperie, quasi attoniti et exanimes effecti, diu super oram speluncae iacuerunt. Cumque a supervenientium inquietudine terrerentur, diffugere voluerunt, sed introitum speluncae minime reperire potuerunt, donec ab eis comprehenderentur.

Now the boy always suffered a sort of weakness and died in a short time. But the girl enjoyed continuing good health. Becoming used to all sorts of food she totally lost her leek-green colour, and gradually recovered the ruddy appearance of her whole body.

She was afterwards regenerated by the cleansing of holy baptism, and stayed for many years in the service of that same knight (as we have often heard from the knight himself and his household); but she remained very wanton and impudent.

Now she was often asked about the people of her country. She claimed that all the inhabitants and all things that existed in that country were dyed with a green colour; they saw no sun, but experienced a sort of light like that which occurs after sunset.

Asked how she and the boy had come into this land, she replied that when they were following the cattle they had come into a certain cavern.

When they entered it, they had heard a beautiful sound of bells. Captivated by the sweetness of the sound they had gone on wandering through the cavern for a very long time, until they reached a way out of it.

When they came out from there they were stunned and struck senseless, as it were, by the brightness of the sun and the unusual warmth of the air, and for a long time they lay at the mouth of the cave. Then they were terrified by the noise of people coming towards them and tried to flee; but they could in no way find the entrance to the cave before they were caught.

Notes

Chapter 1: An Introduction

1. A phrase borrowed from an anonymous reviewer of an early draft of this text.
2. <https://museumoflondon.academia.edu/JohnClark> [accessed 11 September 2023].
3. 'The finest work on the Green Children of Woolpit, for example, is a sixty-thousand-word book, available in pdf form on academia.edu; it also happens to be one of the more interesting works brought out on fairies in recent years' (Young 2018a: 186).

Chapter 2: The Story and its Legacy

1. Some writers have suggested that a third author, Gervase of Tilbury, also gives an account of the Green Children (noted for example by Harris 1998: 86). There is no such account in Gervase's work (Gervase of Tilbury 2002). This confusion may have first arisen with Harold Wilkins, who in a popular book on *Mysteries Solved and Unsolved* (1959: 190–91) attributed to Gervase what seems to be no more than a garbled extract from William of Newburgh. It may have persisted because of the lack, until 2002, of a reliable English translation of Gervase's text to consult.
2. The term 'folk-lore' (the Lore of the People) was coined in 1846. The story of the Green Children presumably gained prominence among folklorists because of the rarity of early medieval evidence of belief in 'fairies' that they could compare to more recent accounts in oral tradition.
3. <https://en.wikipedia.org/wiki/Green_children_of_Woolpit> [accessed 12 June 2023].
4. These recent papers acknowledge and draw on an early draft of this present text, formerly posted on the academia.edu website (Clark 2018). I have in turn cited and quoted from both papers elsewhere in this much enlarged and updated version.

5.   I am grateful to Jon Howe for drawing my attention to this publication. For the history and significance of this extraordinary magazine, see Round (2019). Internal evidence suggests that the main source used by the unnamed writer of the 'Green Children' story was, directly or indirectly, Harold Wilkins's version, published in his *Mysteries Solved and Unsolved* (1959). I owe to Julia Round the suggestion (pers. comm.) that the writer was Malcolm Shaw, *Misty*'s editor, whose wife later commented 'He used to have all these reference books ... like *Tales of the British Isles* [...] spooky stories, legends, and myths' (Round 2019, 41).

6.   The duo, Milla Sunde and Marlow Bevan, specialize in 'ethereal Electro-Pop for the soul'. Their song 'Encounter' (2010, available on YouTube at https://www.youtube.com/watch?v=qCIouuXyCjk) is about a meeting with 'a strangely coloured boy and girl'. The back cover of the original CD album of the same name (Spinside Records SPNR 07275-7) comprised a photograph of two oddly dressed children (looking very much like younger incarnations of the singers themselves) standing at the entrance of a cave.

Chapter 3: Transmission

1.   British Library Stowe MS 62, a manuscript of William of Newburgh's *Historia Rerum Anglicarum* dating to about 1200, has been scanned and digitized and is available online: <https://www.bl.uk/manuscripts/Viewer.aspx?ref=stowe_ms_62_f002r> with the story of the Green Children on ff. 24r–24v [accessed 11 September 2023].

2.   Ralph of Coggeshall's *Chronicon*, from British Library Cotton MS Vespasian D X, is online at <https://www.bl.uk/manuscripts/Viewer.aspx?ref=cotton_ms_vespasian_d_x_f046r> with the Green Children episode on ff. 91v–92r [accessed 11 September 2023].

3.   Martène and Durand printed what are effectively no more than extracts from Ralph's complete work (from a manuscript then in the abbey of Saint-Victor in Paris) in two sections under two distinct titles: *Chronicon Anglicanum ab anno MLXVI ad MCC* ('English Chronicle from 1066 to 1200') and *Libellus de motibus Anglicanis sub Joanne rege* ('A little book about English events under King John'). The former ends with a mandate from Pope Innocent III about the planned Crusade (as printed in Ralph of Coggeshall 1875: 113–17), thus stopping just before the first of Ralph's accounts of a 'wonder', the 'wild man' of Orford; the second resumes with events in 1213 (ibid.: 165).

4.   Oxford, Bodleian Libraries MSS. Top. gen. c. 1–4.

5.   Centerwall's discussion of the relationship between Wild Man and Green Man in sixteenth-century pageantry and imagery (1997) may be relevant, although scientific attempts in the seventeenth century to define 'satyrs' either as men

with tails or as a species of ape are perhaps equally significant (Wittkower 1987: 68–69).

6. In 1584 David Powel, author of *The Historie of Cambria*, listed Ralph of Coggeshall among authors whose manuscript works were then in the possession of John Stow, 'who deserueth commendation for getting together the ancient writers of the histories of this land' (Stow 1908: lxxxvii). This is confirmed by John Joscelyn (chaplain to Archbishop Matthew Parker) in a note he added (at some time after 1567) to an entry on Ralph of Coggeshall in a list of writers on English History: '*Habet Joannes Stowe*'—'John Stow has [it]' (Graham and Watson 1998: 88). Annotations in Stow's handwriting have been identified on a copy of Ralph's work now in the collection of the College of Arms (MS Arundel 11) (Roberts and Watson 1990: 171, no DM84); this copy was at one time owned by Dr John Dee.

7. Lawton (1931: 39) confessed himself unable to identify these authors, and surmised that they or their works might be fictitious. However, the first is presumably Iñigo López de Mendoza, Marquis de Mondéjar, governor of Granada, who led an army against Moorish rebels in Granada in 1569 and wrote an account of the campaign justifying his actions to King Philip I (printed by Alfred Morel-Fatio (1878: 1–56)), but did *not* it seems write a 'description of *Nueva Granata*' as cited by Godwin (Clark 2007: 168 note 2). Joseph Desia de Carana, author, according to Godwin, of a history of Mexico, I have not identified. Poole (in Godwin 2009: 114 note 2) concludes that both works are fictitious.

8. 'The Naturall Historie of Wiltshire, 1685' Volume 1, the rough draft by John Aubrey, in two volumes, now in the Bodleian Library (Bodleian MS Aubrey 1 and 2). For Aubrey's text quoted here, see the digitized manuscript at <https://digital.bodleian.ox.ac.uk/objects/341b7478-3028-4d06-a142-47fceef91b81/surfaces/ce764bf0-6b9c-44c4-a30a-a0ef35217591/> [accessed 12 July 2022].

9. A notice once displayed (summer 2001) in Woolpit village and a booklet sold locally (Cockayne n.d., 3) may be read to imply that Robert Reyce had incorporated William of Newburgh's account in his *Breviary of Suffolk* in 1618. In fact, the text appears only in Lord Francis Hervey's discursive notes added to his 1902 edition of Reyce's previously unpublished work (Reyce 1902: 267–69)—Reyce himself had done no more than include Woolpit in a transcript of a list of Suffolk manors dating from 1315 (ibid.: 119).

10. The Hon. Algernon Herbert (1792–1855), fourth son of the Earl of Carnarvon, was an antiquary and lawyer, and author of 'a variety of publications which were abstruse and often inconclusive' (Boase 2004). They were also unorthodox. In a later work *Cyclops Christianus: Or, An Argument to Disprove the Supposed Antiquity of the Stonehenge and Other Megalithic Erections in England and Britanny* [sic] (Herbert 1849) he concluded that Stonehenge was erected in the fifth century CE.

11. Herbert took the phrase '*virides Britanni*' from verse by the Roman poet Ovid (*Amores* 2.16, l. 39). Herbert assures us that woad can be used to produce a *green*

dye as well as the normal blue colour (which seems not to be true), and that the Britons who dyed themselves green were of higher status than those who wore blue ([Herbert] 1836–1841: 1:lvi). However, as we shall see later, and confusingly, the Latin adjective *'viridis'* originally had a range of meanings that could embrace the colour blue.

12. Picard's text was presumably derived from the manuscript of Ralph's *Chronicon* then in the abbey of Saint-Victor, Paris (where Picard was himself a canon, as his title page tells us). This manuscript is now in the Bibliothèque nationale in Paris (BnF Ms. lat. 15076; Delisle 1869: 70). It was also the source of Martène and Durand's printed partial edition of 1724–1733, and is an early copy of the manuscript in the British Library (Gransden 1974: 323). The Woolpit story is on ff. 29v–30r of this manuscript, and *does* include the green girl's claim that the children had thought the food they were offered was 'inedible'. See <https://gallica.bnf.fr/ark:/12148/btv1b9066689n/f32.item> [accessed 10 June 2023]. Thus it was indeed Picard who first omitted the phrase!

13. Watton and Wayland Wood are about 14½ miles (23.3 km) north-east of Thetford.

14. I am grateful to the Rev. Ruth Farrell, Rector of Woolpit and Drinkstone, for identifying her predecessor.

15. Quoted in part on the website *Hidden East Anglia* <http://www.hiddenea.com/norfolks.htm> [accessed 31 August 2016]. The writer was presumably Michael Sidney Tyler-Whittle, later notable as author of biographies of Queen Victoria and Richard III, books on ancient Greece and on early botanists, and a children's guide to Norwich Cathedral.

16. <http://woolpit-festival.com/events/the-green-children/> [accessed 15 October 2023]. School plays or activities based on the Green Children seem to be frequent events in the area.

17. Haslam (2002) comments: 'Despite the obvious fact the story was a re-write, many authors picked up Macklin's story and repeated the account, often changing details further ... the name of the children's saviour, Ricardo da Calno, is not repeated in any of the further re-tellings of the story, for example. This means that at least one of the authors repeating the Banjos story realized it was a fake, but chose to disguise this fact by removing a detail that would be a dead giveaway.'

18. For discussion of these later uses of the story of the Green Children by writers of fiction, see also Clark (2006a), an earlier and shorter version of the present text.

19. See <https://www.imdb.com/title/tt0776149/> [accessed 29 June 2022].

20. Falkiner (2016: 788 note 52) suggests that this might have been Harold Wilkins's *Mysteries Solved and Unsolved* (Wilkins 1959—to which we shall return), which was reprinted in paperback in 1961.

21. Crozier also told Stow about Crossley-Holland's new book. Stow later wrote: 'I was somewhat put out by this, but got the book and liked it very much, and it doesn't really affect my plans or compete in the least' (Falkiner 2016: 502).

22. According to Falkiner, Stow sent a copy of the libretto to his friend, the poet Tom Shapcott (b. 1935), which Shapcott kept among his papers.

23. As ever, I am grateful to James Plumtree for alerting me to this publication.

24. As we shall see, the naming of the green girl 'Agnes' is significant.

25. The epigraph beginning 'The sun does not rise upon our countrymen' is taken from Joseph Stevenson's 1861 translation of William of Newburgh. Writing about the significance of the epigraph and analysing the poem in 2002, N.H. Reeve (who is sparing with references) was apparently unaware of the source of the translation, and cites only the occurrence of the Latin text in the 1902 edition of Robert Reyce's *The Breviary of Suffolk* (Reeve 2002: 29–30).

26. Reprinted as 'Green Children' in her collection *How to Fracture a Fairy Tale* (2018: 272–73).

27. The CD *The Green Children & Other Poems* (Private Label MN+THB001CD) was issued in 2016.

28. I owe my knowledge of this book to Wikipedia.

29. Once again, readers of website pages on the Green Children, or of Duncan Lunan's book *Children from the Sky* (2012), will recognize the source of the name 'Agnes' shared by the village girl heroine and the green girl in J. Anderson Coats's story.

30. And see 'The Green Children as science fiction' below.

31. On the publication of the book and its reception by reviewers, see Falkiner (2016: 615–17). For Stow's 'medievalism' and his use of medieval sources, see Duckworth (2011) and Lynch (2011).

32. I am grateful to James Plumtree for advising me of this publication. I owe my knowledge of its content to a French translation—published before the Polish original (Tokarczuk 2016).

33. Carolyne Larrington had earlier included an account of the Green Children in her book on the mythology of the British Isles *The Land of the Green Man* (2015: 209–12).

34. My thanks to Sonia Overall for drawing my attention to Daisy Johnson's story and also to her own work cited next.

Chapter 4: Interpretations

1. The article is signed 'W.A.D.', but Francis Young is surely correct in identifying this as William A. Dutt (1870–1939), journalist and prolific author of guidebooks to Suffolk and Norfolk. As we have already noted, he had included an account of the Green Children in his 1904 guidebook to Suffolk (Dutt 1904: 307).

2.   The subtitle of the familiar motif index is *A Classification of Narrative Elements in Folktales, Ballads, Medieval Romances, Exempla, Fabliaux, Jest-Books and Local Legends*. It would seem justifiable to establish a 'narrative element' on the basis of a single occurrence in any one of these sources—it does not necessarily imply it is or was 'traditional', although that is perhaps how it is usually interpreted.

3.   Partner's 'if anything' is perhaps particularly galling to those of us who have an interest in 'what really happened'!

4.   Until, that is, the autumn of 2023, with the appearance of Paul Dutton's important but brief discussion of the Green Children (Dutton 2023: 11–53). This appeared too late for me to incorporate any comment on or response to Dutton's conclusions in this book.

5.   My own research note '"Agnes Barre": Green Child of Woolpit or historical fantasy?' was uploaded to my academia.edu account in 2018: <https://www.academia.edu/23411354/Agnes_Barre_Green_Child_of_Woolpit_or_historical_fantasy> [accessed 5 February 2023]. See also, in Chapter 6, 'Who was Agnes Barre?'

6.   This subtitle 'A Speculative Treatment of a Medieval Mystery—the Green Children of Woolpit' is on the title page. It appears as 'A Speculative Interpretation ...' on the cover. For more on Lunan's conclusions, see 'Who was Agnes Barre?' below. His scientifically detailed exploration of the possibility of the children's origin on another planet seems to have attracted little attention—his identification of the girl as 'Agnes Barre', however, seems to have met with general acceptance among contributors to pages on the internet, and authors of fictional retellings such as Martin Newell (2015), J. Anderson Coats (2019), Edward Carey (2019) and Don Nigro (2021), who all call the girl 'Agnes'.

7.   Art Evans, editor of *Science Fiction Studies*, drew this to my attention, and agreed that the overlap with my own work was not so great as to preclude publication of my paper.

8.   British readers of a certain age will also recall the 7-foot tall green-skinned Treens encountered by Dan Dare on Venus, and their evil mastermind the Mekon, himself surely an archetypal '*little* green man' with diminutive body and spindly limbs, and an oversized head housing an enlarged brain.

9.   Green fairies and the so-called Green Man are debatable entities to be considered further below in our section 'And were fairies green?'.

10.   Usually as 'a time of barbarism and backwardness' we gather (Kears and Paz 2016b, 23).

11.   In 1966, Randolph Stow, working on his proposed collaboration with Peter Maxwell Davies on a 'Green Children' opera, had perceptively described it as 'a sort of medieval science fiction story' (Falkiner 2016: 465).

12.   Davis (1983: 9) comments: 'when the words "fact" and "fiction" are used, they are not defining two distinct and unimpeachable categories. They are more properly extremes of a continuum.'

13. *The Life and Strange Surprizing Adventures of Robinson Crusoe, of York, Mariner ...*
14. For the text and this translation, see the Appendix.
15. The full title of the magazine in which Duncan Lunan first published his conclusions about the extraterrestrial origins of the Green Children is of course *Analog: Science Fiction, Science Fact* (Lunan 1996).

Chapter 5: The Chroniclers and the Texts

1. On William's sources and his methods, see also Staunton (2017: 82–94).
2. See now also Staunton (2017: 117–27). See Gransden (1974: 323–24) and Carpenter (1998: 1210–16) for fuller discussions of the sequence of composition.
3. The anonymous author tells us that he heard the story from Thurkill's own mouth—'*ab eius ore audivimus*' (Ralph of Coggeshall 1978: 4). Such a claim, indeed the very phrase, is a commonplace among Anglo-Norman chroniclers (Watkins 2001: 95)—Ralph of Coggeshall uses identical wording when describing how he heard from Gervase of Tilbury about strange events in which Gervase had been involved in France (to which we shall return) (Ralph of Coggeshall 1875: 122). Yet Ralph was certainly ideally placed in Coggeshall to hear a report straight from the mouth of Thurkill, from the neighbouring village of Stisted.
4. Le Goff (1984) considers the nature and the significance of these influences. He notes 'how learned culture tends to manipulate folklore, that is, the objects of popular culture. [...] provided one can actually discern the "popular" datum under its learned or half-learned disguise' (ibid.: 31)—a reminder, if one were needed, that Ralph of Coggeshall and William of Newburgh were not modern folklorists; they did not attempt to transcribe traditional oral narratives with scientific accuracy and truth to the original.
5. In her personification of 'troublesome intruders' Otter echoes, no doubt unwittingly, the opening of Charles Fort's first book, *The Book of the Damned*: 'A procession of the damned. By the damned, I mean the excluded. We shall have a procession of data that Science has excluded' (Fort 1974: 3).
6. In a similar vein, perhaps, in the nineteenth century the Rev. J.C. Atkinson concluded of one of his elderly Yorkshire parishioners who told him tales of local fairies, 'it was impossible to doubt for a moment her perfect good faith. She told all with the most utter simplicity, and the most evident conviction that what she was telling was matter of faith, and not at all the flimsy structure of fancy or fable' (Atkinson 1891: 57).
7. However, an anonymous reviewer comments: 'the idea that there was communication between Newburgh and Ixworth because they were both Augustinian houses is a bit thin. Most Augustinian houses were essentially independent; they were only an "order" in the sense that they followed the same rule, not in

the substantial sense that the Cistercians were an order centrally governed by a General Chapter.'

Chapter 6: The Framing Narrative

1. As he says: 'They are reported to have said these and many other things, too long to relate.'
2. Powicke (1906: 286) also identified a change in the handwriting in the manuscript of the Coggeshall text at this point. Gransden (1974: 323 n.22) disputed this, recognizing a change in the ink but not in the hand, and suggested that Ralph was writing his text sporadically.
3. I have not discovered who first identified Richard de Calne and his manor at Wykes. Suffolk writers Eric Rayner (1966: 341) and Norman Scarfe (1986: 166–67) take the identification for granted. Other commentators, perhaps less familiar with the area, have assumed that the landowner in question was a Sir Richard de *Colne*, of Wakes Colne in Essex, which indeed lies less than 5 miles (8 km) from Ralph's abbey at Coggeshall but a full 25 miles (40 km) from Woolpit (Oman 1944: 10; Gransden 1974: 331).
4. Perhaps the versions of the story that reached William of Newburgh, far away in Yorkshire, did not include this local detail. Or possibly, even, a mishearing or misreading of a phrase such as Ralph's *'apud uuikes'* ('in Wykes'), with its unfamiliar place-name, as a more familiar *'apud uicum'* ('in the village') may have led William to assume that Sir Richard's home was in Woolpit itself, and that it was to the village that the children were taken—as indeed he puts it, *'ducti sunt in vicum'*.
5. But see 'Who was Agnes Barre?'.
6. A landowner with property in both Suffolk and Essex, if travelling between his two holdings, might well have broken his journey at Coggeshall—providing opportunities for Ralph to hear the story of the Green Children.
7. Although we shall see evidence later that suggests that Richard's son Walter was already dead, leaving an orphan daughter, by 1185, before the death of his own father (Round 1913: 77; Walmsley 2006: 114–15). Within the widespread de Calne family the names Walter and Richard recur with confusing frequency, and perhaps the Walter of the 1187/88 Pipe Rolls was not Richard's son.
8. We may also note the remarkable case of Maud de Bidun, already married and then widowed by the age of ten in 1185, who eventually died in 1255 at the age of eighty, still in possession of her original dowry (Round 1913: xxxvi–vii)!
9. According to Bond (1995: 313), large-seeded *Vicia faba* beans were unknown before about 500 CE. It is not clear to me whether it is known when the large-seeded variety was first grown in England, or when the distinction between human and animal consumption arose. Certainly Bond and others point out that

smaller beans of the field bean type are widely eaten elsewhere in the world. Indeed 'a significant proportion of the [British] crop [of field beans] is exported to North Africa for human consumption' (Garden Organic 2022).

10. For example there were '*Rodberd filius Willelmi et Edricus et Ricardus filius Ernoldi*' and '*Osbertus filius Hurketel*'. The fathers (William, Ernold and Hurketel) of those recorded as '*filius*' ('son of') in the 1180s could well be of the generation that first discovered the Green Children, if our dating of the event is correct.

11. However, the authoritative *Gazetteer of Markets and Fairs in England and Wales* (Letters 2013) does *not* confirm this early date for a fair at Woolpit, citing a date of 1481–1482 as the earliest reference to it and commenting 'Woolpit may have developed relatively late as a commercial centre […] and there is no medieval reference to its market.'

12. The spring and the moat comprise a Scheduled Ancient Monument (SF201) (Suffolk Historic Environment Record 2023: WPT 002).

13. I am again indebted to an anonymous reviewer for this reference.

14. I am very grateful to Keith Briggs for discussion of the place-name and its significance, and for a sight of his draft of the full entry for Woolpit that will appear in the definitive English Place-Name Society volume on the place-names of Suffolk.

15. A wolf duly appears in silhouette on the Woolpit village sign (Fig. 5). There is, however, an alternative suggestion known locally that the village derived its name from that same Earl Ulfketel who had granted it to Bury St Edmunds Abbey in 1005 (Anon. 2022c). The local Woolpit website suggests that the name 'Ulfketel' can literally be translated 'wolf-pit'—this seems unlikely, the word 'ketel' normally meaning 'cauldron' or indeed 'kettle'. I am glad to have Suffolk place-name specialist Keith Briggs's advice that 'The Ulfketel etymology is absurd.'

16. Rackham (1986: 35) notes the existence of 'two-legged wolves, symbolic wolves and wolves spiritual'—citing for example the use of *Wulf* as an element in Anglo-Saxon personal names, and the designation of an outlaw as 'wolf's-head'.

17. The *Dictionary of Medieval Latin from British Sources* also suggests a meaning 'trap' in such cases as an eleventh-century reference to '*luporum fovea*'.

18. There is no reference to Woolpit in a modern account of the archaeology of Suffolk in Roman times (Moore et al. 1988), although a few scattered Roman finds are noted in the Suffolk Historic Environment Record (2023: search terms parish 'Woolpit' and time period 'Roman'). However, a recent archaeological investigation on the edge of Elmswell village just north-east of Woolpit (and close to the course of the 'Franchise Bank' discussed below) identified an enclosure of early Roman date and a probable Roman pottery kiln; the report also notes earlier scattered finds of Roman material from the area (Cotswold Archaeology 2016).

19. As I have noted above, Keightley's version was reprinted by Hartland (1890: 132–34) and Briggs (1971: 1:262), and more recently by Harris (1998: 82–33), and drawn on by writers such as Herbert Read and Kevin Crossley-Holland.

20. '[T]he three estates: those who normally fought spoke French, those who worked, English, and those who prayed, Latin' (Hogg and Denison 2006: 273).

21. These languages also have another word for English 'green' overlapping in significance with *glas*—Welsh *gwyrdd* and Irish *uaine* (Dineen 1927: 1283; Bevan et al. 1967–2002: 1782).

22. The term 'fairy', from French 'faierie', seems to begin to replace English 'elf' (from Old English 'ælf') in the early fourteenth century (Wade 2011: 4)—at least as an adjectival designation of origin 'from the land of the *fées*' (Green 2016: 4–5, 208 n.18).

23. And Jeremy Harte's forthcoming book *Fairy Encounters in Medieval England* must be added to the list of new contributions to this study (Harte 2024).

24. Gervase, like William of Newburgh, uses the term *daemones*, though he adds 'I not know whether I should call them *daemones*, or mysterious *effigies* [ghosts?] of unknown origin' (Gervase of Tilbury 2002: 675).

25. Little Malekin of Dagworth, as we shall see, had been stolen by an 'other' woman from her mother—whether she had been replaced by a substitute 'changeling', a term not recorded before the sixteenth century (Simpson and Roud 2000: 53–54; Hall 2007: 117–18; Hutton 2014: 1146; Green 2016: 111–12) is unknown. As Hutton points out (2014: 1136), some folklorists have tended to assume that elements recorded from oral tradition in later times may be of immeasurable antiquity. On medieval beliefs about changelings and child substitution now see Sawyer (2023).

26. Alaric Hall (2007: 88–95) concludes that elves were already seen as figures of unearthly female beauty in the late Anglo-Saxon period.

27. The fairies' colour green, and in particular 'even their flesh', is something we question.

28. I shall adopt the more generally recognized term 'fairy/fairies' for the rest of this book!

29. Harms (2018: 194) also draws attention to a reference in William Camden's *Britannia* (1586) to an Irish cunning-woman who used charms against illness caused by 'wood-fayries, white redde, blacke, & c.'.

30. On the tendency of early modern fairies to come in 'sets' of up to four colours, see Clark (2022).

31. They later offered him a mysterious drink in a *green* horn, which he wisely refused to drink (Wade 2008: 18; Craster 1951: 102). Or was it merely a drinking vessel made of 'green-horn', defined by the *Oxford English Dictionary* as 'Horn which has been made translucent by a process of heating and impregnation with oils or fats, used as a material for manufacture'?

32. Thus at least in the familiar traditional ballad—the fuller 'romance' versions, although devoting much space to the lady's unearthly beauty, her jewellery and the extravagant equipment of her horse, say nothing of the colour of her dress (John Murray 1875: 2–5).

33. The Rev. J.C. Atkinson was informed by an old Yorkshire parishioner that she had often seen 'a little green man, with a queer sort of a cap on him' disappearing into a culvert near her cottage (Atkinson 1891: 52–53).

34. Many of these fairies are described as wearing clothing in natural shades of green and brown—appropriately since many of Johnson's informants seem to have envisaged them as nature spirits or elementals; others were dressed in brighter colours, such as red jackets or caps.

35. I am grateful to Simon Young for drawing this particular case to my attention. One should note that the date, the 1950s, was far too early for the witness to have been influenced by Kevin Crossley-Holland's first retelling for children of the story of the Green Children (1966).

36. See further Clark (2006b).

37. On the origin, ramifications, academic downfall but popular currency of 'Lady Raglan's construct', see now Hutton (2022: 159–92). He similarly identifies 'the modern Green Man' as 'a divinity-like being who has appeared in response to modern needs and within a post-Christian society' (ibid.: 192).

38. Here as elsewhere Godwin is presumably inspired by William of Newburgh's account of the Green Children (Clark 2006a, 212–15).

39. No green fairies seen in Suffolk were reported to or by Marjorie Johnson (2014), and Simon Young (2018: 97–98) provides only three recent reports from Suffolk of fairy sightings—none of them of green fairies (nor admittedly any of Hollingsworth's 'Stowmarket' type).

40. *Lanaham* seems to be an unusual form of this place-name, though the similar *Laneham* is recorded (Copinger 1904: 4:17).

41. See Thompson (1955–1958) Motif F379.3: 'Man lives with fairies seven years'. Seven years was of course the length of time that Thomas of Erceldoune was required to spend in the Otherworld, according to the traditional ballad (John Murray 1875: liv, l. 27; lv, ll. 91–92), although manuscripts of the longer romance version specify variously 'three year and more' or 'seven year and more' (ibid.: 16, l. 286).

42. Westwood and Simpson (2005: 691) comment 'She may have been obliged to do so because of the old belief that perpetual captivity in the Otherworld arose from accepting its food'—cf. Stith Thompson (1955–1958) Motif C211: 'Tabu on eating in other world' and Motif C661: 'Girl from elfland must eat earthly food in order to remain [among mortals]'.

43. Compare Thompson's Motif F352, and migratory legend ML6045 in Christiansen (1958: 168–77).

44. Thomas Wright (1861: 1:35) reports that a 'debased version' of William of Newburgh's story was still current among the local 'peasantry' in his own time.

45. For more on Ketellus see Clark (2024). Ketellus shared this gift of second sight with a contemporary Welshman Meilyr, who saw 'unclean spirits' ('*spirites immundi*') and *incubi* in the form of huntsmen with hunting horns, who hunted the souls of men, but also aided him to foresee the future and to identify liars (Gerald of Wales 1868: 57–61; 1978: 116–21).

46. However, the root meaning 'to immerse something in liquid' gave rise to a specific usage in the medieval Church: 'to baptize' (Niermeyer 1976: 1341; *Dictionary of Medieval Latin from British Sources* 2018: s.v.).

47. And thus, as Lunan points out, the children would refuse any food they perceived as being the 'wrong' colour, until by chance seeing the fresh green bean-plants that were brought in <13–15>.

48. I am grateful to a member of the audience at one of my talks who directed my attention to William Morris.

49. I am most grateful to Frances Pritchard for advice on this issue, and to Debbie Bamford and John Stoker of The Mulberry Dyer (Rochdale, Greater Manchester) for discussion of this process and for their demonstration of woad dyeing—and for a hank of wool thread dyed with woad and weld to a good '*prassinus*' green colour!

50. The theory seems already to have been in circulation in 1966, when a resident of Woolpit told author Randolph Stow, later to incorporate the Green Children in his novel *The Girl Green as Elderflower* (1980), that a local doctor had suggested the children 'were suffering from a kind of anaemia that caused their skin to seem green' (Richards 2014: 7; Falkiner 2016: 472).

51. In a report to the British Medieval Association Scientific Grants Committee in 1897, pathologist Ernest Lloyd Jones presented the results of his analyses of the blood of those suffering from what he categorized as 'the special anæmia of young women' (Jones 1897). He noted the success of treatment with iron: 'iron has long been recognized as a specific for chlorosis' (ibid.: 63–67).

52. For contemporary medical views on the effects of tightly laced corsets in cases of chlorosis, see Taylor et al. (1896: 720–21). Dixon (1995) discusses 'chlorosis' within a wider range of 'women's diseases' with similar symptoms, to which earlier medical practitioners had applied such terms as '*furor uterinus*', 'suffocation of the womb' and 'hysteria' (in its original sense of a disease related to the womb).

53. Although Varandal writes of 'the disease of virgins, which we, from Hippocrates, call Chlorosis', the word 'chlorosis' cannot be found in any work attributed to Hippocrates (H. King 2004: 43–45).

54. Yet a reader's letter published in *Fortean Times*, prompted by an earlier reference to chlorosis, has provided a modern first-hand account of a young woman in Germany who, normally very pale, turned 'a pale, mottled, but not entirely

unattractive green' on two occasions in the course of a morning's English lesson (Cribben 2001). No explanation is offered.

55. One wonders how far the apparent colour might be affected by the underlying natural complexion of the patient—Perdahl-Wallace and Schwartz's patient was, they tell us, of mixed Mediterranean and Filipino descent (2006: 187). And Dr Frederick Taylor noted that some believed the green tint 'is only recognisable in those of dark complexion' (Taylor et al. 1896: 720).

56. I am grateful to Jelena Bekvalac of the Museum of London's Centre for Human Bioarchaeology for advice on this topic. A table published by Roberts and Cox (2003: 234–35, table 5.4) comprises results of the study of over 5,000 skeletons from thirty-three sites, covering the period 1050–1500, and indicates an average of 11 per cent (rising to over 50 per cent on one site) showing *cribra orbitalia* (porous lesions on the upper part of the eye sockets), the result of iron-deficiency anaemia in early childhood.

57. I note (November 2023) that Dutton (2023: 45–49) has independently considered the 'favism' option to explain the children's coloration, and argues strongly in favour of it.

58. Beans or bean flour were also a major constituent of baked 'horse-bread', a staple of the diet of medieval horses, apparently also eaten by the poor in time of need (Rubel 2006).

59. In Kevin Crossley-Holland's 1994 version of the story, told in the words of the green girl, she explains: 'And the beans … They were strange. There was nothing in the stalks but froth [...] Who has ever heard of beans inside a pod!' (Crossley-Holland and Marks 1994: n.p.).

60. For more on this and other possible reasons for the Pythagorean ban on beans, see Gainsford (2016).

61. A seventeenth-century report from the Greek island of Amorgos of five or six *vrykolakes* (vampire-like animated corpses) seen eating beans in a bean-field (Lawson 1910: 368) is hardly evidence for widespread belief that the dead ate beans.

62. Citing Bond (1995: 314), who notes that Homer described beans as black seeded.

63. I am grateful to Roy Vickery for drawing my attention to Simoons's work, and to Caroline Oates for directing me to the next book referred to, that by Per Binde.

64. Binde (1998: 191) says: 'The symbolic association between beggars and the dead has been documented in Europe since antiquity', citing Oexle (1983: 52f).

65. Gerald presented a copy of his *Gemma Ecclesiastica* to Pope Innocent in Rome, where he had gone seeking consecration as bishop of St David's, so he must have considered his advice on the efficacy of baptism by lay persons to be wholly orthodox and not something that would harm his claim to high ecclesiastical office (Gerald of Wales 1979: xv–xvi).

66. A number of different forms in Latin of the name of Lynn (such as *Lena*, *Linna* or *Lynna*) appear in written sources from Domesday Book onwards (Ekwall 1960:

310). The specific form employed by William of Newburgh here, *Lenna* (although he uses the spelling *Linna* elsewhere), is found in other twelfth-century texts (Hunter 1844b: 44 and 50; Pipe Roll Society 1884b: 5).

67. As a corollary to his view of the 'extraterrestrial' origins of the children, Lunan takes this to be 'the 12th century view of a woman from a more sophisticated culture, someone we'd describe as liberated' (Lunan 2012: 388).

68. I am most grateful to Samuel Gillis Hogan for drawing attention to this possibility ('an attempt to connect her to the depiction of fairies/sylvaticae as sexual temptresses') during discussion following my lecture on the Green Children to the Folklore Society in April 2022. It is an aspect of Ralph's account I had not considered in this context previously.

69. For example, a website called 'Ancient Code', devoted to 'ancient mysteries', includes an article 'Do descendants of the mysterious Green Children of Woolpit exist today?'. It tells us that 'Agnes was baptized and lived and worked for Sir Richard and later was married to the archdeacon of Ely, Richard Barre. The couple had at least one child, thus her descendants may exist today.' See <https://www.ancient-code.com/do-descendants-of-the-mysterious-green-children-of-woolpit-exist-today/> [accessed 1 September 2021].

70. Most websites that repeat the identification of the Green Girl as 'Agnes' and her marriage to Richard Barre do *not* mention Lunan's 'extraterrestrial' theories.

71. For the life and career of Richard Barre (*c*.1130–*c*.1202) (but no mention of a marriage or of a wife called Agnes), see Rigg (2004).

72. At the time Lunan was writing, this was Robert Washington Shirley, 13th Earl Ferrers (1929–2012) (Lunan 2012: 277–79). On his death in 2012 his son Robert William Saswalo Shirley (b. 1952), succeeded to the title of Earl Ferrers but not to the seat in the House of Lords.

73. In assigning 'Ricardus clericus' to *Stafford*, Lunan seems to have misread the medieval scribe's abbreviation for 'Stratford' (Hunter 1835: 216)—that is, Water Stratford in Buckinghamshire (Page 1927: 260, where this same reference in Hunter is cited).

74. I am grateful to Duncan Lunan for providing the detailed reference for this case, which was inadvertently omitted in his book.

75. At the foot of the record is the annotation 'Bedeford' (that is, the county of Bedford), and neither editor had any hesitation in including it among their records from Bedfordshire.

76. The relationship between the Red and Black Books is beyond my competence to comment on. Historian J.H. Round severely criticized Hall's edition of the Red Book of the Exchequer (Round [1898]: 17–66). I do not believe that this affects the interpretation of this record.

77. Baughman's only exemplum of this motif (1966: 214) comes from the Rev. J.C. Atkinson's *Forty Years in a Moorland Parish* (1891: 53–54). Atkinson's informant had known a lass who was raking in the hayfield and had raked over a 'fairy

bairn'—'liggin' in a swathe of the half made hay' (another of those perilous harvest fields for human and fairy children!). However, 'it did not stay lang wi' t' lass at fun' (found) it. It a sort o' dwinied away, and she aimed (supposed) the fairy-mother couldn't deea wivout it any langer.' So, strangely, and unlike the green boy, the child both pined away *and* returned to its mother.

78. It was presumably the influence of stories such as 'Skillywidden' (Briggs 1971: 1:355–56) embodying Motif F329.4.3 'Fairy captured by mortal escapes' that led Rose (1996: 131) to write of the Green Children that 'In one version of the story, their parents found them and took them away.' The only versions of the story that I am aware of in which either of the Green Children returns home are Herbert Read's 'romance' *The Green Child* (1935) and Adrian Mitchell's retelling (1996), in which the green girl eventually finds her way through the caves and across the dividing river to the land she left as a child—to which one may now add J. Anderson Coats's retelling (2019) in which the relationship between the inhabitants of our world and 'Those Good People' of the Otherworld is a continuing one.

79. There is no indication whether the 'other woman' who took Malekin away left a sickly 'changeling' child in her place.

80. I am grateful to Simon Young for drawing this case to my attention.

81. However, several contributors to a discussion on an online 'British folklore' group have pointed out that the dangers and the anxieties of harvest time were practical ones. Mothers joining their neighbours in the vital and hard work of bringing the harvest in had either to leave the baby at home or to take it with them and, like Malekin's mother, anxiously leave it unattended at the side of the field.

82. And see the same author's contribution on 'Harvest festivals and rituals' in Lindahl et al. (2000: 466): 'Is this an embroidered account of the discovery of actual feral children, or is it a garbled account of an archaic harvest ritual translated into legend form? It could be either, but it may well be that the Corn Spirit […] is peeking through as a palimpsest in the records of elite culture.'

Chapter 7: The Children's Story

1. However, I do not believe we need to go as far as Lunan (1996: 48–49; 2012: 132–39) in envisaging a formal trial or investigation by the church authorities.

2. William of Newburgh specifies 'when they had the use of *our* language (*nostrae usum loquelae*)'—and William had, in the very first sentence of his *Historia*, identified himself as English when he wrote of '*our* race, that is, the English (*gentis nostrae, id est Anglorum*)' (William of Newburgh 1988: 28–29). William regarded himself as English (rather than as one of the French-speaking Norman rulers), and we may assume it was English rather than the Anglo-Norman French

of Richard de Calne or the Latin of the Church that the children learnt and in which they responded to questions.

3. This is an early example of the folkloric concept of 'proto-ostension': 'Proto-ostension occurs when, to gain attention, persons take a story alleged to have happened to someone else and claim it as a personal experience of their own' (Ellis 2000: 163; and see Dégh and Vázsonyi 1983: 19–20).

4. Ladurie and Zysberg (1983: 1308–09), although citing different numbers, confirm the preponderance of 'Saint-Martin' among the names of French communes.

5. Victorian economic historian William Cunningham put forward the theory that Flemings who had settled in England in the twelfth century initiated a new cloth-making industry and that the weavers' gilds established in several towns were associations of Flemish craftsmen. He further suggested that Flemings who had arrived as mercenary troops 'were able and willing to take up the trade of weaving' (Cunningham 1922: 648–55). His views do not seem to have gained general acceptance: 'the argument is unfortunately replete with assumptions that do not hold up in the light of modern scholarship' (Oksanen 2012: 208–09).

6. For the significance of the battle in the context of the Earl of Leicester's East Anglian campaign, and the fate of the Flemish mercenaries, see Matthew Strickland (2016: 173–78).

7. For a recent account of this battle and its outcome, and the treatment of the defeated Flemings, see Hosler (2017: especially 44–58).

8. Discussed also in Clark (2006b).

9. Thurkill's vision, like that of the monk of Wenlock, includes a perilous bridge across which the souls of the dead must struggle to pass, but we are given no description of the river or valley that it spans (Ralph of Coggeshall 1978: 12, 16; Ward 1875: 432–33).

10. I am grateful to an anonymous reviewer for pointing out the implications of the geology and the presence of chalk caverns under Bury St Edmunds.

11. In the context, one trusts that the land 'al grene' is merely verdant, rather than that all things there were coloured green, as we are told of the Green Children's home <R32>!

12. Although Gervase's identification of the land with that of the Antipodes appears explicitly only in the chapter heading 'De Antipodibus et eorum terra' ('Concerning the Antipodes and their land'), the words are Gervase's own, not a later interpolation or editorial gloss. The heading appears in the earliest extant manuscript, thought to be in Gervase's own hand (Caldwell 1957; 1962: 31; Gervase of Tilbury 2002: lxxix–lxxxii).

13. 'Hanc inhabitare phylosophi antipodes autumant; quos a nobis diversitate temporum diversos asserunt. Nam cum aestate torremur, illi frigore congelantur.' On a mappa mundi illustrating Lambert of Saint-Omer's Liber Floridus (Fig. 20).

14. Loomis (1941: 294–95) and Gautier Dalché (1989: 105) also note that Gerald of Wales (1868: 76), in his tale of young Elidurus's Otherworld adventures, refers to our own world as both '*nostrum hemisphaerium*' ('our hemisphere') and '*superius hemisphaerium*' ('the upper hemisphere'). Gautier Dalché (1989: 113–14) concludes that Gerald, like Gervase, although less confidently and explicitly, was prepared to identify a mysterious country reached through subterranean passages as the geographers' land of the Antipodes.

15. 'Queer character at Woodbridge', *East Anglian Daily Times*, Ipswich, 13 January 1905: 2. Fort's text of the report from Scotland Yard (1974: 691) differs slightly—but not significantly—from that in the original newspaper account.

Chapter 8: Excursions

1. And I have suggested previously that William may have confused a reference to 'uuikes' (Wykes) with the word '*uicus*' (village) and may have assumed the house the children were taken to was in Woolpit village.

2. Charles Fort would certainly have approved of twelfth-century writers' reliance on testimony rather than on laws of probability!

Chapter 9: Strangers in a Strange Land

1. On the powerful effects of 'narrative causality', see Terry Pratchett (especially Pratchett 1991 *passim*).

Appendix: The Sources

1. Harris reprinted Keightley's translation of Ralph of Coggeshall's text. The translation of William of Newburgh's text that he used had previously been published in the *Bulletin* of the Ipswich Geological Group (William of Newburgh 1976), where it was attributed to R. Wingfield of Pakenham.

2. I note (November 2023) that Paul Dutton's new discussion of the Green Children (Dutton 2023) also includes texts and translations.

3. Except where, as with *fovea* and *fossa*, or *thyrsus* and *stipes*, the different choice of words seems significant—as I have discussed earlier.

Bibliography

Adam of Bremen. 1846. 'Mag. Adami gesta hammenburgensis ecclesiae pontificum', ed. by J.M. Lappenberg, in *Monumenta Germaniae historica: Scriptorum* 7, ed. by G.H. Pertz (Hannover: Deutsches Institut für Erforschung des Mittelalters), 267–389

———. 1959. *History of the Archbishops of Hamburg-Bremen*, trans. by Francis J. Tschan. Records of Civilisation: Sources and Studies 53 (New York: Columbia University Press)

Anderson, Earl. 2003. *Folk-Taxonomies in Early English* (Madison, NJ: Fairleigh Dickinson University Press/London: Associated University Presses)

André, Jacques. 1949. *Étude sur les termes de couleur dans la langue latine* (Paris: Klincksieck)

Anon. 1566. *The Examination of John Walsh, before Maister Thomas Williams, Commissary to the Reuerend father in God William bishop of Excester, vpon certayne Interrogatories touchyng Wytchcrafte and Sorcerye ...* (London: John Awdely)

———. 2022a. 'Woolpit Museum'. *Welcome to Woolpit* <https://www.woolpit.org/information-2/museum/> [accessed 15 April 2022]

———. 2022b. 'Green Children'. *Welcome to Woolpit* <https://www.woolpit.org/information-2/green-children/> [accessed 15 April 2022]

———. 2022c. 'A short history'. *Welcome to Woolpit* <https://www.woolpit.org/information-2/a-short-history/> [accessed 15 April 2022]

ap Gwilym, Dafydd. 2001. *Dafydd ap Gwilym: His Poems*, trans. by Gwyn Thomas (Cardiff: University of Wales Press)

Arnold, Thomas (ed.). 1890. *Memorials of St Edmund's Abbey* (Rolls Series 96), Vol. 1 (London: Longman & Co.)

———. 1896. *Memorials of St Edmund's Abbey* (Rolls Series 96), Vol. 3 (London: Longman & Co.)

Atkinson, Rev. J.C. 1891. *Forty Years in a Moorland Parish: Reminiscences and Researches in Danby in Cleveland* (London: Macmillan and Co.)

Attwater, Donald. 1965. *The Penguin Dictionary of Saints* (Harmondsworth: Penguin)

Aybes, C., and D.W. Yalden. 1995. 'Place-name evidence for the former distribution and status of Wolves and Beavers in Britain', *Mammal Review*, 25: 201–27 https://doi.org/10.1111/j.1365-2907.1995.tb00444.x

Bailey, Mark. 1989. *A Marginal Economy? East Anglian Breckland in the Later Middle Ages*, Cambridge Studies in Medieval Life and Thought: Fourth Series (Cambridge: Cambridge University Press) https://doi.org/10.1017/CBO9780511896477

Baker, Alan. 2000. *The Encyclopaedia of Alien Encounters* (London: Virgin Publishing)

Baldwin, Patrice. 2009. *School Improvement through Drama: A Creative Whole School, Whole Class Approach* (London: Network Continuum)

Bane, Theresa. 2013. *Encyclopedia of Fairies in World Folklore and Mythology* (Jefferson, NC: McFarland & Company)

Barker, Robert. 1977. 'Sources of Herbert Read's *The Green Child*', *Notes and Queries* 222.5 (October): 455–57

——. 1980. 'Sources of Herbert Read's *The Green Child*—II', *Notes and Queries* 225.6 (December): 531–33 https://doi.org/10.1093/nq/27.6.531-c

Bartholomew, Mark. 2006a. *Whispers in the Woods*, illus. by Jan Evans (Blackburn: Eprint)

——. 2006b. *Chaos in the Cathedral*, illus. by Jan Evans (Blackburn: Eprint)

——. 2007. *Swords in the Summer*, illus. by Jan Evans (Blackburn: Eprint)

Bartlett, Robert. 1982. *Gerald of Wales 1146–1223* (Oxford: Clarendon Press)

——. 2000. *England under the Norman and Angevin Kings, 1075–1225* (Oxford: Oxford University Press)

Baughman, E.W. 1966. *Type and Motif-Index of the Folktales of England and North America* (The Hague: Mouton and Co.) https://doi.org/10.1515/9783111402772

Belsey, Mark A. 1973. 'The epidemiology of favism', *Bulletin of the World Health Organization*, 48: 1–13

Benson, Larry D. 1965. *Art and Tradition in* Sir Gawain and the Green Knight (New Brunswick, NJ: Rutgers University Press)

Berlitz, Charles. 1991. *Charles Berlitz's World of the Incredible but True* (New York: Fleming H. Revell Co.)

Bevan, Gareth A., P.J. Donovan and Avery Goldman (eds). 1967–2002. *Geiriadur Prifysgol Cymru. A Dictionary of the Welsh Language*, 4 vols (Caerdydd: Gwasg Prifysgol Cymru/University of Wales Press)

Beyer, Jürgen. 1999. 'On the transformation of apparition stories in Scandinavia and Germany, *c.*1350–1700', *Folklore*, 110: 39–47. https://doi.org/10.1080/0015587X.1999.9715979

Biddle, Anthony J. 2017. *Peas and Beans* (Wallingford: CABI). https://doi.org/10.1079/9781780640914.0000

Biggam, C.P. 1997. *Blue in Old English: An Interdisciplinary Semantic Study.* Costerus New Series, 110 (Amsterdam: Rodopi) https://doi.org/10.1163/9789004489486

Biggs, Tony. 1999. *Growing Vegetables.* Royal Horticultural Society Encyclopedia of Practical Gardening, new edn. (London: Mitchell Beazley)

Bignell, Shirley J. 2000. *Suffolk Tales 1: The Wild Man of Orford; The Green Children*, narrated by Peter Davison [audio CD with teachers' notes] (Debenham: Big Toe Audio)

Bildhauer, Bettina, and Robert Mills (eds). 2001a. *The Monstrous Middle Ages* (Cardiff: University of Wales Press)

——. 2001b. 'Introduction: conceptualizing the monstrous', in Bildhauer and Mills 2001a: 1–27

Binde, Per. 1999. *Bodies of Vital Matter: Notions of Life Force and Transcendence in Traditional Southern Italy*. Gothenberg Studies in Social Anthropology (Göteborg: Acta Universitatis Gothoburgensis)

Boase, G.C. 2004. 'Herbert, Algernon (1792–1855)', revised by Joanne Potier, in *Oxford Dictionary of National Biography* (Oxford: Oxford University Press), online edn, ed. by David Cannadine <https://www.oxforddnb.com/view/article/13016> [accessed 12 Oct 2016] https://doi.org/10.1093/ref:odnb/13016

Bond, D.A. 1995. 'Faba bean Vicia faba', in *Evolution of Crop Plants*, ed. by J. Smartt and N.W. Simmonds, 2nd edn (Harlow: Longman Scientific and Technical), 312–16

Bord, Janet. 1997. *Fairies: Real Encounters with the Little People* (London: Michael O'Mara Books)

Breeze, Andrew. 1995. 'Chaucer's "Malkin" and Dafydd ap Gwylim's "Mald y Cwd"', *Notes and Queries*, 240.2 (June): 159–60. https://doi.org/10.1093/notesj/42.2.159

Brewer, Derek. 1997. 'The colour green', in *A Companion to the Gawain Poet*, ed. by Derek Brewer and Jonathan Gibson (Cambridge: D.S. Brewer), 181–90

Briggs, Katharine M. 1959. *The Anatomy of Puck: An Examination of Fairy Beliefs among Shakespeare's Contemporaries and Successors* (London: Routledge and Kegan Paul)

———. 1962. *Pale Hecate's Team: An Examination of the Beliefs on Witchcraft and Magic among Shakespeare's Contemporaries and His Immediate Successors* (London: Routledge and Kegan Paul)

———. 1967. *The Fairies in English Tradition and Literature* (London: Routledge and Kegan Paul)

———. 1971. *A Dictionary of British Folk-Tales in the English Language. Incorporating the F.J. Norton Collection. Part B Folk Legends*, 2 vols (London: Routledge and Kegan Paul)

———. 1976. *A Dictionary of Fairies, Hobgoblins, Brownies, Bogies and Other Supernatural Creatures* (London: Allen Lane)

Briggs, Keith, and Kelly Kilpatrick. 2016. *A Dictionary of Suffolk Place-Names*. English Place-Name Society, Popular Series 6 (Nottingham: English Place-Name Society)

Brockmeier, Kevin. 2003. *The Truth about Celia: A Novel* (New York: Pantheon Books)

Brodu, Jean-Louis. 1995. 'Magonia: a re-evaluation', in *Fortean Studies*, Vol. 2, ed. by Steve Moore (London: John Brown Publishing), 198–215

Bromwich, Rachel. 2006. *Trioedd Ynys Prydein: The Welsh Triads of the Island of Britain*, 3rd edn. (Cardiff: University of Wales Press)

Brown, Arthur C.L. 1947. *The Origin of the Grail Legend* (Cambridge, MA: Harvard University Press)

Bruce, Scott G. 2019. '"Sunt altera nobis sidera, sunt omnes orbes alii": imagining subterranean peoples and places in medieval Latin literature', *Mediaevistik*, 32: 105–118 https://doi.org/10.3726/med.2019.01.04

Brumbaugh, Robert, and Jessica Schwartz. 1980. 'Pythagoreans and beans: a medical explanation', *Classical World*, 73: 421–22 https://doi.org/10.2307/4349235

Burton, Marianne. 2013. *She Inserts the Key* (Bridgend: Seren)

Burton, Robert. 1989. *The Anatomy of Melancholy*, Vol. 1, ed. by Thomas C. Faulkner, Nicolas K. Kiessling and Rhonda L. Blair (Oxford: Clarendon Press) https://doi.org/10.1093/actrade/9780198124481.book.1

———. 1990. *The Anatomy of Melancholy*, Vol. 2, ed. by Nicolas K. Kiessling, Thomas C. Faulkner and Rhonda L. Blair (Oxford: Clarendon Press) https://doi.org/10.1093/actrade/9780198123309.book.1

Bury Free Press. 1941. 'Death of the Rev. G.F.H. Page: Rector of Woolpit since 1914', *Bury Free Press* 8973 (17 May): 5

———. 1956. 'Woolpit legend on stage'. *Bury Free Press* 9654 (5 October): 7

Caldwell, James R. 1957. 'The autograph manuscript of Gervase of Tilbury (Vatican, Vat. Lat. 933)', *Scriptorium*, 11: 87–98 https://doi.org/10.3406/scrip.1957.2923

———. 1962. 'Manuscripts of Gervase of Tilbury's *Otia Imperialia*', *Scriptorium*, 16: 28–45 https://doi.org/10.3406/scrip.1962.3110

Cam, Helen M. 1944. 'The King's government as administered by the greater abbots of East Anglia', in *Liberties & Communities in Medieval England: Collected Studies in Local Administration and Topography* (Cambridge: Cambridge University Press), 183–205

Camden, William. 1586. *Britannia. Siue florentissimorum regnorum, Angliae, Scotiae, Hiberniae, et Insularum adiacentium ex Intima antiquitate Chorographica descriptio* (London: Ralph Newbery)

———. 1610. *Britain, or a Chorographicall Description of the Most Flourishing Kingdomes, England, Scotland, and Ireland, and the Islands Adjoyning, Out of the Depth of Antiquitie*, trans. by Philemon Holland (London: George Bishop and John Norton)

———. 1722. *Britannia. Or a Chorographical Description of Great Britain and Ireland, Together with the Adjacent Islands ... Translated into English, with Additions and Improvements*, 2nd edn. rev. by Edmund Gibson. 2 vols (London: Awnsham Churchill)

Cameron, Alan. 1976. *Circus Factions: Blues and Greens at Rome and Byzantium* (Oxford: Oxford University Press)

Camille, Michael. 1992. *Image on the Edge: The Margins of Medieval Art* (London: Reaktion)

Campbell, Mary Baine. 1999. *Wonder & Science: Imagining Worlds in Early Modern Europe* (Ithaca, NY: Cornell University Press)

———. 2016. '"Those two green children which Nubrigensis speaks of in his time, that fell from heaven", or the origins of science fiction', in Kears and Paz 2016a: 117–32

Camporesi, Piero. 1993. *The Magic Harvest: Food, Folklore and Society* (Cambridge: Polity Press)

Cardon, Dominique. 2007. *Natural Dyes: Sources, Tradition, Technology and Science* (London: Archetype)

Carey, Edward. 2019. 'These our monsters', in *These Our Monsters: The English Heritage Book of New Folktale, Myth and Legend*, ed. by Katherine Davey (London: English Heritage), 31–42

Carey, John. 1989. 'Ireland and the Antipodes: the heterodoxy of Virgil of Salzburg', *Speculum*, 64.1: 1–10 https://doi.org/10.2307/2852184

Carozzi, Claude. 1994. *Le Voyage de l'âme dans l'au-delà d'après la literature latine (Ve–XIIIe siècle)*. Collection de l'École française de Rome, 189 (Rome: École française de Rome)

Carpenter, D.A. 1998. 'Abbot Ralph of Coggeshall's account of the last years of King Richard and the first years of King John', *English Historical Review*, 113, no 454 (November): 1210–30 https://doi.org/10.1093/ehr/113.454.1210

Carr, J.L. 1976. *The Green Children of the Woods* (London: Longman)

Carroll, Lewis. 1962. *The Annotated Snark*, ed. by Martin Gardner (Harmondsworth: Penguin)

Caufield, Catherine. 1981. *The Emperor of the United States of America and Other Magnificent British Eccentrics* (New York: St Martin's Press)

Cavendish, Margaret, Duchess of Newcastle. 1992. *The Description of a New World Called the Blazing World and Other Writings*, ed. by Kate Lilley (London: William Pickering)

Centerwall, Brandon S. 1997. 'The name of the Green Man', *Folklore*, 108: 25–33 https://doi.org/10.1080/0015587X.1997.9715933

C[harleston], R.J. 1959. '"The Luck of Edenhall": a notable acquisition for the nation'. *The Connoisseur*, 143, no 575 (February): 34–35

Christiansen, Reidar Thoralf. 1958. *The Migratory Legends: A Proposed List of Types with a Systematic Catalogue of the Norwegian Variants* (Helsinki: FF Communications 175)

Clark, Jerome. 1993. *Encyclopedia of Strange and Unexplained Physical Phenomena* (Detroit, Washington, DC, and London: Gale Research Inc.)

Clark, John. 1981. 'Trinovantum—the evolution of a legend', *Journal of Medieval History*, 7: 135–51 https://doi.org/10.1016/0304-4181(81)90024-5

——. 1999. 'The Green Children: a cautionary tale', in *Fortean Studies*, Vol. 6, ed. by Steve Moore (London: John Brown Publishing), 270–77

——. 2006a. '"Small, vulnerable ETs": the Green Children of Woolpit', *Science Fiction Studies*, 33.2 (July): 209–29

——. 2006b. 'Martin and the Green Children', *Folklore*, 117.2 (August): 207–14 https://doi.org/10.1080/00155870600707904

——. 2007. 'Bishop Godwin's *The Man in the Moone*: the other Martin', *Science Fiction Studies*, 34.1 (March): 164–69

——. 2018. *The Green Children of Woolpit* <https://www.academia.edu/10089626/The_Green_Children_of_Woolpit> [now withdrawn]

——. 2022. 'Colour-coded fairies?', *Fairy Investigation Society Newsletter*, n.s. 16 (June): 32–33

——. 2024. 'Ketil and the *daemones*: the Second Sight in medieval Yorkshire', *Fairy Investigation Society Newsletter*, n.s. 19 (January): 119–225

Clarke, Catherine A.M. 2009. 'Signs and wonders: writing trauma in twelfth-century England', *Reading Medieval Studies*, 35: 55–77

Clute, John, and John Grant (eds). 1997. *The Encyclopedia of Fantasy* (London: Orbit)

Clute, John, and Peter Nicholls (eds). 1993. *The Encyclopedia of Science Fiction* (London: Orbit)

Coats, J. Anderson. 2019. *The Green Children of Woolpit* (New York: Atheneum Books)

Cockayne, Elizabeth. n.d. *The Green Children of Woolpit* (Woolpit: [Woolpit Museum])

Cohen, Jeffrey Jerome. 2008. 'Green children from another world, or the archipelago in England', in *Cultural Diversity in the British Middle Ages: Archipelago, Island, England*, ed. by Jeffrey Jerome Cohen (New York: Palgrave Macmillan), 75–94 https://doi.org/10.1057/9780230614123_5

Colwell, Eileen. 1972. *Round About and Long Ago: Tales from the English Counties* (London: Longman Young Books)

Copinger, W.A. 1904. *County of Suffolk: Its History as Disclosed by Existing Records and Other Documents.* 5 vols (London: Henry Sotheran)

———. 1905–1911. *The Manors of Suffolk: Notes on their History and Devolution.* 7 vols (London: T. Fisher Unwin; Manchester: Taylor, Garrett, Evans)

Cotswold Archaeology. 2016. *Land adjoining Wetherden Road, Elmswell, Suffolk: Archaeological Evaluation.* CA Report 16497 (Andover, Cirencester, Exeter, Milton Keynes: Cotswold Archaeology) <http://reports.cotswoldarchaeology.co.uk/content/uploads/2017/01/660766-Land-Adjoining-Wetherden-Road-Elmswell-Suffolk-draft-evaluation-report-Final.pdf> [accessed 14 October 2023]

Council for Subject Associations. [2009?]. 'Drama. Resource 4: the Green Children of Woolpit'. *A Voice for Subjects.* <http://www.subjectassociation.org.uk/index.php?page=101> [accessed 22 June 2012]—no longer accessible (July 2019) but see <https://patricebaldwin.files.wordpress.com/2015/08/nd-1-the-green-children-v2.doc> and Baldwin 2009 above

Craster, Edmund. 1951. 'The miracles of Farne', *Archaeologia Aeliana* 4th ser., 29: 93–107

Cribben, Lise. 2001. 'Green girl'. *Fortean Times* 150 (September): 52

Crosby, William H. 1987. 'Whatever became of chlorosis?', *JAMA: Journal of the American Medical Association*, 257.20 (22 May): 2799–800 https://doi.org/10.1001/jama.257.20.2799

Cross, Tom Peete. 1952. *Motif-Index of Early Irish Literature* (Bloomington, IN: Indiana University Press; repr. New York: Kraus, 1969)

Crossley-Holland, Kevin. 1966. *The Green Children*, illus. by Margaret Gordon (London: Macmillan)

———. 1982. *The Dead Moon and Other Tales from East Anglia and the Fen Country*, illus. by Shirley Felts (London: André Deutsch)

———. 1997. *The Old Stories: Folk Tales from East Anglia and the Fen Country*, illus. by John Lawrence (Cambridge: Colt Books)

———. 2005. *Outsiders*, illus. by Christian Birmingham (London: Orion)

———. 2012. 'A visit from Kevin Crossley-Holland', *The History Girls* blog <http://the-history-girls.blogspot.com/2012/03/visit-from-kevin-crossley-holland.html> [accessed 5 October 2023]

———. 2018. *Between Worlds: Folktales of Britain & Ireland*, illus. by Frances Castle (London: Walker Books)

Crossley-Holland, Kevin, and Alan Marks. 1994. *The Green Children* (Oxford: Oxford University Press)

Crowley, John. 1981. 'The green child', in *Elsewhere*, ed. by Terri Windling and Mark Allen Arnold (New York: Ace Books), 1–5. [Repr. in John Crowley *Novelties and Souvenirs: Collected Short Fiction* (New York: Perennial, 2004), 32–7]

Cunningham, William. 1922. *The Growth of English Industry and Commerce During the Early and Middle Ages.* 5th edn. (Cambridge: Cambridge University Press)

Curta, Florin. 2004. 'Colour perception, dyestuffs, and colour terms in twelfth-century French literature', *Medium Ævum*, 73.1: 43–65 https://doi.org/10.2307/43630698

Dane, Clemence. 1938. *The Moon is Feminine* (London and Toronto: Heinemann)

Darby, H.C. (ed.). 1936. *An Historical Geography of England before A.D. 1800* (Cambridge: Cambridge University Press)

Datlow, Ellen, Kelly Link and Gavin Grant (eds). 2003. *Year's Best Fantasy & Horror. Sixteenth Annual Collection* (New York: St. Martin's Press)

Davies, Glyn. 2010. 'New light on the Luck of Edenhall', *Burlington Magazine* 152, no 1282 (January): 4–7

Davis, Lennard. 1983. *Factual Fiction: The Origins of the English Novel* (New York: Columbia University Press)

Davis, R.H.C. 1954. *The Kalendar of Abbot Samson of Bury St. Edmunds and Related Documents* (London: Camden Third Series 84) https://doi.org/10.1017/S204217100000203X

Defoe, Daniel. 1927. *The Life & Strange Surprizing Adventures of Robinson Crusoe ...* 3 vols. The Shakespeare Head Edition of the Novels and Selected Writings of Daniel Defoe (Oxford: Basil Blackwell)

Dégh, Linda, and Andrew Vázsonyi. 1983. 'Does the word "dog" bite? Ostensive action: a means of legend-telling', *Journal of Folklore Research*, 20.1 (May): 5–34

Delisle, Léopold. 1869. 'Inventaire des manuscrits latins de Saint-Victor conservés à la Bibliothèque impériale sous les numéros 14232–156175'. *Bibliothèque de l'École des Chartes*, 6th series, 5: 1–79 https://doi.org/10.3406/bec.1869.446252

Diceto, Ralph de. 1876. *Radulfi de Diceto decani Lundoniensis opera historica. The Historical Works of Master Ralph de Diceto, Dean of London* (Rolls Series 68), ed. by William Stubbs. 2 vols (London: Longman & Co.; Trübner & Co.)

Dictionary of Medieval Latin from British Sources. 2018. Ed. by R.K. Ashdowne, D.R. Howlett and R.E. Latham (Oxford: British Academy), online edn. <http://www.dmlbs.ox.ac.uk/web/online.html> [accessed 11 September 2023]

Dineen, Patrick S. (ed.). 1927. *Foclóir Gaedelige agus Béarla: An Irish-English Dictionary* (Dublin: Irish Texts Society/Educational Company of Ireland)

Dinzelbacher, Peter. 1986. 'The way to the other world in medieval literature and art', *Folklore*, 97.1: 70–87 https://doi.org/10.1080/0015587X.1986.9716368

Diss Express. 1957. 'Folk-lore is so fascinating says author of "Green Children"', *Diss Express* 4813 (8 March): 7

Dixon, Laurinda S. 1995. *Perilous Chastity: Women and Illness in Pre-Enlightenment Art and Medicine* (Ithaca, NY, and London: Cornell University Press) https://doi.org/10.7591/9781501735769

Dodwell, Barbara (ed.). 1958. *Feet of Fines for the County of Norfolk for the Reign of King John, 1201–1215; for the County of Suffolk for the Reign of King John, 1199–1214* (London: Publications of the Pipe Roll Society 70 (n.s. 32))

Douglas, D.C. 1932. *Feudal Documents from the Abbey of Bury St. Edmunds.* Records of the Social and Economic History of England and Wales 8 (London: British Academy/Oxford University Press)

Du Cange, Charles du Fresne, et al. 1886. *Glossarium mediae et infimae latinitatis*, Vol. 6 (Niort: L. Favre)

Duckworth, Melanie. 2011. 'Grievous music: Randolph Stow's Middle Ages', *Australian Literary Studies*, 26.3–4: 102–14 https://doi.org/10.20314/als.e8d9ec4f7b

Dunne, John S. 1999. *The Mystic Road of Love* (Notre Dame, IN: University of Notre Dame Press)

Dutt, William A. 1904. *Suffolk* (London: Methuen)

—— ['W.A.D.']. 1909. 'Suffolk Fairies', *East Anglian Daily Times* 12,787 (Thursday 18 November): 4

Dutton, Paul Edward. 2023. *Micro Middle Ages*. The New Middle Ages (Cham: Palgrave Macmillan)

Dymond, David and Edward Martin (eds). 1989. *An Historical Atlas of Suffolk*. 2nd edn (Ipswich: Suffolk County Council Planning Department)

Edinburgh Festival Fringe. 1996. *Edinburgh Festival Fringe Programme (11–31 August 1996)* (Edinburgh: Edinburgh Festival Fringe Society Ltd) <https://issuu.com/edinburgh_festival_fringe/docs/1996_fringe_programme> [accessed 5 May 2022]

Ekwall, Eilert. 1960. *The Concise Oxford Dictionary of English Place-Names*. 4th edn (Oxford: Clarendon Press)

Ellis, Bill. 2000. *Aliens, Ghosts, and Cults: Legends We Live* (Jackson, MS: University Press of Mississippi)

Falkiner, Suzanne. 2016. *Mick: A Life of Randolph Stow* (Crawley, Western Australia: University of Western Australia Publishing)

Fanthorpe, Lionel and Patricia. 1997. *The World's Greatest Unsolved Mysteries* (Toronto and London: Hounslow Press)

Fantosme, Jordan. 1981. *Jordan Fantosme's Chronicle*, ed. and trans. by R.C. Johnston (Oxford: Clarendon Press) https://doi.org/10.1093/actrade/9780198157588.book.1

Faral, Edmond. 1929. *La Légende arthurienne. Études et documents*. 3 vols. Bibliothèque de l'École des Hautes Études fascs 255–57 (Paris: Honoré Champion; repr. 1969)

Fisher, J.D.C. 1965. *Christian Initiation: Baptism in the Medieval West: A Study in the Disintegration of the Primitive Rite of Initiation*. Alcuin Club Collections, 47 (London: S.P.C.K.)

Fleming, J. Arnold. 1930. *Flemish Influence in Britain*. 2 vols (Glasgow: Jackson Wylie)

Fort, Charles. 1974. *The Complete Books of Charles Fort* (New York: Dover Publications)

Freeman, Elizabeth. 2000. 'Wonders, prodigies and marvels: unusual bodies and the fear of heresy in Ralph of Coggeshall's *Chronicon Anglicanum*', *Journal of Medieval History*, 26.2: 127–43 https://doi.org/10.1016/S0304-4181(99)00019-6

——. 2002. *Narratives of a New Order. Cistercian Historical Writing in England, 1150–1220*. Medieval Church Studies 2 (Turnhout: Brepols) https://doi.org/10.1484/M.MCS-EB.5.112712

Gage, John. 1999. *Colour and Meaning. Art, Science and Symbolism* (London: Thames & Hudson)

Gainsford, Peter. 2016. 'Pythagoras and the beans #2: why ban beans?'. *Kiwi Hellenist* <http://kiwihellenist.blogspot.com/2016/12/pythagoras-and-beans-2-why-ban-beans.html> [accessed 15 April 2022]

Gane, A.J., J.M. King and G.P. Gent. 1975. *Pea & Bean Growing Handbook, Vol. 2: Beans* (Peterborough: Processors and Growers Research Organisation)

Garden Organic. 2022. 'Growing field beans for human consumption'. Garden Organic (Henry Doubleday Research Association) <https://www.gardenorganic.org.uk/growing-field-beans-human-consumption> [accessed 3 May 2022]

Gardner, Martin. 1957. *Fads and Fallacies in the Name of Science*, revised edn (New York: Dover Publications)

Gautier Dalché, Patrick. 1989. 'Entre le folklore et la science: la légende des antipodes chez Giraud de Cambrie et Gervais de Tilbury', in *La Leyenda. Antropología, Historia, Literatura. Actas del coloquio celebrado en la Casa de Velásquez* (Madrid: Casa de Velásquez) 103–14; repr. in Gautier Dalché, Patrick. *Géographie et Culture: La représentation de l'espace du VIe au XIIe siècle*, Essay XI, with original pagination (Aldershot: Ashgate, 1997)

Gay, Nicola (ed.). 2016. *The Anthology of English Folk Tales* (Stroud: History Press)

Gennep, Arnold van. 1960. *The Rites of Passage*, trans. by Monika B. Vizedomand and Gabrielle L. Caffee (London: Routledge & Kegan Paul)

Geoffrey of Monmouth. 1973. *Life of Merlin: Vita Merlini*, ed. and trans. by Basil Clarke (Cardiff: University of Wales Press)

———. 2007. *The History of the Kings of Britain. An Edition and Translation of* De gestis Britonum [Historia Regum Britanniae], ed. by Michael D. Reeve, trans. by Neil Wright. Arthurian Studies 69 (Woodbridge: Boydell Press) https://doi.org/10.1017/9781846155567

Gerald of Wales. 1867. *Giraldi Cambrensis Opera. Vol. V. Topographia Hibernica et Expugnatio Hibernica* (Rolls Series 21), ed. by James F. Dimock (London: Longmans, Green, Reader and Dyer)

———. 1868. *Giraldi Cambrensis Opera. Vol. VI. Itinerarium Kambriae et Descriptio Kambriae* (Rolls Series 21), ed. by James F. Dimock (London: Longman & Co.)

———. 1978. *The Journey through Wales and The Description of Wales*, trans. by Lewis Thorpe (Harmondsworth: Penguin)

———. 1979. *The Jewel of the Church: A Translation of* Gemma Ecclesiastica *by Giraldus Cambrensis*, trans. by John J. Hagen. Davis Medieval Texts and Studies 2 (Leiden: E.J. Brill) https://doi.org/10.1163/9789004625761

Gervase of Tilbury. 2002. *Otia Imperialia. Recreation for an Emperor*, ed. and trans. by S.E. Banks and J.W. Binns (Oxford: Oxford University Press) https://doi.org/10.1093/actrade/9780198202882.book.1

Gervers, Michael (ed.). 1982. *The Cartulary of the Knights of St John of Jerusalem in England: Secunda Camera Essex*. Records of Social and Economic History n.s. 6 (Oxford: British Academy/Oxford University Press)

Gibson, Marion. 2000. *Early Modern Witches: Witchcraft Cases in Contemporary Writing* (London/New York: Routledge)

[Godwin, Francis]. 1638. *The Man in the Moone: or a Discovrse of a Voyage Thither, by Domingo Gonsales* (London: John Norton)

———. 2009. *The Man in the Moone*, ed. by William Poole (Peterborough, Ontario: Broadview)

Gomme, George Laurence (ed.). 1885. *The Gentleman's Magazine Library: English Traditional Lore: To Which is Added Customs of Foreign Countries and Peoples* (London: Elliot Stock)

Graham, Timothy, and Andrew G. Watson. 1998. *The Recovery of the Past in Early Elizabethan England: Documents by John Bale and John Joscelyn from the Circle of Matthew Parker.* Cambridge Bibliographical Society Monograph 13 (Cambridge: Cambridge University Library)

Gransden, Antonia. 1974. *Historical Writing in England c.550–c.1307* (London: Routledge and Kegan Paul)

Green, Richard Firth. 2016. *Elf Queens and Holy Friars: Fairy Beliefs and the Medieval Church* (Philadelphia, PA: University of Pennsylvania Press) https://doi.org/10.9783/9780812293166

Green, Thomas A. (ed.). 1997. *Folklore. An Encyclopedia of Beliefs, Customs, Tales, Music, and Art.* 2 vols (Santa Barbara, CA: ABC-CLIO)

Grillandus, Paulus. 1536. *Tractatus de hereticis: et sortilegiis omnifariam coitu: eorumque penis* ... (Lyons)

Grinsell, L.V. 1976. *Folklore of Prehistoric Sites in Britain* (Newton Abbot: David & Charles)

Grose, Francis. 1788. *A Classical Dictionary of the Vulgar Tongue.* 2nd edn (London: S. Hooper)

Gurdon, Lady Eveline Camilla (ed.). 1893. *County Folk-Lore: Printed Extracts No. 2, Suffolk* (London: Folk-Lore Society; facsimile Felinfach: Llanerch/Folklore Society, 1997)

Gurevich, Aaron J. 1984. 'Oral and written culture of the Middle Ages: two "peasant visions" of the late twelfth–early thirteenth centuries', trans. Ann Shukman, *New Literary History*, 16.1 (*Oral and Written Traditions in the Middle Ages*) (Autumn): 51–66 https://doi.org/10.2307/468775

Hall, Alaric. 2007. *Elves in Anglo-Saxon England: Matters of Belief, Health, Gender and Identity* (Woodbridge: Boydell Press)

Hall, Hubert (ed.). 1896. *The Red Book of the Exchequer* (Rolls Series 99), 3 parts (London: HMSO/Eyre and Spottiswoode)

Hall, Marshall. 1827. *Commentaries on Some of the More Important of the Diseases of Females* (London: Longman, Rees, Orme, Brown and Green)

Harder, Worth T. 1973. 'The crystal source: Herbert Read's *The Green Child*', *Sewanee Review*, 81.4 (Autumn): 714–38

Harms, Dan. 2018. '"Of Fairies": An excerpt from a seventeenth-century magical manuscript', *Folklore*, 129.2 (June): 192–98 https://doi.org/10.1080/0015587X.2018.1447888

Harris, Paul. 1991. 'The Green Children of Woolpit', *Fortean Times*, 57 (Spring): 39–41

——. 1998. 'The Green Children of Woolpit: a 12th century mystery and its possible solution', in *Fortean Studies*, Vol. 4, ed. by Steve Moore (London: John Brown Publishing), 81–95

——. 1999. 'St Martin's Land. Land of the Green Children—an alternative possibility'. In *Fortean Studies*, Vol. 6, ed. Steve Moore (London: John Brown Publishing), 267–69

Harte, Jeremy. 2008. *English Holy Wells: A Sourcebook* (Loughborough: Heart of Albion Press)

———. 2024. *Fairy Encounters in Medieval England: Landscape, Folklore and the Supernatural* (Exeter: University of Exeter Press)

Hartland, Edwin Sidney (ed.). [1890]. *English Fairy and Other Folk Tales* (London: Walter Scott)

———. 1891. *The Science of Fairy Tales: An Inquiry into Fairy Mythology* (London: Walter Scott)

Hartsiotis, Kirsty. 2013. *Suffolk Folk Tales* (Stroud: History Press)

Haslam, Garth. 2002. 'Extra: the Green Children of Banjos?', in *Anomalies: The Green Children of Woolpit*, 11–12 <http://anomalyinfo.com/sites/default/files/patrons/Green_Children_of_Woolpit.pdf > [accessed 14 October 2023]

Hassall, Anthony J. 1986. *Strange Country: A Study of Randolph Stow* (St Lucia, London, New York: University of Queensland Press)

Haughton, Brian. 2007. *Hidden History: Lost Civilizations, Secret Knowledge, and Ancient Mysteries* (Franklin Lakes, NJ: Career Press)

Henisch, Bridget Ann. 1999. *The Medieval Calendar Year* (University Park, PA: Pennsylvania State University Press)

Henken, Elissa R. 2001. 'Contemporary legend in the works of Gerald of Wales', *Contemporary Legend*, n.s. 4: 93–107

Herbermann, C.G., Edward A. Pace, Condé B. Pallen, Thomas J. Shahan and John J. Wynne (eds). 1907–1918. *The Catholic Encyclopedia. An International Work of Reference on the Constitution, Doctrine, Discipline, and History of the Catholic Church.* 17 vols (New York: Robert Appleton)

[Herbert, Algernon]. 1836–1841. *Britannia after the Romans: Being an Attempt to Illustrate the Religious and Political Revolutions of that Province in the Fifth and Succeeding Centuries ...* 2 vols (London: H.G. Bohn)

———. 1849. *Cyclops Christianus: Or, An Argument to Disprove the Supposed Antiquity of the Stonehenge and Other Megalithic Erections in England and Britanny* (London: John Petheram)

Heritage Gateway. 2012. 'Willie Howe', in *Heritage Gateway: Historic England Research Records* (Swindon: Historic England) <https://www.heritagegateway.org.uk/Gateway/Results_Single.aspx?uid=79831&resourceID=19191> [accessed 12 November 2023]

Hervey, Francis (ed.). 1925. *The Pinchbeck Register Relating to the Abbey of Bury St Edmunds, &c.* 2 vols (Brighton: Farncombe)

Heywood, Thomas. 1635. *The Hierarchie of the Blessed Angells* (London: A. Islip; facsimile Amsterdam: Theatrum Orbis Terrarum; New York: Da Capo Press, 1973)

Hiatt, Alfred. 2008. *Terra Incognita: Mapping the Antipodes before 1600* (London: British Library)

Hoffmann-Krayer, E., and Hanns Bächtold-Stäubli (eds). 1927–42. *Handwörterbuch des deutschen Aberglaubens*. 10 vols (Berlin, Leipzig: Walter de Gruyter & Co.) https://doi.org/10.1515/9783110840148

Hogg, Richard, and David Denison (eds). 2006. *A History of the English Language* (Cambridge: Cambridge University Press) https://doi.org/10.1017/CBO9780511791154

Holden, Lynn. 2000. *Encyclopedia of Taboos* (Oxford: ABC-CLIO)

Hole, Christina. 1977. *Witchcraft in England*. New edn (London: Batsford)

Hollingsworth, A.G.H. 1844. *The History of Stowmarket, the Ancient County Town of Suffolk: With Some Notices of the Hundred of Stow* (Ipswich: F. Pawsey; repr. Stowmarket: Mike Durrant/imaginaire, 2002)

Hosler, John D. 2017. 'Chivalric carnage? Fighting, capturing and killing at the Battles of Dol and Fornham in 1173', in *Prowess, Piety, and Public Order in Medieval Society: Studies in Honor of Richard W. Kaeuper*, Later Medieval Europe 14, ed. by Craig M. Nakashian and Daniel P. Franke (Leiden, Boston: Brill), 36–61 https://doi.org/10.1163/9789004341098_004

Howlett, Richard (ed.). 1884. *Chronicles of the Reigns of Stephen, Henry II, and Richard I* (Rolls Series 82), Vol. 1 (London: Longman & Co.)

———. 1885. *Chronicles of the Reigns of Stephen, Henry II, and Richard I* (Rolls Series 82), Vol. 2 (London: Longman & Co.)

Humphreys, Margaret. 1997. 'Chlorosis: "The Virgin's Disease"', in *Plague, Pox and Pestilence: Disease in History*, ed. by Kenneth F. Kiple (London: Weidenfield and Nicolson), 160–65

Hunter, Joseph (ed.). 1835. *Fines, sive Pedes finium: sive, finales concordiæ in Curia Domini Regis, ab anno septimo regni Regis Ricardi I ad annum decimum sextum Regis Johannis. A.D. 1195–1214*, Vol. 1 (London: Eyre and Spottiswoode)

———. 1844a. *Fines, sive Pedes finium: sive, finales concordiæ in Curia Domini Regis, ab anno septimo regni Regis Ricardi I ad annum decimum sextum Regis Johannis. A.D. 1195–1214*, Vol. 2 (London: Eyre and Spottiswoode)

———. 1844b. *The Great Roll of the Pipe for the First Year of the Reign of King Richard the First, A.D. 1189–1190* (London: Eyre and Spottiswoode)

Hurry, Jamieson B. 1930. *The Woad Plant and its Dye* (London: Oxford University Press)

Hutchings, John. 1997. 'Folklore and symbolism of green', *Folklore*, 108: 55–64 https://doi.org/10.1080/0015587X.1997.9715937

Hutton, Ronald. 2014. 'The making of the Early Modern British fairy tradition', *The Historical Journal*, 57.4: 1157–75 https://doi.org/10.1017/S0018246X14000351

———. 2022. *Queens of the Wild: Pagan Goddesses in Christian Europe: An Investigation* (New Haven, CT, and London: Yale University Press) https://doi.org/10.12987/9780300265279

Huxley, A., M. Griffiths and M. Levy. 1992. *The New Royal Horticultural Society Dictionary of Gardening*. 4 vols (London: Macmillan)

Ibbotson, Eva. 1994. *The Secret of Platform 13* (London: Macmillan)

Istituto Giovanni XXIII. 1967. *Bibliotheca Sanctorum*, Vol. 8 (Roma: Città Nuova Editrice)

Iyengar, Sujata. 2005. *Shades of Difference: Mythologies of Skin Color in Early Modern England* (Philadelphia, PA: University of Pennsylvania Press) https://doi.org/10.9783/9780812202335

James, M.R. 1930. *Suffolk and Norfolk: A Perambulation of the Two Counties with Notices of their History and their Ancient Buildings* ... (London & Toronto: J.M. Dent & Sons)

Jarman, A.O.H. 1960. *The Legend of Merlin. An Inaugural Lecture Delivered at University College, Cardiff, 10th March, 1959* (Cardiff: University of Wales Press)

———. 1991. 'The Merlin legend and the Welsh tradition of prophecy', in *The Arthur of the Welsh: The Arthurian Legend in Medieval Welsh Literature*, ed. by Rachel Bromwich, A.O.H. Jarman and Brynley F. Roberts (Cardiff: University of Wales Press), 117–46

Jocelin of Brakelond. 1840. *Chronica Jocelini de Brakelonda, de rebus gestis Samsonis Abbatis Monasterii Sancti Edmundi*, ed. by John Gage Rokewode (London: Camden Society Old Series 13) https://doi.org/10.1017/S2042169900011615

———. 1989. *Chronicle of the Abbey of Bury St Edmunds*, trans. by Diana Greenway and Jane Sayers (Oxford: Oxford University Press)

Johnson, Daisy. 2020. 'A Retelling', in *Hag: Forgotten Folktales Retold* (London: Virago Press), 15–36

Johnson, Marjorie T. 2014. *Seeing Fairies: From the Lost Archives of the Fairy Investigation Society, Authentic Reports of Fairies in Modern Times* (San Antonio, TX: Anomalist Books)

Jones, E. Lloyd. 1897. *Chlorosis: The Special Anæmia of Young Women: Its Causes, Pathology, and Treatment* (London: Baillière, Tindall and Cox)

Jonson, Ben. 1975. *The Complete Masques*, ed. by Stephen Orgel (New Haven, CT, and London: Yale University Press)

Joynes, Andrew. 2001. *Medieval Ghost Stories* (Woodbridge: Boydell Press) https://doi.org/10.1515/9781846154928

Kears, Carl, and James Paz (eds). 2016a. *Medieval Science Fiction*. King's College London Medieval Studies 24 (London: King's College London, Centre for Late Antique & Medieval Studies)

———. 2016b. 'Medieval science fiction; an impossible fantasy?', in Kears and Paz 2016a: 1–35

Keats-Rohan, K.S.B. 1999. *Domesday People: A Prosopography of Persons Occurring in English Documents 1066–1166. I. Domesday Book* (Woodbridge: Boydell Press) https://doi.org/10.2307/j.ctv136bx0q

———. 2002. *Domesday Descendants: A Prosopography of Persons Occurring in English Documents 1066–1166. II. Pipe Rolls to Cartae Baronum* (Woodbridge: Boydell Press) https://doi.org/10.2307/j.ctv25m8d6r

[Keightley, Thomas] 'T.K'. 1828. *The Fairy Mythology*. 2 vols (London: W. Harrison Ainsworth)

Keightley, Thomas. 1850. *The Fairy Mythology, Illustrative of the Romance and Superstition of Various Countries ... A New Edition, Revised and Greatly Enlarged* (London: Bohn's Antiquarian Library)

Kendrick, T.D. 1950. *British Antiquity* (London: Methuen; repr. New York: Barnes & Noble; London: Methuen, 1970)

King, Edmund. 2004. 'Peverel, William (*b. c.*1090, *d.* after 1155)', in *Oxford Dictionary of National Biography* (Oxford: Oxford University Press) online edn, ed. by David Cannadine <https://www.oxforddnb.com/view/article/22076> [accessed 14 October 2023] https://doi.org/10.1093/ref:odnb/22076

King, Helen. 2004. *The Disease of Virgins: Green Sickness, Chlorosis and the Problems of Puberty* (London: Routledge)

King, James. 1990. *The Last Modern: A Life of Herbert Read* (London: Weidenfeld and Nicolson)

[King, Richard J.] 1875. *Handbook for Essex, Suffolk, Norfolk, and Cambridgeshire*. 2nd edn (London: John Murray)

Kirby, John. 1735. *The Suffolk Traveller or, a Journey through Suffolk* (Ipswich: John Bagnall)

Kircher, Athanasius. 1678. *Mundus Subterraneus, in XII libros digestus* ... 2 vols (Amsterdam: J.J. Waesberge)

Kittredge, George Lyman. 1916. *A Study of Gawain and the Green Knight* (Cambridge, MA: Harvard University Press) https://doi.org/10.4159/harvard.9780674598973

Knight, Damon. 1971. *Charles Fort, Prophet of the Unexplained* (London: Victor Gollancz)

Knott, C.M., A.J. Brill and B.M. McKeown. 1994. *The PGRO Field Bean Handbook* (Peterborough: Processors and Growers Research Organisation)

La Fontaine, J.S. 1997. *Speak of the Devil: Tales of Satanic Abuse in Contemporary England* (Cambridge: Cambridge University Press) https://doi.org/10.1017/CBO9780511621758

Lacy, Norris J. (ed.). 1988. *The Arthurian Encyclopedia* (Woodbridge: Boydell)

Ladurie, Emmanuel le Roy, and André Zysberg. 1983. 'Géographie des hagioto-ponymes en France', *Annales: Histoire, Sciences Sociales*, 38 (6): 1304–35 https://doi.org/10.3406/ahess.1983.411022

Lang, Andrew. 1901. *Magic and Religion* (London: Longmans, Green, and Co.)

Lange, Johannes. 1554. *Medicinalium epistolarum miscellanea* (Basel: J. Oporinus)

Larrington, Carolyne. 2015. *The Land of the Green Man: A Journey Through the Supernatural Landscapes of the British Isles* (London: I.B. Tauris) https://doi.org/10.5040/9780755621606

——. 2020. 'Preface', in *Hag: Forgotten Folktales Retold* (London: Virago Press), 1–14

Lawson, John Cuthbert. 1910. *Modern Greek Folklore and Ancient Greek Religion: A Study in Survivals* (Cambridge: Cambridge University Press)

Lawton, H.W. 1931. 'Bishop Godwin's *Man in the Moone*', *Review of English Studies*, 7: 23–55 https://doi.org/10.1093/res/os-VII.25.23

Lea, Henry Charles. 1939. *Materials towards a History of Witchcraft*, ed. by Arthur C. Howland (Philadelphia, PA: Pennsylvania University Press)

Lecoy de la Marche, A. 1881. *Saint Martin* (Tours: Alfred Mame)

LeFanu, Nicola, and Kevin Crossley-Holland. 1990. *The Green Children: An Opera in Two Acts* (London: Novello)

Le Goff, Jacques. 1984. 'The learned and popular dimensions of journeys in the otherworld in the Middle Ages', in *Understanding Popular Culture. Europe from the Middle Ages to the Nineteenth Century*, ed. by Steven L. Kaplan (Berlin, New York, Amsterdam: Mouton), 19–37 https://doi.org/10.1515/9783110854305.19

——. 1990. *The Birth of Purgatory*, trans. by Arthur Goldhammer (Aldershot: Scolar Press)

Leland, John. 1715. *Johannis Lelandi antiquarii de rebus Britannicis collectanea*. Ed. by Thomas Hearne. 6 vols (Oxford: E Theatro Sheldoniano)

——. 1906–1910. *The Itinerary of John Leland in or about the Years 1535–1543*. Ed. by Lucy Toulmin Smith. 5 vols (London: George Bell and Sons; reissue, with a foreword by Sir Thomas Kendrick, London: Centaur Press, 1964)

Letters, Samantha. 2013. *Gazetteer of Markets and Fairs in England and Wales to 1516* (London: Centre for Metropolitan History). Last updated 16 December 2013 <https://www.history.ac.uk/cmh/gaz/gazweb2.html> [accessed 15 April 2022]

Lewis, Charlton Thomas, and Charles Short. 1879. *A Latin Dictionary Founded on Andrews' Edition of Freund's Latin Dictionary* (Oxford: Clarendon Press)

Lewis, Mary E. 2007. *The Bioarchaeology of Children* (Cambridge: Cambridge University Press)

Lindahl, Carl, John McNamara and John Lindow (eds). 2000. *Medieval Folklore. An Encyclopedia of Myths, Legends, Tales, Beliefs, and Customs*. 2 vols (Santa Barbara, CA: ABC-CLIO)

Lloyd, T.H. 1977. *The English Wool Trade in the Middle Ages* (Cambridge: Cambridge University Press) https://doi.org/10.1017/CBO9780511561214

Lobel, Mary D. 1935. *The Borough of Bury St Edmunds* (Oxford: Clarendon Press)

Loomis, R.S. 1941. 'King Arthur and the Antipodes', *Modern Philology*, 38: 289–304 https://doi.org/10.1086/388484

Lot, Ferdinand (ed.). 1934. *Nennius et l'*Historia Brittonum*, étude critique*. 2 vols. Bibliothèque de l'École des Hautes Études fasc. 263 (Paris: Honoré Champion)

Loudon, Irvine. 1984. 'The diseases called chlorosis', *Psychological Medicine*, 14: 27–36 https://doi.org/10.1017/S0033291700003056

Lunan, Duncan. 1996. 'Children from the sky'. *Analog: Science Fiction, Science Fact*, 116:11 (September): 39–53

——. 2012. *Children from the Sky: A Speculative Treatment of a Medieval Mystery—the Green Children of Woolpit* (London: Mutus Liber)

Lynch, Andrew. 2011. '"I have so many truths to tell": Randolph Stow's *Visitants* and *The Girl Green as Elderflower*', *Australian Literary Studies*, 26.1: 20–32 https://doi.org/10.20314/als.ddb41c538d

Lysaght, Patricia. 1991. 'Fairylore from the Midlands of Ireland', in Narváez 1991a: 22–46

McColley, Grant. 1937. 'The date of Godwin's *Domingo Gonsales*', *Modern Philology*, 35.2: 47–60 https://doi.org/10.1086/388279

MacCulloch, Diarmaid (ed.). 1976. *The Chorography of Suffolk* (Ipswich: Boydell Press/ Suffolk Records Society)

MacKillop, James. 1998. *A Dictionary of Celtic Mythology* (Oxford: Oxford University Press)

Macklin, John. 1965. *Strange Destinies* (New York: Ace Books)

Macpherson, Gordon (ed.). 1999. *Black's Medical Dictionary*, 39th edn (London: A. & C. Black)

MacRitchie, David. 1890. *The Testimony of Tradition* (London: Kegan Paul)

——. 1895. *Fians, Fairies and Picts* (London: Kegan Paul)

Madej, Michał. 2020. 'The story about the Green Children of Woolpit according to the medieval chronicles of William of Newburgh and Ralph of Coggeshall', *Res Historica*, 49: 117–132 https://doi.org/10.17951/rh.2020.49.117-132

Malvenda, Thomas. 1604. *De Antichristo Libri Vndecim* (Rome: apud C. Vulliettum)

———. 1647. *De Antichristo* (Lyon: Societas Bibliopolarum)

Map, Walter. 1983. *De Nugis Curialium: Courtiers' Trifles*, ed. and trans. by M.R. James; revised by. C.N.L. Brooke and R.A.B. Mynors (Oxford: Clarendon Press)

Martène, Edmond, and Ursin Durand (eds). 1724–1733. *Veterum scriptorum et monumentorum, historicorum, dogmaticorum, moralium, amplissima collectio*. 9 vols (Paris)

Maxwell, Donald. 1926. *Unknown Suffolk* (London: John Lane Bodley Head)

Maxwell, Glyn. 1996. *Wolfpit: The Tale of the Green Children of Suffolk* (Todmorden: ARC)

Mays, Simon. 2016. 'The ghostly child in medieval Northwest Europe', *Childhood in the Past*, 9.2 (September): 109–119 https://doi.org/10.1080/17585716.2016.1205341

Melville, Robert. 1944. 'The first sixty-six pages of *The Green Child*', in *Herbert Read: An Introduction to his Work by Various Hands*, ed. by Henry Treece (London: Faber and Faber), 81–90

Meurger, Michel. 1996. 'Surgeons from outside', in *Fortean Studies*, Vol. 3, ed. by Steve Moore (London: John Brown Publishing), 308–21

Meyer, Kuno. 1889. 'The adventures of Nera', *Revue Celtique*, 10: 212–28

Michell, John and Robert J.M. Rickard. 1977. *Phenomena: A Book of Wonders* (London: Thames and Hudson)

Middle English Dictionary. 1952–2001. Ed. by Robert E. Lewis et al. (Ann Arbor: University of Michigan Press). Online edition in *Middle English Compendium*, ed. by Frances McSparran et al. (Ann Arbor: University of Michigan Library, 2000–2018) <http://quod.lib.umich.edu/m/middle-english-dictionary/> [accessed 26 April 2022]

Miller, Benjamin F. 1997. *Miller-Keane Encyclopedia and Dictionary of Medicine, Nursing, and Allied Health*, ed. by Marie T. O'Toole (Philadelphia, PA, London, etc: W.B. Saunders Co.)

Miller, Konrad. 1895. *Mappaemundi. Die ältesten Weltkarten, Vol. 3: Die kleineren Weltkarten* (Stuttgart: J. Roth'sche)

Millett, Bella. 1994. 'How green is the Green Knight?', *Nottingham Medieval Studies*, 38: 138–51 https://doi.org/10.1484/J.NMS.3.231

Minyak, Otto. 2000. [Review of *Fortean Studies* 6], *Fortean Times*, 132 (March): 56

'Mr X.' 1989. 'The aparacido and the death of Gómez Pérez Dasmariñas', *Fortean Times*, 52 (Summer): 55–59

Misty. 1980. 'The Green Children', *Misty Holiday Special* (Summer): unpaginated

Mitchell, Adrian. 1996. *Maudie and the Green Children* (London and Vancouver: Tradewind)

Mitchell, Donald, Philip Reed and Mervyn Cooke (eds). 2004. *Letters from a Life: the Selected Letters of Benjamin Britten 1913–1976, Volume 3 1946–1951* (London: Faber and Faber)

Mittman, Asa Simon. 2001. 'The other close at hand: Gerald of Wales and the "Marvels of the West"', in Bildhauer and Mills 2001a: 97–112

Moore, Ellen Wedermeyer. 1985. *Fairs of Medieval England. An Introductory Study* (Toronto: Pontifical Institute of Mediaeval Studies)

Moore, Ivan E., Judith Plouviez and Stanley West. 1988. *The Archaeology of Roman Suffolk* (Ipswich: Suffolk Archaeological Unit)

Morel-Fatio, Alfred (ed.). 1878. *L'Espagne au XVIe et au XVIIe siècle, documents historiques et littéraires* (Heilbronn: Henninger Frères)

Morris, William. 1893. 'Of dyeing as an art', in *Arts and Crafts Essays by Members of the Arts and Crafts Exhibition Society* (London: Rivington, Percival and Co.), 196–211

Munro, John H. 2003. 'Medieval woollens: textile technology and industrial organisation, c.800–1500', in *The Cambridge History of Western Textiles*, ed. by David Jenkins (Cambridge: Cambridge University Press), 181–227

Murray, James A.H. (ed). 1875. *The Romance and Prophecies of Thomas of Erceldoune Printed from Five Manuscripts*. Early English Text Society 61 (London: N. Trübner)

Narváez, Peter (ed.). 1991a. *The Good People. New Fairylore Essays* (New York & London: Garland)

———. 1991b. 'Newfoundland berry pickers "in the fairies"', in Narváez 1991a: 336–67

Newell, Martin. 2015. *The Green Children* (Wivenhoe: Jardine Press)

Nicolson, Marjorie Hope. 1960. *Voyages to the Moon* (London: Macmillan)

Niermeyer, J.F. 1976. *Mediae latinitatis lexicon minus* (Leiden: E.J. Brill)

Nigro, Don. 2021. *Pirandello and Other Plays* (London: Samuel French)

Ó Giolláin, Diarmaid. 1991. 'The fairy belief and official religion in Ireland', in Narváez 1991a: 199–214

Oexle, Otto G. 1983. 'Die Gegenwart der Toten', in *Death in the Middle Ages*, ed. by Herman Braet and Werner Verbeke (Leuven: Leuven University Press), 19–77

Oksanen, Eljas. 2012. *Flanders and the Anglo-Norman World, 1066–1216*. Cambridge Studies in Medieval Life and Thought: Fourth Series (Cambridge: Cambridge University Press) https://doi.org/10.1017/CBO9781139032322

Oman, C.C. 1944. 'The English folklore of Gervase of Tilbury', *Folk-Lore*, 55: 2–15 https://doi.org/10.1080/0015587X.1944.9717702

Orme, Nicholas. 1995. 'The culture of children in medieval England', *Past and Present*, 148: 48–88 https://doi.org/10.1093/past/148.1.48

———. 2001. *Medieval Children* (New Haven, CT, and London: Yale University Press)

Otter, Monika. 1996. *Inventiones: Fiction and Referentiality in Twelfth-Century English Historical Writing* (Chapel Hill, NC, and London: University of North Carolina Press)

Overall, Sonia. 2021. 'Green is the colour', *Neon*, 52 (Spring): 38–41

Padel, O.J. 2006. 'Geoffrey of Monmouth and the development of the Merlin Legend', *Cambrian Medieval Celtic Studies*, 51 (Summer): 37–65

Page, William (ed.). 1907. *The Victoria History of the County of Suffolk*, Vol. 2 (London: Archibald Constable) https://doi.org/10.5962/bhl.title.17548

———. 1911. *The Victoria History of the County of Suffolk*, Vol. 1 (London: Archibald Constable) https://doi.org/10.5962/bhl.title.26388

———. 1912. *The Victoria History of the County of Bedford*, Vol. 3 (London: Archibald Constable)

——. 1927. *The Victoria History of the County of Buckingham*, Vol. 4 (London: St. Catherine Press)

Paine, Clive. 1993. 'The chapel and well of Our Lady of Woolpit', *Proceedings of Suffolk Institute of Archaeology and History*, 38.1: 8–12

Parker, Vanessa. 1971. *The Making of Kings Lynn: Secular Buildings from the 11th to the 17th Century* (London and Chichester: Phillimore)

Partner, Nancy F. 1977. *Serious Entertainments: The Writing of History in Twelfth-Century England* (Chicago: University of Chicago Press)

Pastoureau, Michel. 2014. *Green: The History of a Color*, trans. by Jody Gladding (Princeton, NJ: Princeton University Press)

Patch, Howard Rollin. 1950. *The Other World: According to Descriptions in Medieval Literature* (Cambridge, MA: Harvard University Press) https://doi.org/10.4159/harvard.9780674183841

Perdahl-Wallace, Eva, and Richard H. Schwartz. 2006. 'A girl with green complexion and iron deficiency: chlorosis revisited', *Clinical Pediatrics*, 45.2 (March): 187–89 https://doi.org/10.1177/000992280604500212

Philmus, Robert M. 1996. 'Murder most fowl: Butler's edition of Francis Godwin', review of *The Man in the Moone*, by Francis Godwin, ed. by John Anthony Butler, *Science Fiction Studies*, 69 (23/2) (July): 260–69

Pipe Roll Society. 1884a. *The Great Roll of the Pipe for the Fifth Year of the Reign of King Henry the Second. A.D. 1158–1159* (London: Publications of the Pipe Roll Society 1)

——. 1884b. *The Great Roll of the Pipe for the Sixth Year of the Reign of King Henry the Second. A.D. 1159–1160* (London: Publications of the Pipe Roll Society 2)

——. 1885. *The Great Roll of the Pipe for the Seventh Year of the Reign of King Henry the Second. A.D. 1160–1161* (London: Publications of the Pipe Roll Society 4)

——. 1898. *Feet of Fines of the Ninth Year of the Reign of King Richard I. A.D. 1197 to A.D. 1198* (London: Publications of the Pipe Roll Society 23)

——. 1925. *The Great Roll of the Pipe for the Thirty-Fourth Year of the Reign of King Henry the Second. A.D. 1187–1188* (London: Publications of the Pipe Roll Society 38)

Plumtree, James. 2022. 'Placing the Green Children of Woolpit', in *Strangers at the Gate! Multidisciplinary Explorations of Communities, Borders, and Othering in Medieval Western Europe*, ed. by Simon C. Thomson. Explorations in Medieval Culture 21 (Leiden: Brill), 202–24 https://doi.org/10.1163/9789004511910_013

Pluskowski, Aleksander. 2006. *Wolves and the Wilderness in the Middle Ages* (Woodbridge: Boydell)

Poole, Austin Lane. 1955. *From Domesday to Magna Carta, 1087–1216* (Oxford: Oxford University Press)

Poole, William. 2005. 'The origins of Francis Godwin's *The Man in the Moone* (1638)', *Philological Quarterly*, 84.2 (Spring): 189–210

Porter, Enid. 1974. *The Folklore of East Anglia* (London: Batsford)

Potter, Ursula. 2002. 'Greensickness in *Romeo and Juliet*: considerations on a sixteenth-century disease of virgins', in *The Premodern Teenager: Youth in Society 1150–1650*, ed. by Konrad Eisenbichler (Toronto: Centre for Reformation and Renaissance Studies, University of Victoria), 271–91

———. 2013. 'Navigating the Dangers of Female Puberty in Renaissance Drama', *Studies in English Literature 1500–1900*, 53.2 (Spring): 421–39 https://doi.org/10.1353/sel.2013.0013

Powell, W.R. (ed.). 1956. *A History of the County of Essex Vol. IV Ongar Hundred.* The Victoria History of the Counties of England (London: Oxford University Press)

Powicke, F.M. 1906. 'Roger of Wendover and the Coggeshall Chronicle', *English Historical Review*, 21, no 82 (April): 286–96 https://doi.org/10.1093/ehr/XXI.LXXXII.286

Pratchett, Terry. 1991. *Witches Abroad* (London: Gollancz)

Prynne, J.H. 1982. 'The land of Saint Martin', in *Poems* (Edinburgh, London: Agneau 2), 265–69

Purkiss, Diane. 2000. *Troublesome Things: A History of Fairies and Fairy Stories* (London: Allen Lane)

Rackham, Oliver. 1986. *The History of the Countryside* (London: Dent)

Ralph of Coggeshall. 1875. *Radulphi de Coggeshall Chronicon Anglicanum* (Rolls Series 66), ed. by Joseph Stevenson (London: Longman & Co.)

———. 1978. *Visio Thurkilli. Relatore, ut videtur, Radulphi de Coggeshall*, ed. by Paul Gerhard Schmidt. Bibliotheca Teubneriana (Leipzig: Teubner)

Rayner, Eric. 1966. 'Woolpit', *East Anglian Magazine*, 25: 340–42

Read, Herbert. 1935. *The Green Child: A Romance* (London: Heinemann)

———. 1945. *The Green Child*, illus. by Felix Kelly (London: Grey Walls Press)

———. 1947. *The Green Child*, intro. by Graham Greene, Century Library 4 (London: Eyre & Spottiswoode)

———. 1952a. *English Prose Style*. New edn (London: G. Bell and Sons)

———. 1952b. *La fanciulla verde*, trans. by Martino Rossi (Milan: Bompiani)

———. 1979. *La niña verde*, trans. by Enrique Pezzoni (Buenos Aires: Minotauro; repr. Barcelona: Duomo Ediciones, 2010)

———. 2004. *Zelenoe ditja*, trans. by Natalya Reinhold (Moscow: BSG-Press)

Reeve, N.H. 2002. 'Twilight Zones: J.H. Prynne's *The Land of Saint Martin*', *English: Journal of the English Association*, 51: 27–44 https://doi.org/10.1093/english/51.199.27

Rey, Alain (ed.). 1993. *Dictionnaire historique de langue française.* 2 vols (Paris: Dictionnaires Le Robert)

Reyce, Robert. 1902. *Suffolk in the XVIIth Century: The Breviary of Suffolk by Robert Reyce, 1618: Now Published for the First Time from the MS. in the British Museum, with Notes by Lord Francis Hervey* (London: John Murray)

Richards, Fiona. 2014. 'The Englishness of Randolph Stow', *Journal of the Association for the Study of Australian Literature*, 14, no 5 <https://openjournals.library.sydney.edu.au/JASAL/issue/view/777> [accessed 20 July 2022]

———. 2018. 'Max & Mick: the partnership of Peter Maxwell Davies and Randolph Stow', *The Musical Times*, 159, no 1943 (Summer): 25–38

Rigg, J.M. 2004. 'Barre, Richard (*b. c.*1130, *d.* in or after 1202)', revised by Ralph V. Turner, in *Oxford Dictionary of National Biography* (Oxford: Oxford University Press). Online edn, ed. by David Cannadine, October 2007 <https://www.oxforddnb.com/view/article/1510> [accessed 14 October 2023]

Roberts, Bob. 1978. *A Slice of Suffolk* (Lavenham: T. Dalton)

Roberts, Charlotte, and Margaret Cox. 2003. *Health & Disease in Britain: From Prehistory to the Present Day* (Stroud: Sutton)

Roberts, Julian, and Andrew G. Watson (eds). 1990. *John Dee's Library Catalogue* (London: Bibliographical Society)

Robertson, Martin. 1977. 'The Green Children of Woolpit', in *A Hot Bath at Bedtime: Poems, 1933–77* (Oxford: Robert Dugdale), 73–75

Roger of Hoveden. 1853. *The Annals of Roger of Hoveden*, trans. by Henry T. Riley, 2 vols (London: H.G. Bohn)

———. 1869. *Chronica Magistri Rogeri de Houedene*, ed. by William Stubbs (Rolls Series 51), Vol. 2 (London: Longman & Co.; Trübner & Co.)

Room, Adrian (rev.). 1999. *Brewer's Dictionary of Phrase and Fable* Millennium Edn. (London: Cassell)

Rose, Carol. 1996. *Spirits, Fairies, Gnomes and Goblins: An Encyclopedia of the Little People* (Santa Barbara, CA: ABC-CLIO)

Rosenberg, Bruce A. 1981. 'Oral literature in the Middle Ages', in *Oral Traditional Literature*, ed. by J.M. Foley (Columbus, OH: Slavica), 440–50

Rosenthal, T.G. 1969. 'Read and the underground Utopia', *New Statesman*, 78 no. 2020 (28 November): 785

Roth, Cecil. 1964. *A History of the Jews in England*, 3rd edn (Oxford: Oxford University Press; repr. 1978)

Round, John Horace. [1898]. *Studies on the Red Book of the Exchequer* (London: Printed for private circulation)

——— (ed.). 1913. *Rotuli de dominabus et pueris et puellis de XII comitatibus, 1185* (London: Publications of the Pipe Roll Society 35)

Round, Julia. 2019. *Gothic for Girls:* Misty *and British Comics* (Jackson, MS: University Press of Mississippi) https://doi.org/10.14325/mississippi/9781496824455.001.0001

Rubel, William. 2006. 'English horse-bread, 1590–1800', *Gastronomica*, 6.3: 40–51 https://doi.org/10.1525/gfc.2006.6.3.40

Ruch, Lisa M. 2013. 'Digression or discourse? William of Newburgh's ghost stories as urban legends', in *The Medieval Chronicle VIII*, ed. by Erick Kooper and Sjoerd Levelt (Amsterdam/New York: Rodopi), 261–72 https://doi.org/10.1163/9789401209885_013

Rye, Walter. 1900. *A Calendar of the Feet of Fines for Suffolk* (Ipswich: Suffolk Institute of Archaeology and Natural History)

Salunkhe, D.K., and S.S. Kadham (eds). 1989. *CRC Handbook of World Food Legumes* (Boca Raton, FL: CRC Press)

Sanders, I.J. 1960. *English Baronies. A Study of Their Origin and Descent, 1086–1327* (Oxford: Oxford University Press)

Sands, Donald B. 1986. *Middle English Verse Romances* (Exeter: University of Exeter Press)

Saunders, Corinne. 2010. *Magic and the Supernatural in Medieval English Romance* (Cambridge: D.S. Brewer) https://doi.org/10.1017/9781846158056

Savage, D.S. 1978. 'Unripeness is all: Herbert Read and *The Green Child*'. *Durham University Journal*, 70.2 (June): 205–24

Sawyer, Andy. 2016. 'The riddle of medieval technology', in Kears and Paz 2016a: 153–75

Sawyer, Rose. 2023. *The Medieval Changeling: Health, Childcare, and the Family Unit* (Cambridge: D.S. Brewer) https://doi.org/10.1017/9781800109285

Scarfe, Norman. 1986. *Suffolk in the Middle Ages* (Woodbridge: Boydell Press)

———. 1987. *The Suffolk Landscape*. Revised edn (Bury St Edmunds: Alastair Press)

Schmidt, Paul Gerhard. 1978. 'The Vision of Thurkill'. *Journal of the Warburg and Courtauld Institutes*, 41: 50–64 https://doi.org/10.2307/750862

Shakespeare, William. 2000. *King Henry VI Part 1*, ed. by Edward Burns (London: Arden Shakespeare)

Shepherd, Stephen H.A. (ed.). 1995. *Middle English Romances* (New York and London: W.W. Norton)

Shuker, Karl P.N. 1996. *The Unexplained: An Illustrated Guide to the World's Natural and Paranormal Mysteries* (London: Carlton)

Silver, Carole G. 1999. *Strange and Secret Peoples: Fairies and Victorian Consciousness* (Oxford: Oxford University Press)

Simoons, Frederick J. 1998. *Plants of Life, Plants of Death* (Madison, WI, London: University of Wisconsin Press)

Simpson, Jacqueline. 2003. 'Repentant soul or walking corpse? Debatable apparitions in medieval England', *Folklore*, 114: 389–402 https://doi.org/10.1080/0015587032000145397

Simpson, Jacqueline, and Steve Roud. 2000. *A Dictionary of English Folklore* (Oxford: Oxford University Press)

Sims-Williams, Patrick. 1990. 'The unseen world: The monk of Wenlock's vision', in *Religion and Literature in Western England, 600–800*, Cambridge Studies in Anglo-Saxon England (Cambridge: Cambridge University Press), 243–72 https://doi.org/10.1017/CBO9780511553042.011

Skelton, R.A., and P.D.A. Harvey (eds). 1986. *Local Maps and Plans from Medieval England* (Oxford: Oxford University Press)

Smedt, Carolus de, Gulielmus van Hooff and Josephus de Backer (eds). 1884. 'De cultu S. Martini apud Turonenses extr. sec. XII epistolae quatuor', *Analecta Bollandiana*, 3: 217–57 https://doi.org/10.1484/J.ABOL.4.00271

Souter, A., et al. (eds). 1968–1982. *Oxford Latin Dictionary* (Oxford: Oxford University Press)

Speed, John. 1611. *The Theatre of the Empire of Great Britaine, presenting an exact geography of the kingdomes of England, Scotland, Ireland and the iles adioyning ...* (London: Iohn Sudbury and Georg Humble)

Speirs, John. 1949. 'Sir Gawain and the Green Knight'. *Scrutiny*, 16: 274–300

Staunton, Michael. 2017. *The Historians of Angevin England* (Oxford: Oxford University Press) https://doi.org/10.1093/oso/9780198769965.001.0001

Stevenson, Joseph (trans.). 1861. *The Church Historians of England. Vol. IV part 2 The History of William of Newburgh; The Chronicles of Robert de Monte* (London: Seeleys)

Stinton, Judith. 1983. *Tom's Tale*, illus. by Janet Duchesne (London: Julia MacRae Books)

Stow, John. 1908. *A Survey of London. Reprinted from the Text of 1603*. Intro. and notes Charles Lethbridge Kingsford. 2 vols (Oxford: Clarendon Press)

Stow, Randolph. 1980. *The Girl Green as Elderflower* (London: Secker and Warburg)

Strickland, Matthew. 2016. *Henry the Young King, 1155–1183* (New Haven, CT, and London: Yale University Press) https://doi.org/10.12987/yale/9780300215519.001.0001

Subcommittee on Arsenic in Drinking Water. 1999. *Arsenic in Drinking Water*. National Research Council, Commission on Life Sciences (Washington, DC: National Academy Press)

Suffolk Historic Environment Record. 2023. *Suffolk Heritage Explorer* (Bury St Edmunds: Suffolk County Council) <https://heritage.suffolk.gov.uk/search> [accessed 15 October 2023]

Tal, Kali. 1996. *Worlds of Hurt: Reading the Literatures of Trauma* (Cambridge: Cambridge University Press)

Tanner, Norman P. (ed.). 1977. *Heresy Trials in the Diocese of Norwich, 1428–31*. Camden Fourth Series 20 (London:, Royal Historical Society) https://doi.org/10.1017/S0068690500004372

Tatlock, J.S.P. 1950. *The Legendary History of Britain. Geoffrey of Monmouth's Historia Regum Britanniae and its Early Vernacular Versions* (Berkeley, CA: University of California Press; repr. New York: Gordian Press, 1974)

Taylor, Christopher. 1979. *Roads and Tracks of Britain* (London: J.M. Dent)

Taylor, Frederick, et al. 1896. 'A discussion on anæmia: its causation, varieties, associated pathology, and treatment', *British Medical Journal*, 1864 (19 September): 719–28

Taylor, Martyn. 2022. *Going Underground Bury St Edmunds* (Stroud: Amberley Publishing)

TGC. 2022. *The Green Children* <https://www.tgcmusic.com> [accessed 15 April 2022]

Theriot, Nancy M. 1996. *Mothers and Daughters in Nineteenth-Century America: The Biosocial Construction of Femininity* (Lexington: University Press of Kentucky)

Thomas, R.J., Gareth A. Bevan and P.J. Donovan (eds). 1967–2002. *Geiriadur Prifysgol Cymru. A Dictionary of the Welsh Language* (Caerdydd: Gwasg Prifysgol Cymru) https://geiriadur.ac.uk/gpc/gpc.html [accessed 14 October 2023]

Thompson, Stith. 1955–1958. *Motif-Index of Folk-Literature: A Classification of Narrative Elements in Folktales, Ballads, Medieval Romances, Exempla, Fabliaux, Jest-Books and Local Legends*. 6 vols (Copenhagen: Rosenkilde and Bagger)

Tobler, Adolf, and Erhard Lommatzsch. 1989–2002. *Altfranzösisches Wörterbuch*, Vol. 11 (Stuttgart: Franz Steiner)

Tokarczuk, Olga. 2016. *Les Enfants verts*, trans. by Margot Carlier. Collection Fictions d'Europe (Lille: La Contre Allée)

———. 2018. 'Zielone Dzieci, czyli Opis dziwnych zdarzeń na Wołyniu sporządzony przez medyka Jego Królewskiej Mości Jana Kazimierza, Williama Davissona', in *Opowiadania Bizarne* (Kraków: Wydawnictwo Literackie), 10–44

Tolkien, J.R.R., and E.V. Gordon (eds). 1925. *Sir Gawain & the Green Knight* (Oxford: Clarendon Press; repr. 1949)

Toller, T. Northcote. 1921. *An Anglo-Saxon Dictionary Based on the Manuscript Collections of the Late J. Bosworth. Supplement* (Oxford: Oxford University Press)

Tolstoy, Nikolai. 1985. *The Quest for Merlin* (London: Hamish Hamilton)

Trench, Brinsley le Poer. 1974. *Secret of the Ages: U.F.O.s from Inside the Earth* (London: Souvenir Press)

Trudel, Jean-Louis. 2005. 'Looking for little green men', *New York Review of Science Fiction*, 207 (November): 1, 6–11

Turner, Daniel. 1714. *De morbis cutaneis: A treatise of diseases incident to the skin* (London: R. Bonwicke et al.)

Tusser, Thomas. 1984. *Five Hundred Points of Good Husbandry* (Oxford: Oxford University Press)

Tyler-Whittle, M.S. 1952. 'Witchcraft', *East Anglian* Magazine, 11.12 (October): 652–56

Tyson, Rachel. 2000. *Medieval Glass Vessels Found in England c.AD 1200–1500*. Council for British Archaeology Research Report 121 (York: Council for British Archaeology)

Union Académique Internationale. 1998. *Novum glossarium mediae latinitatis ab anno DCCC usque ad annum MCC*. Fascicule *Per–Perlysus*, ed. by François Dolben (Copenhagen: Ejnar Munksgaard)

Uytven, Raymond van. 1983. 'Cloth in the medieval literature of Western Europe', in *Cloth and Clothing in Medieval Europe: Essays in Memory of Professor E.M. Carus-Wilson*, ed. by N.B. Harte and K.G. Ponting (London: Heinemann Educational), 151–85

Vallée, Jacques. 1970. *Passport to Magonia: From Folklore to Flying Saucers* (London: Neville Spearman)

Vickery, Roy. 2019. *Vickery's Folk Flora: An A–Z of the Folklore and Uses of British and Irish Plants* (London: Weidenfeld & Nicolson)

Vries, Ad de. 1974. *Dictionary of Symbols and Images* (Amsterdam: North-Holland Publishing Co.)

Wade, James. 2008. 'Abduction, surgery, madness: an account of a little red man in Thomas Walsingham's *Chronica Maiora*', *Medium Aevum*, 77.1: 10–29 https://doi.org/10.2307/43630593

———. 2011. *Fairies in Medieval Romance* (New York: Palgrave Macmillan) https://doi.org/10.1057/9780230119154

Wakefield, Walter L., and Austin P. Evans. 1969. *Heresies of the High Middle Ages: Selected Sources Translated and Annotated*. Records of Civilisation. Sources and Studies 81 (New York: Columbia University Press)

Walmsley, John (ed. and trans.). 2006. *Widows, Heirs, and Heiresses in the Late Twelfth Century. The Rotuli de dominabus et pueris et puellis* (Tempe, AZ: Arizona Center for Medieval and Renaissance Studies)

Walsh, Martin W. 2000. 'Medieval English *Martinmesse*: the archaeology of a forgotten festival', *Folklore*, 111: 231–54 https://doi.org/10.1080/00155870020004620

Ward, H.L.D. 1875. 'The Vision of Thurkill, probably by Ralph of Coggeshall', *Journal of the British Archaeological Association*, 31: 420–59 https://doi.org/10.1080/00681288.1875.11904357

Warner, Richmond. 2019. *The Green Children: A Foxfield Railway Story*, illus. by Sarah-Leigh Wills (Whitley Bay: UK Book Publishing)

Warner, Sylvia Townsend. 1979. *Kingdoms of Elfin* (Harmondsworth: Penguin)

Warren, Nick. 2001. 'Disappearing diseases', *Fortean Times*, 148 (July): 17

Watkins, Carl. 2001. 'Memories of the marvellous in the Anglo-Norman realm', in *Medieval Memories: Men, Women and the Past, 700–1300*, ed. by Elisabeth van Houts (Harlow: Pearson Education), 92–112 https://doi.org/10.4324/9781315839097-6

——. 2002. 'Sin, penance and purgatory in the Anglo-Norman realm: the evidence of visions and ghost stories', *Past and Present*, 175.1: 3–33 https://doi.org/10.1093/past/175.1.3

——. 2007. *History and the Supernatural in Medieval England* (Cambridge: Cambridge University Press) https://doi.org/10.1017/CBO9780511496257

Westwood, Jennifer. 1985. *Albion: A Guide to Legendary Britain* (London: Grafton Books)

Westwood, Jennifer, and Jacqueline Simpson. 2005. *The Lore of the Land: A Guide to England's Legends, from Spring-Heeled Jack to the Witches of Warboys* (London: Penguin)

White, William J. 1988. *Skeletal Remains from the Cemetery of St. Nicholas Shambles, City of London*. London and Middlesex Archaeological Society Special Paper 9 (London: London and Middlesex Archaeological Society)

Wilkins, Harold T. 1959. *Mysteries Solved and Unsolved* (London: Odhams Press; repr. London: Paul Elek, 1961)

William of Newburgh. 1610. *Guillelmi Neubrigensis Angli, […] de rebus Anglicis suis temporis, libri quinque*, ed. by Jean Picard (Paris: C. Sevestre et al.)

——. 1719. *Guilielmi Neubrigensis Historia sive Chronica rerum Anglicarum, libris quinque …*, ed. by Thomas Hearne (Oxford: E Theatro Sheldoniano)

——. 1976. 'The Green Children of Woolpit', trans. by R. Wingfield, *Ipswich Geological Group Bulletin*, 18 (September): 4–5 <http://geosuffolk.co.uk/images/ipswich-geological-group/iggbulletin18a.pdf> [accessed 14 October 2023]

——. 1988. *The History of English Affairs, Book I*, ed. and trans. by P.G. Walsh and M.J. Kennedy (Warminster: Aris and Phillips)

——. 2007. *The History of English Affairs, Book II*, ed. and trans. by P.G. Walsh and M.J. Kennedy (Oxford: Aris and Phillips)

Windling, Terri (ed.). 1995. *The Armless Maiden and Other Tales of Childhood's Survivors* (New York: Tor)

Witte, Anne E. 1988. 'St Martin: seasonal and legendary aspects'. *Mediaevalia*, 14: 63–74

Wittkower, Rudolph. 1987. 'Marvels of the East: a study in the history of monsters', in *Allegory and the Migration of Symbols* (New York: Thames and Hudson), 45–74

Woolf, D.R. 2004. 'Godwin, Francis (1562–1633)', in *Oxford Dictionary of National Biography* (Oxford: Oxford University Press); online edn, ed. by David Cannadine <https://www.oxforddnb.com/view/article/10890> [accessed 15 April 2022]

Wright, John Kirtland. 1925. *The Geographical Lore of the Time of the Crusades: A Study in the History of Medieval Science and Tradition in Western Europe* (New York: American Geographical Society Research Series 15)

Wright, Thomas. 1861. *Essays on Archæological Subjects, and on Various Questions Connected with the History of Art, Science, and Literature in the Middle Ages*, 2 vols (London: John Russell Smith)

Yolen, Jane. 1993. 'The Green Children', *Asimov's SF*, 17.8 (July): 47 <https://
   endicottstudio.typepad.com/poetrylist/green-children-by-jane-yolen.html>
   [accessed 15 April 2022]

——. 2018. *How to Fracture a Fairy Tale* (San Francisco: Tachyon Publications)

Youmans, Marly. 2001. *The Wolf Pit: A Novel* (New York: Farrar, Straus and Giroux)

Young, Francis. 2006. '"An horrid popish plot": the failure of Catholic aspirations in
   Bury St. Edmunds 1685–88', *Proceedings of Suffolk Institute of Archaeology and History*,
   41.2: 209–25

——. 2019. *Suffolk Fairylore* (Norwich: Lasse Press)

——. 2023. *Twilight of the Godlings: The Shadowy Beginnings of Britain's Supernatural Beings*
   (Cambridge: Cambridge University Press) https://doi.org/10.1017/9781009330343

Young, Simon. 2012. 'Three notes on West Yorkshire fairies in the nineteenth century',
   Folklore, 123.2: 223–30 https://doi.org/10.1080/0015587X.2012.682493

——. 2018a. 'And a Historical Folklore Survey? A Reply to John Widdowson's
   "New Beginnings"', *Folklore*, 129.2: 181–91 https://doi.org/10.1080/0015587X.
   2018.1441948

——(ed.). 2018b. *Fairy Census, 2014–2017*. https://www.fairyist.com/wp-content/
   uploads/2014/10/The-Fairy-Census-2014-2017-1.pdf [accessed 14 October 2023]

——. 2022. 'Fairies, folklore and forteana: It's not easy being green', *Fortean Times*,
   422 (September): 25

——. 2023. 'Changelings and harvest', *Fairy Investigation Society Newsletter*, n.s. 17
   (January): 97–108

Zaleski, Carol. 1987. *Otherworld Journeys: Accounts of Near-Death Experience in Medieval and
   Modern Times* (Oxford: Oxford University Press)

Zipes, Jack (ed.). 2000. *The Oxford Companion to Fairy Tales* (Oxford: Oxford University
   Press)

Retellings, Reworkings and Reimaginings: A Chronological Listing

1638

Godwin, Francis. *The Man in the Moone: or a Discovrse of a Voyage Thither, by Domingo Gonsales* (London: John Norton)

1935

Read, Herbert. *The Green Child: A Romance* (London: Heinemann)

1938

Dane, Clemence. *The Moon is Feminine* (London and Toronto: Heinemann)

1966

Crossley-Holland, Kevin. *The Green Children*, illus. by Margaret Gordon (London: Macmillan) [This retelling has been reprinted several times in collections, most recently in *Between Worlds: Folktales of Britain & Ireland* (London: Walker Books, 2018). Crossley-Holland also returned to the theme with fresh texts in 1990 and 1994, see below.]

1972

Colwell, Eileen. 1972. *Round About and Long Ago: Tales from the English Counties* (London: Longman Young Books)

1976

Carr, J.L. *The Green Children of the Woods* (London: Longman)

1977

Robertson, Martin. 'The Green Children of Woolpit' [poem], in *A Hot Bath at Bedtime: Poems, 1933–77* (Oxford: Robert Dugdale), 73–75

1979

Warner, Sylvia Townsend. 'Elphenor and Weasel', in *Kingdoms of Elfin* (Harmondsworth: Penguin), 23–37

1980

Misty. 'The Green Children' [picture story], *Misty Holiday Special* (Summer): unpaginated
Stow, Randolph. *The Girl Green as Elderflower* (London: Secker and Warburg)

1981

Crowley, John. 'The green child', in *Elsewhere*, ed. by Terri Windling and Mark Allen Arnold (New York: Ace Books), 1–5. [Repr. 2004, in Crowley, John. *Novelties and Souvenirs. Collected Short Fiction* (New York: Perennial), 32–37]

1982

Prynne, J.H. 'The land of Saint Martin' [poem], in *Poems* (Edinburgh, London: Agneau 2), 265–69

1983

Stinton, Judith. *Tom's Tale*, illus. by Janet Duchesne (London: Julia MacRae Books)

1990

LeFanu, Nicola, and Kevin Crossley-Holland. *The Green Children: An Opera in Two Acts* [opera] (London: Novello)

1993

Yolen, Jane. 'The Green Children' [poem], *Asimov's SF* 17.8 (July): 47. [Reprinted 2018, as 'Green Children', in Yolen, Jane. *How to Fracture a Fairy Tale* (San Francisco: Tachyon Publications), 272–73]

1994

Crossley-Holland, Kevin, and Alan Marks. *The Green Children* (Oxford: Oxford University Press)

1995

Windling, Terri. 'The Green Children', in *The Armless Maiden and Other Tales of Childhood's Survivors*, ed. by Terri Windling (New York: Tor), 269–74

1996

Maxwell, Glyn. *Wolfpit: The Tale of the Green Children of Suffolk* [play] (Todmorden: ARC)

Mitchell, Adrian. *Maudie and the Green Children*, illus. by Sigune Hamann (London and Vancouver: Tradewind)

2000

Bignell, Shirley J. *Suffolk Tales 1: The Wild Man of Orford; The Green Children*, narrated by Peter Davison [audio CD with teachers' notes] (Debenham: Big Toe Audio)

2001

Youmans, Marly. *The Wolf Pit: A Novel* (New York: Farrar, Straus and Giroux)

2003

Brockmeier, Kevin. 'The Green Children', in *The Truth about Celia: A Novel* (New York: Pantheon Books), 55–76

2006–7

Bartholomew, Mark. *Whispers in the Woods* (2006); *Chaos in the Cathedral* (2006); *Swords in the Summer* (2007), all illus. by Jan Evans (Blackburn: Eprint)

2010

The Green Children (TGC). 'Encounter' [song], on CD *Encounter* (Spinside Records SPNR 07275-7). Available on YouTube https://www.youtube.com/watch?v=qCIouuXyCjk)

2013

Burton, Marianne. 'The Green Girl's Husband', [poem], in *She Inserts the Key* (Bridgend: Seren), 15

Hartsiotis, Kirsty. 'The Green Children', in *Suffolk Folk Tales* (Stroud: History Press), 14–17

2015

Newell, Martin. *The Green Children* [poem] (Wivenhoe: Jardine Press). [Recorded with music by the Hosepipe Band, on CD *The Green Children & Other Poems* (Private Label MN+THB001CD) 2016]

2016

Tokarczuk, Olga. *Les Enfants verts*, [French] trans. by Margot Carlier (Lille: La Contre Allée)

2018

Tokarczuk, Olga. [Original Polish version.] 'Zielone Dzieci, czyli Opis dziwnych zdarzeń na Wołyniu sporządzony przez medyka Jego Królewskiej Mości Jana Kazimierza, Williama Davissona', in *Opowiadania Bizarne* (Kraków: Wydawnictwo Literackie), 10–44

2019

Carey, Edward. 'These our monsters', in *These Our Monsters: The English Heritage Book of New Folktale, Myth and Legend*, ed. by Katherine Davey (London: English Heritage), 31–42

Coats, J. Anderson. *The Green Children of Woolpit* (New York: Atheneum Books)

Warner, Richmond. *The Green Children: A Foxfield Railway Story*, illus. by Sarah-Leigh Wills (Whitley Bay: UK Book Publishing)

2020

Johnson, Daisy. 'A Retelling', in *Hag: Forgotten Folktales Retold* (London: Virago Press)

2021

Nigro, Don. *The Recollection of Green Rain* [play], in *Pirandello and Other Plays* (London: Samuel French), 73–88

Overall, Sonia. 'Green is the colour', *Neon* 52 (Spring 2021): 38–41

Index

www.ingramcontent.com/pod-product-compliance
Lightning Source LLC
Chambersburg PA
CBHW021812270326
41932CB00007B/152